Staking Out The Terrain

Staking Out The Terrain

Power and Performance among
Natural Resource Agencies

SECOND EDITION

Jeanne Nienaber Clarke
and
Daniel C. McCool

State University of New York Press

Published by
State University of New York Press, Albany

© 1996 State University of New York

For information, address the State University of New York
Press, State University Plaza, Albany, NY 12246

Production by Marilyn Semerad
Marketing by Dana E. Yanulavich

Library of Congress Cataloging-in-Publication Data

Clarke, Jeanne Nienaber, 1943-
    Staking out the terrain : power and performance among natural
resource agencies / Jeanne Nienaber Clarke and Daniel C.
McCool. — 2nd ed.
        p.   cm. — (SUNY series in environmental politics and policy)
    Includes bibliographical references and index.
    ISBN 0-7914-2945-8 (hc : alk. paper). — ISBN 0-7914-2946-6 (pb :
alk. paper)
    1. Natural resources—Government policy—United States.
2. Environmental policy—United States. 3. Administrative agencies–
–United States. 4. Bureaucracy—United States. I. McCool, Daniel,
1950–   . II. Title. III. Series.
HC103.7.C53 1996
333.7'0973—dc20
                                                                95-45344
                                                                      CIP

10 9 8 7 6 5 4 3 2

Still for Jim and Michael
(J.N.C.)
To Olivia and Jack McCool
(D.C.M.)

Contents

List of Illustrations

List of Tables

Acknowledgments
The Second Edition

No one deserves more credit for bringing out the second edition of *Staking Out the Terrain* than Clay Morgan, our editor at the State University of New York Press. Since 1992, when we first suggested the project to him, he has been endlessly patient and unflagging in his support. Due to a variety of misfortunes that were visited upon both authors, the project took longer than we thought. It also became attenuated because we ended up rewriting the entire book. (At least one of us thus discovered that it is easier to write a book from scratch than to rewrite one.) Although we suspect that Clay had doubts about whether the revised version would ever be completed, he kindly kept them to himself. All authors should be so fortunate.

Several colleagues, friends, and family members—some of whom helped with the original edition—assisted us in our research this time around. Special thanks are due to Dorotha Bradley, Shmuel Burmil, James Clarke, Hanna Cortner, Susan and Wendell Fletcher, Perry Hagenstein, Don Hanson, Helen Ingram, Robert Jacobs, Richard Linford, Judy May, John Mumma, Beryl Radin, Lettie Wenner, and Ervin Zube.

In preparing this edition we were assisted by three graduate students: Andrea Gerlak and Jamal Hosseini of the University of Arizona, and Michael McCoy of the University of Utah. We are grateful for their help, as well as that of Trisha Morris, manuscript specialist for the University of Arizona's Political Science Department. She good-naturedly bailed us out on more than one occasion, when, it seemed, all else had failed. Denise Allyn, also of the Political Science Department, made important contributions too.

Finally, we again want to thank the many agency officials whom we contacted and/or interviewed. With few exceptions, our queries were promptly and graciously met. Since we promised anonymity, we must acknowledge the contributions of these individuals in that way. Needless to say, without their help this study could not have been done.

Two individuals, however, went far beyond the call of duty in helping us with this project. Kyle Schilling, director of the Corps of

Engineers' Institute for Water Resources, and Eugene Stakhiv, IWR's Policy Studies branch chief, not only granted us extended interviews, but they provided us with literally boxloads of material on water resources policy. They also helped us in scheduling interviews with other agency officials.

Our fifteen-year-long study of these seven federal agencies has caused us to be more, not less, impressed with the nation's natural resources managers. Although there is always room for improvement, on the whole they have done an exceptionally good job, under the most trying political circumstances.

Of course, the usual assignment of responsibility applies for this book. The errors and weaknesses contained herein are the responsibility of my co-author.

Differentials in Agency Power

INTRODUCTION

A resurgence in interest in natural resources issues characterizes the last decade of the twentieth century. From the May 1994 signing of an international agreement to protect wildflowers at the Botanical Gardens in Washington, D.C., to the September 1994 world conference on population control in Cairo, worldwide attention is focused on how well we humans have carried out our stewardship role on this planet.

This is by no means a novel concern. Such an interest can be traced back to biblical times, to classical Greece, to Confucius' China. A reading of the great books and the great philosophers of recorded history shows that the relationship between humans and nature has been of concern to virtually all societies. So it is with the United States. But it has been a fluctuating and cyclical concern. As Anthony Downs stated some twenty years ago, public issues in modern media-driven societies go through an "issue-attention cycle."[1] In the United States, in this century alone, there have been four distinct periods when citizens and their governments grappled with conservation and environmental concerns: during the presidency of Theodore Roosevelt (1901–9), during FDR's New Deal (1933–39), during the tumultuous ten years of the Johnson and Nixon presidencies (1964–74), and most recently during the Bush-Clinton regimes.

It is when public attention is at its most intense that the opportunity for enacting new legislation is maximized. It is, however, a relatively narrow window of opportunity, since public attention to any given issue is generally short-lived. To take the example of the 1964–74 period, there occurred a flurry of legislative activity in response to off-shore oil spills, smog-producing temperature inversions, and tension-filled summers in overcrowded metropolitan centers. Washington's response included enactment of the 1964 Wilderness Act, more stringent clean air and water legislation, the National Environmental Policy Act of 1969 (NEPA), and the Endangered Species Act of 1973. Taken together, it was an impressive statutory record.

As interest in environmental quality issues inevitably began to wane during this period, a new, albeit related, issue came to the forefront of national attention. Uncertainty over the adequacy of energy supplies was dramatically felt by many Americans during the winter of 1973–74, as drivers waited in long stationary lines at local gasoline stations.

Familiar themes were reiterated during this latest crisis: Were we running out of oil and other valuable energy resources? Had our natural resources been grossly mismanaged, possibly squandered away by short-sighted entrepreneurs operating in both the public and private sectors? Was it necessary to devise more rational policies for the coming worldwide era of frugality? One presidential ship of state was largely wrecked on the shoals of the energy crisis, and another was swept into office by the tide of popular sentiment favoring fiscal conservatism—particularly as it pertained to the federal government. Scarcity and frugality were the key political concepts of the 1970s, and by the middle of the decade the environmental crisis had evolved almost imperceptibly into the energy crisis. As had been the case with the environmental issue, the federal government acted on the public's concern over energy shortages by passing several pieces of legislation designed to alleviate the energy crunch.[2] And, again, resource-managing agencies found themselves the foci for much of this public attention.

The formulation of new public policies through the legislative process and by executive order is by no means the end of the story, however. In fact, the scholarly and journalistic attention accorded the implementation stage of policymaking since Pressman and Wildavsky's seminal book on the subject makes it appear as though new federal legislation is virtually the beginning of the process rather than, as we used to think, its conclusion. In some respects this is so: How policies get twisted, changed, modified, distorted, and even at times successfully executed has become the subject matter of a flourishing subfield within the disciplines of political science and public administration.

Even a single piece of legislation—for instance NEPA—is subjected to microscopic analysis by students of the policy process. (It was possible to refer to oneself in the 1970s as a "NEPA specialist".) At least as important a step as deciding on a goal or objective is, then, how it gets implemented in the policy process.

When the focus is on implementation one is inevitably drawn into the milieu of the federal bureaucracy, for it is a bureaucratic organization(s) that nearly always is given the responsibility of executing federal laws.[3] In a book on the presidency Francis Rourke noted, "It is important also to remember that while the White House staff may be very good at designing broad-gauge programs, these programs must be carried out by some bureaucratic organization."[4] Whether policies succeed or fail in their objectives is largely dependent upon the nature of the organization mandated to carry out those policies. Those natures differ. The flora and fauna of what is commonly referred to as "the federal bureaucracy" is actually rich in its diversity and complexity. Although it appears monolithic when viewed from the outside, or from a distance, that vast executive branch establishment headquartered in Washington, D.C. and its environs is actually a collection of hundreds of agencies, bureaus, departments, councils, and commissions. By one count, the executive branch is composed of something like eighteen hundred of these subunits.[5]

It is the thesis of this study that the characteristics that distinguish one organization from another in the federal bureaucracy can be as significant as those elements that they hold in common. By and large, the scholarship on bureaucracy has stressed, beginning with the influential work of Max Weber, the common features of bureaucratic organizations. Without trying to minimize these important generalizations, this study will emphasize the idiosyncratic. We wish to examine what accounts for the performance differences that exist among certain federal agencies—for that which makes one agency rich, powerful, and influential in the governmental process and another one impoverished, impotent, and inconsequential. Our intention is thus to provide a detailed examination of what Rourke has called "differentials in agency power,"[6] and to discuss why these differentials are important in the policy process.

The scholarship on NEPA is a good illustration of how agency differences come into play in policymaking and policy implementation.

Once enacted in 1969, NEPA quickly became a celebrated and much-studied piece of legislation. Because one of its principal intentions was to force agencies to change established patterns of behavior (through Section 102(2) (c) of the act), the statute provided an uncommon opportunity for social scientists to observe the dynamics of organizational change. Several things were discovered. First, it was learned that the discipline lacked universal indicators of organizational change. A measurement problem surfaced. What yardsticks could be used to assess the extent of change within an organization? Many had to admit that such measures did not exist, and so they had to be constructed. Observation thus became intertwined, as is inevitable in the social sciences, with evaluation. The result was that to a certain extent the units of measurement varied from study to study.

A second important discovery, though, had to do with the fact that federal agencies did not respond in a uniform manner to the new NEPA goals and objectives. Notwithstanding a certain degree of imprecision, as we just mentioned, in the measurement techniques being used, most observers discerned rather clear differences among agencies with respect to their willingness to change. Some agencies simply responded more quickly, more effectively, and more thoroughly than did others. Many wondered why.

Third, certain paradoxes emerged with respect to the bureaucratic response to NEPA. All who studied the act admitted that it contained a pro-environment, pro-conservation, and hence an anti-development or anti-public works bias. A good guess would have been that those agencies whose missions were most congruent with the basic philosophy of the act would have been the agencies with the best, or better, response records. Agencies like the National Park Service and the U.S. Fish and Wildlife Service ought to have responded more quickly to NEPA than, for example, pro-development agencies like the Corps of Engineers and the U.S. Forest Service. This was found not to be the case. In three separate studies on the implementation of NEPA, the researchers found little or no correlation between the nature of the agency's mission and its response to new environmental requirements. For example, Allen F. Wichelman, in his study of NEPA,[7] found the Corps of Engineers to have as good a response record as the U.S. Forest Service, and a better track record than the National Park Service. A study done by Richard Andrews, *Environmental Policy and Administrative Change,*[8] compared the Corps of Engineers with the Soil Conservation Service (SCS) in the Agriculture Department; the former agency came out far ahead of the SCS. Finally, Richard Liroff's book evaluated the Corps of Engineers' implementation record and labeled it "extremely well" to "best of all."[9] Other agencies did not fare so well: The Bureau of Reclamation did poorly, and the National Park Service and the Fish and Wildlife Service both were "slow" to implement requirements that, ostensibly, fit in nicely with their existing programs and policies.

The point to be emphasized is that there exist observable and significant differences in how federal resource managers perform under similar circumstances. This is seen not only in the implementation of NEPA, but in the way agencies have responded to a whole series of changes in their immediate external environments; it must be remembered that the ecology movement not only produced NEPA and its EIS (Environmental Impact Statement) requirement, but scores of other new requirements as well. The energy crisis of the 1970s, for instance, had several impacts on agency behavior, from stepped-up minerals exploration on the public lands to a renewed interest in and funding for the energy benefits derived from federal hydroelectric projects. We argue in this study that what accounts for these performance differences is a set of organizational and political conditions that have produced different types of agencies within the executive establishment. Consequently, these varying types of organizations manifest different patterns of response to essentially the same stimuli, and so there is produced a situation wherein certain organizations have what amounts to "favored agency status" relative to other agencies. The adage that nothing succeeds like success thus has a certain relevance and even poignancy to the world of bureaucratic politics, especially as that world has become more populated, more complex, and more differentiated in the twentieth century.[10]

What exactly are these political and organizational factors that act as sources of agency power? And what kinds of agencies have been produced as a result? In answer to the first question, the literature on bureaucratic behavior suggests that organizations have two primary sources of power. In *Bureaucracy, Politics, and Public Policy* Francis Rourke noted that agency resources include (1) the expertise, knowledge, and information an agency has at its disposal, and (2) the clientele and other external support an agency can muster in support of its programs.[11]

The classic research by Weber stressed the element of expertise as the bureaucracy's primary source of power:

> Under normal conditions, the power position of a fully developed bureaucracy is always overtowering. The 'political master' finds himself in the role of the 'dilettante' who stands opposite the 'expert,' facing the trained official who stands within the management of administration. This holds whether the 'master' whom the bureaucracy serves is a 'people,' equipped with the weapons of 'legislative initiative,' the 'referendum,' and the right to remove officials, or a parliament, elected on a more aristocratic or more 'democratic' basis and equipped with the right to vote a lack of confidence. It holds whether the master is an aristocratic, collegiate body, legally or actually based on self-recruitment, or whether he is a popularly-elected president, a hereditary and 'absolute' or a 'constitutional' monarch.[12]

Our own research into the histories and behavior of seven federal resource agencies corroborates these analyses. The display of expertise and the mobilization of political support are crucial to an analysis of agency behavior. However, we also found that for purposes of comparing one agency's power base and performance with others, it is necessary to look at the several dimensions that go to make up expertise and political clout. In other words, these two broadly defined resources can be broken down into their constituent parts. We see the first resource, expertise and the control of information, as being composed of: (1a) the nature of the mission originally given the agency; (1b) the extent to which the agency embodies a highly-regarded profession; (1c) the degree to which the leadership of the agency can capitalize on the knowledge base of the organization; and (1d) whether a sense of esprit de corps permeates the organization. The second variable, political support, includes such characteristics as: (2a) the existence of an optimal-size constituency on which the agency generally can count; (2b) the extent to which the agency's mission is linked to identifiable economic interests in society; (2c) whether it is a service or regulatory agency; and (2d) the organization's position vis-à-vis its executive branch superiors and the U.S. Congress. These characteristics are displayed in table 1.1.

Each of these factors has been extensively studied elsewhere, so we wish here to simply summarize what is meant by each of them, why they are significant determinants of agency behavior, and how they relate to our seven-agency study. In the three chapters that follow, we expand upon the argument presented here by tracing the historical development of each of these seven resource-managing agencies, with emphasis on how the agency's power base has molded its subsequent behavior.

Table 1.1 Sources of Agency Power

1. Expertise/Control of Information			
1a Nature of Mission	1b Dominant, Established Profession	1c Astute leadership	1d *Espirt de Corps*
+pro-development; multiple-use; utilitarian values +created by an organic act +contains a mission that is expandable	+scientific, legal, military bases of expertise -interdisciplinary; melting pot or professions	+scientific, legal or military leadership +strong founder +recruitment from within -political appointments to head agency	+coherent public image +well-defined agency character +integrated organization -servile attitude; inferiority complex -lack of a competitive edge

0 age of organization			
-the product of executive orders or re-organizations -narrow or esoteric mission; dominant use; preservationist values			

2. Political/Constituency Support			
2a Constituency Size	2bLinkages to Majoritarian Interests	2c Service or Regulatory	2d Intra-governmental Support
+large; evenly distributed +well-educated, well-funded -narrow exotic interest -broad, amorphous interest	+concrete, economic interests +defense contractors -the poor; ethnic minorities	+service orientation and functions -regulatory functions	+congressional support +presidential support -judicial oversight

Note: + = positive influence or characteristic; - = negative influence or characteristic; 0 = no discernible effect.

THE EXPERTISE FACTOR AND ITS CONSTITUENT PARTS

It is often observed that "knowledge is power," and bureaucracies in the modern state are the acknowledged repositories of vast amounts of data and expertise. For Weber, as well as for more contemporary students of organizational behavior, collecting and using information are the *sine qua non* of all bureaucracies. (In some ways even our second broad variable, constituency support, can be viewed as flowing from the first.)

But not all agencies share equally in this power source. As sociological research has shown, some professions or areas of expertise are more valued by members of society than are others. Generally speaking, the most highly regarded professions today are those of science, engineering, medicine, and the law. Hence, if an agency's mission substantially involves any of these areas, its advantage in the political process is enhanced. Rourke summarizes this point:

> As a source of power, expertise reaches its fullest development in those organizations which have skills related to the survival of society. Scientists and military officers, for example, are in a highly advantageous position today to command respect for their particular talents.[13]

These generalizations must be qualified by the recognition that Americans have become less enamored with experts and professionals of all kinds than they once were. To employ Ellis and Wildavsky's terminology, an anti-leadership mood developed out of the Vietnam and Watergate crises of the 1960s and 1970s. It has gathered momentum since then, and it now touches virtually all societal institutions.[14] The result is a crisis in governance, abundantly evident to even the casual newspaper reader or television news viewer.

Public cynicism poses particular problems for bureaucracies, for their very existence is linked to expertise. There is no question that bureaucrats in the 1990s have a much harder time convincing people that they know best, whether it is the forester making decisions on the Flathead National Forest in Montana, or the hydrologist redesigning water flows on Florida's Kissimmee River. As we discuss in detail later, officials in all of the seven agencies examined in this book are grappling with this changed environment. However, despite all of the challenges to the traditional bases of bureaucratic authority, it is hard to imagine American society without bureaucrats and experts of some sort making decisions for the collective good. All things being equal, resource managing agencies still need, and benefit from, a competent professional workforce, even though those professionals may reflect newly emerging disciplines. As a top official in the Forest Service told us recently, "The agency needs a new dominant profession."

The skills of a particular bureau are inextricably intertwined with its mission. Some organizations are blessed with having an original purpose (in most concrete terms, an "organic act") which is highly valued and/or in accord with dominant societal values. For example, both the Army Corps of Engineers and the U.S. Forest Service derive much of their potency from espousing a multiple-use, utilitarian philosophy that allows them to contribute in a material way to the economic development of the nation. This kind of mission contrasts sharply with one that is so broad that it is supposed to control everything—for example, the Environmental Protection Agency[15]—or so narrow that it is perceived to be at best peripheral and at worst a hindrance to our national well-being. Such has been the fate of the U.S. Fish and Wildlife Service for a good part of its one-hundred-twenty year history.

Linked to an agency's mission are the conditions surrounding its creation. For instance, was the agency originally set in motion by a legislative statute—an organic act—or through an executive order? One might think this distinction slight, but according to some of Kaufman's research a statutory base is a more secure foundation for an agency than is creation by departmental or executive order.[16] The latter can more easily be repealed. Also, some agencies do evolve from an executive order to a statutory base but often are the objects of several reorganizations along the way. Frequent reorganizations sap strength. Whatever the benefits to presidents and congresspersons of them, there is little doubt that from an agency's point of view their costs outweigh their benefits. Thus the evidence seems to favor, as we show in the succeeding chapters, agencies which are given a statutory base at the time of their creation, or shortly thereafter. It tends to extend their longevity as well as enhance their influence in the political process by giving them a definite identity to work with and from.

Just as having Congress "present at the creation" is an advantage to an agency, so is having a mission that is flexible enough to allow the agency room to grow. Agencies that have grown powerful over the years are those that slowly but surely add on new functions, without completely sacrificing old ones, as they move along in life. These organizations actively sniff out new opportunities to expand their missions by continuously monitoring their external environment, in hopes of finding problem areas which might conceivably fall under their original flexible purpose. There has been considerable criticism of such a concept as "multiple use," but from the organization's standpoint, it is a wonderfully flexible management philosophy. Other agencies may get trapped by having a contradictory mission, one that is fulfilled in a relatively short time, or one that is so narrow that the organization finds little room for maneuvering in the bureaucratic jungle.

As Rourke noted above, deference is accorded to military and scientific experts in this society. Our research amplifies this observation by arguing that resource-managing agencies which have a dominant, scientifically-based profession develop into stronger organizations. The classic illustration is the Army Corps of Engineers, an organization that is able to capitalize both on the military and engineering mystiques. Until quite recently, professional forestry also served the Forest Service well. Agencies that are interdisciplinary—a melting pot of professions—generally encounter greater difficulties in developing into a cohesive organization. One may find our argument here somewhat contradictory in that we claim that a flexible mission leads to greater success while the dominance of a single profession within an agency also contributes to its stature. Though at first glance it might appear illogical, we believe that the historical records of our seven-agency sample bear out these assertions. A multiple-use mission, together with a well-established profession, is a potent combination.

Agencies that have a strong sense of their own identities and of their mission—often referred to as organizational zeal or *esprit de corps*—have an edge over those that do not. Just as we can sense when we are in the presence of a particularly strong, charismatic personality, so, too, are there agencies which know so well what they are about that they exude a sense of self-confidence in their relationships with others. Though it is a difficult factor to quantify, it is nonetheless a real source of power for an organization. For political power is as much a matter of reputation as it is budget size, size of work force, and other more easily measurable indicators. The agency with *esprit de corps* can both better maintain the loyalty of its members and the support of its outside constituencies.

Along these lines, much was written in the 1980s comparing the U.S. automobile industry with that of the Japanese, and it was concluded that the latter's success could be attributed in great part to the community spirit actively cultivated by Toyota, Nissan and other Japanese car manufacturers with respect to their labor forces. Governmental organizations are no different in this regard.

Finally, leadership of the organization must be considered as a part of its information base. Astute or far-sighted leadership is never guaranteed to an agency throughout its existence, yet there do exist certain conditions pertaining to its top management that aid an agency rather than hinder it. Those agencies that can recruit to their leadership positions from within the organization rather than have a political appointee thrust upon them have an advantage. Also there is some evidence to suggest that a strong founder, who starts an agency off on the right foot, is a power source for the agency later on. Something like a "founder's myth" does exist and does give organizational benefits. For example, the exalted status of the Federal Bureau of Investigation from its inception in the 1920s to the late 1960s was due in large part to the leadership of its one director, J. Edgar Hoover, during that entire period of time. Hoover was not only instrumental in creating the bureau, but in capitalizing on the public's continual concern about crime control by fashioning and maintaining a cohesive organizational unit to combat a highly visible social ill.

THE SEVERAL DIMENSIONS OF CONSTITUENCY SUPPORT

Like expertise, political support can be conceived of as being a composite of several factors. A review of the existing literature combined with our own research into the histories of these seven agencies yield four clusters of factors which are most important to understanding differentials in bureaucratic power in this area. They concern the size of the constituency, the nature of the interests clustering around the organization, the nature of the agency's mission, and the extent of intragovernmental support for the organization.

The simplest taxonomy of federal organizations divides them into two types: service and regulatory. Service-oriented agencies are those which generate "benefits rather than restrictions on the public";[17] regulatory agencies have the essentially thankless task of restricting some economic, social, or political activity. It is quite evident that service-oriented bureaus are advantaged vis-à-vis those whose purpose in life frequently puts them in a position to incur the wrath of influential segments of the public as well as influential policymakers in Washington. Regulatory agencies thus face budget cuts, personnel reductions, and diminutions in their scope and authority more frequently than do their service-oriented cohorts. During the Carter and Reagan administrations we witnessed an increase in the level of dissatisfaction with governmental regulation, both among the American public and among our national leaders, with the result that several regulatory bureaus fell by the wayside in an effort to whittle down the power of the federal bureaucracy.

Regulators like the Environmental Protection Agency (EPA), the Federal Trade Commission, and the Occupational Safety and Health Administration must continuously face a critical environment. Their support is diffuse while their opposition is better organized and better funded. The EPA in this regard is an interesting case, and at first glance it appears as the exception to the rule. It managed to survive a hostile environment under former President Reagan to become a "major player" in the Bush and Clinton administrations. It did so, we think, at least in part because it transformed itself from a regulatory agency to a service-oriented one: One that services predominantly white, middle-class lawyers who have earned a lot of money from litigating environmental clean-up efforts. The EPA also dispenses a great deal of research money.

Among the sample of agencies which we discuss in this study none is of the pure regulatory variety, although some agencies are a mixture of both. In actuality, most federal agencies do some of both: They regulate certain activities, like the Corps' disposal permit program, while at the same time providing benefits to others—the design and construction of new municipal wastewater treatment facilities. The generalization still holds, however; the more regulating an organization does, the less popular it will be. Most organizations thus try to keep their regulatory activities to a minimum in order to avoid being perceived, as has been the case at times with the Fish and Wildlife Service, as a producer of bureaucratic red tape.

The size, nature, and type of interest group support are critical variables affecting an agency's power base. A broad-based, but organized, clientele is preferable to either a distinctly narrow constituency (historic preservationists, bird watchers) or to a constituency that is so broad that it cannot be mobilized easily. The fate of the nationwide consumers' movement is illustrative of what happens with an amorphous clientele. Since it includes virtually everyone in American society, it has proven to be exceedingly difficult to organize either a permanent interest group or a bureaucracy around it. To date, congress has hesitated before launching a Consumer Protection Agency whose mandate conceivably would be broader, more abstract, and more open to administrative interpretation and discretion than are existing statutes which have created similar federal regulatory agencies.

But optimal size is only one factor to consider in measuring constituency support. What also must be considered is how evenly distributed, both in a geographic and a socioeconomic sense, is the agency's interest group support. Organizations that are spatially limited, like the Bureau of Reclamation, whose organic act allows it to operate only in the seventeen Western states of the nation, find themselves competing with a handicap. This holds also for those agencies like the now-defunct Office of Economic Opportunity, whose clientele happened to consist of the most economically disadvantaged groups in American society.

Compared with the education lobby, for instance, or the forest products industry, these more limited constituencies can offer an agency little real support. We turn again to Rourke to provide a summary of the ideal association from an agency's viewpoint:

> it can be said that the ideal administrative constituency is large and well distributed throughout all strata of society or in every geographical section of the community. It should include devoted supporters who derive tangible benefits from the services an agency provides. However, an administrative

agency should not be excessively dependent upon the support of any segment of its constituency, nor should it carry on activities that threaten the interests of substantial outside groups. Finally, the economic or social activities in which a constituency engages should be in accord with the most highly-ranked values in society.[18]

Federal agencies not only cultivate interest group support for their activities, but they must also jockey for position among the power centers in the nation's capital. Like it or not, political executives must continuously seek congressional and/or presidential support for their programs in an increasingly competitive and populated bureaucratic milieu. For a variety of reasons, some agencies are better at this than are others and so they have the budgets, workforce, and prestige associated with intragovernmental support.

Generally speaking, agencies may look to the president, to Congress, or even sometimes to both for protection and assistance. There are some agencies that have been the darlings of presidents, like Kennedy's Peace Corps in the early 1960s, Johnson's Office of Economic Opportunity (OEO) and the Civil Rights Division in the Justice Department, and Reagan's Defense Department. When chief executives take a special interest in a particular organization it usually fares well in the policymaking and budget process; generally the Congress will defer, at least for a time, to the president's pet programs. However, the other side of the coin is that presidents come and go with greater frequency than do members of Congress, and so being a favorite son or daughter of the president is a relatively less secure position than being a Congressional favorite. Consider, for example, the fate of the Peace Corps and the OEO—organizations that were, for a while, in the limelight but which have since faded into obscurity or have been abolished. The OEO survived less than ten years.

Those tight little iron triangles that presidents and their top administrators rail against are, of course, an agency's best hedge against bad times. Former Secretary of Health, Education and Welfare Joseph Califano called it "molecular government," and it is the bane of anyone wishing to make significant changes in the existing power structure. The three-cornered triangle of agency, congressional committee or subcommittee, and lobby proves highly resistant to intrusion and influence even from the president of the United States.

The classic example of this relationship has been the Army Corps of Engineers, described by Arthur Maass in 1951 as the construction and engineering arm of the U.S. Congress.[19] The Corps' unusually close association with Congress allowed it to fend off harsh criticism, bad publicity, and attacks to its sovereignty by even presidents and Supreme Court justices. And, as our research will show, the agency flourished in the process.

Over the last two decades the influence of the judicial branch of government on the bureaucracy has grown. Whereas at one time the federal courts had minimal impact on executive branch agencies and bureaus, those happy days for bureaucrats have disappeared. Judicial review of administrative decision-making is a key feature of the contemporary political process, and some scholars even have posited the existence of a "judicial iron triangle," composed of district court, federal agency, and interest groups, to rival the influence of the congress-based iron triangle.

Litigation is a weapon often used today by all sides in environmental disputes. For agency officials, the usual result of judicial review is delay and/or stalemate. Although few challenge the legitimacy of the courts micro-managing the bureaucracy, their involvement clearly has been frustrating to the majority of resource managers. They see it as contributing to the pathological condition known as governmental gridlock. For these reasons we have labelled judicial oversight in table 1.1 as having an overall negative influence on an agency's power base. Having federal judges constantly looking over one's shoulder is not a comfortable situation.

SUMMARY

Our purpose in this chapter has been to discuss briefly the several sources of power which agencies can exploit, and further to suggest that, over time, different kinds of organizations have been produced as a result of this continuous interaction between the agency and its environment. Our research into the histories of seven federal resource-managing agencies has uncovered three fairly distinct types of organizations, each of which displays a characteristic mode of behavior. Our sample of agencies consists of: The U. S. Army Corps of Engineers, the Bureau of Land Management, the Bureau of Reclamation, the U.S. Fish and Wildlife Service, the U. S. Forest Service, the National Park Service, and the Soil Conservation Service, which in 1994 became the Natural Resources and Conservation Service. Four are Department of the Interior agencies, two are housed in the Agriculture Department, and one is located in the Department of Defense. But their formal position in the executive branch is a less important determination in molding agency behavior than are the factors which we discussed above.

What are the types of agencies which this research has discovered? We posit three categories:[20] What we call bureaucratic superstars; agencies that muddle through; and organizational shooting stars. Two agencies, whose histories we discuss in chapter 2, fall into the first category. They are the Corps of Engineers and the Forest Service. Next, those agencies which have found a relatively secure niche in the bureaucratic environment, and which show only modest variations in behavior from year to year, are discussed in chapter 3. To borrow a concept from Lindblom, they "muddle through."[21] These agencies are the National Park Service, the Natural Resources and Conservation Service, and the Fish and Wildlife Service. Our third category includes the Bureau of Reclamation and the Bureau of Land Management, the shooting stars of the federal establishment. They are the agencies that burn brightly for short periods of time; they rise quickly only to face a relatively precarious future. We discuss them in chapter 4.

In the following three chapters, we expand upon the ideas and the model presented here. Chapter 5 presents further measures of agency power. Chapter 6 contains our conclusions, in which we speculate about the future of these federal agencies and environmental policy generally as we approach the new millennium.

Bureaucratic Superstars:

The Army Corps of Engineers and The U.S. Forest Service

THE CORPS OF ENGINEERS

No civil function has been more important in the history of westward expansion than the development of an inland, water-based transportation system. For over a century, from the founding of the Republic in 1789 to the "closing" of the great American frontier in the 1890s, the United States was embarked upon the development and expansion of its national economy. That expansion was dependent in turn upon transportation, on "the need to move people and goods to and from the ever-advancing frontier."[1] If ever an organization mirrored the economic history of a nation it is the Army Corps of Engineers. The nearly two-hundred year history of the agency is thus inextricably intertwined with the political and economic development of the country. Small wonder, then, that the Corps of Engineers continues to enjoy in the 1990s a reputation for power and influence among the federal establishment. It is among the oldest surviving organizations, and its record of achievements is perhaps unmatched by any other federal agency.

The Corps of Engineers was established by Congressional statute on the 16th of March in the year 1802. There is nothing remarkable about the Corps' beginnings—nothing, in other words, that would presage its unusual development. Congress in 1802 simply stated:

> And be it further enacted, that the President of the United States is hereby authorized and empowered to organize and establish a corps of engineers,

to consist of one engineer, with the pay, rank and emoluments of a major; two assistant engineers, with the pay, rank and emoluments of captains; two other assistant engineers, with the pay, rank and emoluments of first lieutenants; two other assistant engineers, with the pay, rank and emoluments of second lieutenants, and ten cadets, with the pay of sixteen dollars per month, and two rations per day: and the President of the United States is, in like manner, authorized to make such promotions in the said corps and so as that the number of the whole corps shall, at no time, exceed twenty officers and cadets.[2]

This ordinary beginning bears resemblance to the headwaters of a mighty river—the Missouri River, for instance, which begins as a small rivulet not more than fifteen feet wide in west-central Montana. As it makes its southeastern descent through the Rockies, flowing down through the Great Plains, it gains momentum and is fed by a number of tributaries which join the main stream. At some point the river, small and insignificant at its source, becomes an impressive natural force that dictates the patterns of habitation for the heartland of America. The river makes transportation, agriculture, industry, and energy production possible.

The Corps' creation coincided with and complemented the era of exploration in the nation's history. From its beginning, with some twenty army engineers, the agency assumed a central role in the protection and utilization of the nation's waterways. The Army Engineers were also the principal agents of the federal government in locating viable wagon and railroad routes in the exploration of the West. It is no coincidence that the most famous expedition in U.S. history, the Lewis and Clark, commenced in 1803, one year after the Corps' inception. After its members were trained in Illinois, just across the Mississippi River from St. Louis, the expedition set out on a three-year investigation of the western territories. In May, 1804, they began their exploration of the Missouri River.

Throughout the nineteenth century, the army engineers distinguished themselves in the exploration of the entire continent: In 1815, Lieutenant Zebulon Pike, after whom Pike's Peak in Colorado is named, explored the Missouri Valley; later, Lieutenant John C. Fremont surveyed the Oregon Trail and parts of California; and other Corps survey parties helped to locate the transcontinental routes—

which generally followed river routes—of the Sante Fe, Union Pacific, Northern and Southern Pacific railroads.

A significant expansion of the Corps' duties occurred in 1824 when Congress passed the first of what came to be called rivers and harbors bills—known to later critics as pork barrel bills. On 24 May 1824, the Eighteenth Congress of the United States authorized the Corps to investigate and improve navigation on the Mississippi and Ohio Rivers, appropriating $75,000 to be used for that purpose:

> And be it further enacted, that, for the purpose of improving the navigation of the Mississippi River, from the mouth of the Missouri to New Orleans, and of the Ohio River from Pittsburgh to its junction with the Mississippi, the President of the United States is hereby authorized to take prompt and effectual measures for the removal of all trees which may be fixed in the bed of said rivers; and, for this purpose, he is authorized to procure and provide, in that way which in his discretion may be most eligible, the requisite water craft, machinery, implements, and force, to raise all such trees, commonly called "planters, sawyers, or snags."[3]

The Corps' interest in navigational improvements persists to the present day in the form of channelization projects, dredge and fill activities, beach erosion control, and the like. Indeed, a major portion of the Corps' ongoing activities are connected with these so-called internal improvements. While there was considerable discussion as to the constitutionality of federal expenditures for the purpose when Congress first began the procedure, an historian of the conservation movement concluded:

> Despite the long series of learned questions about the constitutionality of federal expenditures for waterways, neither the Congress nor the executive ever forced a clear-cut court test; they simply accepted the responsibility gradually over the years.[4]

Constitutional or not, the function was so necessary to the economic development of the country that the Corps never really faced a serious attempt to halt these activities once they were set in motion. Though the agency has been criticized recently by environmentalists for the self-serving aspect of its programs, it has operated too much in the mainstream of America's overall objectives to risk losing these functions. As a member of the appropriations subcommittee on public works said in 1974:

> We do not want the Corps to go out of business. In times like these, when unemployment is going up a number of public works projects on the shelf ready to go into construction is a good thing to have.[5]

A similar sentiment has been voiced in the 104th Congress.

Early in the Corps' history it became apparent that this was to be a versatile organization rather than an agency dedicated to a single mission. The major dichotomy within the Army Engineers is between civil and military functions. The fact that the Corps today is still an agency directed by military engineers should not be minimized, for the military aura lent to all of its functions serves to add to the agency's prestige. Looking only at the civil functions of the agency, however, one is impressed by the wide array of activities engaged in by the Corps. Over the span of a hundred and seventy years, from 1824 to the present, this accretion of functions has been gradual, but complimentary, in nature. The Corps rarely turns down an opportunity to expand its horizons. Even when confronted by a direct challenge to its activities, such as the National Environmental Policy Act of 1969 and the environmental impact statement requirement, the Corps manages to find a silver lining. As Andrews showed in his comparison of the performances of the Corps and the Soil Conservation Service[6], unlike the Service the Corps puts the best face on any new restrictions and requirements. For example, despite considerable urging from numerous congressmen, the Corps never was willing to state openly that it resented or felt hindered by NEPA requirements. On the contrary, the act always was discussed in public as a step forward; any difficulties the organization experienced from it were of no significance in the long run. The agency would, in fact, be better off for having been put to the test.

In 1850, Congress added another function to the Corps' growing repertoire. It authorized the agency to survey the Mississippi River valley to "determine the most practical plan" for flood prevention. In 1879 the Mississippi River Commission was established, with the Corps directing it, to investigate and improve both navigation and flood control aspects of the river basin. With the addition of these new responsibilities, flood control and intergovernmental coordination, the

Corps became involved in the concept of river basin planning — a concept that became increasingly important to its mission in the twentieth century.

In 1909 there was another responsibility added to the agency's activities. That year's rivers and harbors bill authorized the Corps to consider the development of hydroelectric power in its project studies. By 1917, the notion of comprehensive water resources development was firmly established. Though the Corps initially was hesitant about the concept of multiple purpose water development, it quickly moved to capture the policy once Congress determined to pursue it. The authorization to construct flood control projects by the agency was extended beyond the Mississippi River valley, and Congress authorized the Corps to embark upon comprehensive water basin studies— including navigation, flood control, and hydroelectric power generation—wherever appropriate. The Flood Control Act of 1936, establishing a national flood control policy, simply gave the agency even greater authority to act in these areas of "national concern." As modified in 1938 and 1941, certain local participation and approval requirements were removed,[7] and the Corps was well on its way to becoming what Arthur Maass described in his 1951 classic study of the agency: the engineer consultants and contractors of the U.S. Congress.[8]

During the New Deal Era and the postwar period new concerns in the natural resources area surfaced. While the nation did not abandon its historic commitment to economic development, nevertheless there developed concern over a possible deterioration in water quality caused by the industrial and municipal practice of dumping untreated wastes into the nation's lakes, streams, rivers, and adjoining oceans. At this time, several bills were introduced in Congress (though none was enacted until the 1960s) to establish a National Water Quality Commission. In 1948, however, the federal interest in water pollution control was set out, albeit on a limited basis, "with enactment of a five-year program of grants to the states for pollution studies, and the establishment of a Public Health Service pollution research facility at Cincinnati."[9]

Responding to this shift in national concern, the Corps claimed that it too had a long-standing, though limited, interest in the area of pollution control. The 1899 Refuse Act had authorized the agency to detect, regulate, and/or prohibit the dumping of wastes into the navigable waterways of the United States. Also, its survey of water pollution in the Ohio River Valley had been instrumental in the attempts to enact water quality legislation during this time. Nevertheless, it wasn't until the 1970s that the agency began to capitalize on its pollution control function, primarily through a new urban studies program and an expanded permits program. In 1945, the Corps, evidencing unusual behavior, chose to take a back seat in this area. Testifying before the Rivers and Harbors Committee, the Deputy Chief of Engineers told Congress:

> as far as the Corps of Engineers is concerned we have no desire to enforce the regulations in regard to pollution. It seems to us that the handling of this pollution business in streams is a matter for the Public Health Service.[10]

Despite some initial hesitancy in regard to enforcing the 1899 Act, in 1969 the Corps nevertheless estimated that of a possible twenty to thirty thousand violations, the agency had been able to pin down and take action against three thousand such incidents. In addition, it assisted in the clean-up of spills whenever possible, although this was not part of its statutory duties.

Though there were attempts by both the Roosevelt and Truman administrations to gain greater executive control over the strong and independent agency,[11] the Corps, together with its Congressional supporters, succeeded in keeping the agency away from control by the Interior Department. Thus, by 1950 the Corps' duties were not only undiminished, but actually had been broadened. For example, in 1944 the Corps was authorized to develop "public use" facilities at its projects, thus giving the agency a role in the creation of recreational facilities throughout the nation. By 1964, the Corps estimated that it spent nearly two percent of its construction budget on recreation facilities and calculated that, in comparison with the National Park Service's 94 million visitors in 1964, the Corps' visitor-use days amounted to 147 million. The 1946 Fish and Wildlife Act also affected the Corps, requiring it to cooperate with the U.S. Fish and Wildlife Service and the various states in preventing and/or mitigating damage to these resources. In 1958 this act was amended to provide that "full consideration" be given to the preservation and enhancement of fish and wildlife in the agency's project planning.

The more recent history of the agency, from 1950 to the present, shows the same pattern of behavior: The Corps rarely turns down an opportunity to expand its areas of responsibility. It even takes challenges to its developmental orientation as opportunities to demonstrate its responsiveness to changing public values. The Corps' response to the environmental movement of the 1960s and 1970s is further demonstration of the agency's flexible, even innovative, style. Several analysts of the Corps' response to NEPA generally reach the same conclusion: The agency's response was sincere, swift, and impressive.[12] It incorporated the environmental issue in a manner which forced the grudging respect of even its most strident critics. Its response record was often better than that of federal agencies with a more overtly conservationist orientation. The authors of one such book on the Corps thus conclude:

> The Corps is noteworthy for managing to go through a change cycle while reconciling or at least juggling seemingly irreconcilable demands for water resource development, environmental protection, and open planning. After making a decision to change, the agency moved expeditiously and rather successfully to accommodate itself to a changing social and political environment. Thus, this study serves as a classic illustration of the process of mutual accommodation that occurs between an agency and its attentive publics in a changing world. In observing this particular example of change, one cannot help but note also that the Army Corps of Engineers has once again proved to be a most politically astute organization.[13]

Due to the incorporation of so many new responsibilities and the continued expansion of traditional ones, the Corps' budget skyrocketed in the late 1970s. The 1980 budget estimate of $3.2 billion included $1.7 billion for the construction of over 200 projects, including river and harbor improvements, locks, dams and canals, intercoastal waterways, flood protection, reservoirs, and hydroelectric power production. The Corps also planned to spend $31 million in 1980 on the construction of recreational amenities in order to prepare for an estimated 523 million recreation days of use at these sites. In addition, after the Teton Dam disaster the Corps was given the responsibility to inspect approximately 6,400 dams for possible safety violations. To accomplish all of these tasks, the Corps employed an army of over 28,000 permanent employees.[14]

The Corps' success in responding to new challenges does not mean it has escaped criticism, however. Significant changes in its political environment began in the 1970s. Traditionally, water projects such as dams, canals, and flood control have been supported by a strong tripartite alliance that consists of congressmen (especially members of the public works and appropriations committees), the federal agencies that build and maintain water projects, and water-user constituency groups. This iron triangle of symbiotic interests has often been accused of authorizing "pork-barrel" projects, and while these projects may be of questionable value in terms of cost-benefit ratios or environmental impacts, there is no question that they solidify constituent support for incumbent congresspersons. A result of this powerful political alliance is the emphasis on structural rather than nonstructural solutions to the country's water problems.

The federal agencies authorized to build or manage water control structures are the Tennessee Valley Authority, the Corps of Engineers, the Bureau of Reclamation, and the Soil Conservation Service. These agencies ally themselves with the dozens of congressional committees and subcommittees that deal with water development as well as with interest groups such as the National Water Resources Association and the Western States Water Council.

An initial challenge to "water politics as usual" came in 1977 when newly elected President James Earl Carter announced that he was cutting federal funds for some eighteen ongoing water projects. His bold action quickly produced a storm of protest from Western governors and powerful Southern and Western congressmen. The president responded by expanding, by one, what came to be known as the "hit list." If left unfunded, this action would have amounted to about a $289 million cut in the 1978 budget. In addition, Carter ordered the review of 320 other projects and stressed that they would be evaluated in terms of economics, environment, and safety. Eleven of the nineteen projects slated for termination were being built by the Corps of Engineers.[15]

The initial congressional response to Carter's proposed reforms came as something of a surprise since, just a week earlier, seventy-four congressmen had sent the president a letter expressing their "support for your efforts to reform the water resources programs of the Army Corps of Engineers and the Bureau of Reclamation."[16] It appeared that Carter—a newcomer to Washington—did not totally appreciate what he was up against. Philip Fradkin described some of the opposition:

there were certain interests at work within the government that were not in sympathy with what the President wanted. They were the bureaucrats in the Corps of Engineers and Bureau of Reclamation whose long careers had been molded by the structural concept of water development.[17]

The difficulties which the Carter administration experienced challenging traditional water policy were exacerbated by three factors. First, the president failed to discuss the proposed cuts with relevant congressmen and governors; thus, the specific cuts came as a surprise to them. Second, all of the projects on Carter's list were projects already underway; that is, a substantial amount of money had already been spent on the projects. After the cuts were announced, the seventy-four congressmen who wrote to Carter explained that they had intended to support Carter in resisting any *new* project starts, but that they did not intend to deauthorize *existing* projects.[18] Third, 1976 and 1977 were severe drought years in the West, so the interest in water development was substantial.

Despite congressional opposition, Carter persevered. On 23 March 1977, he announced that fourteen more projects would be reviewed, ten of which were Corps of Engineers projects. But on that same date he reinstated funding for three Corps projects which were on the original cut list.[19] A month later Carter created a revised list of twenty-nine projects; full funding was restored for 8 of these projects (5 of them Corps projects), 5 projects were partially funded (2 Corps projects), and 14 projects—11 of them being built by the Corps of Engineers—were still slated for termination.[20]

By early May the battle over the water projects reached a new plateau. The Congress—always a stronghold of support for water development—vehemently resisted the administration's cuts. The House appropriations subcommittee on public works voted to fund seventeen of the eighteen projects on the original cut list. The previous week a resolution passed by the full House called for full funding of all ongoing projects.[21] In June the Senate attempted a compromise by voting to cut funding for half of the eighteen projects in question. Of the nine projects approved by the Senate, eight of them were in states whose senators were on the full appropriations committee, and seven of them were in states whose senators were on the appropriations subcommittee on public works.

The political power of the Corps of Engineers at that time becomes evident when the membership of relevant committees is compared to the list of Corps projects judged by the Carter administration to be expendable. As tables 2.1 and 2.2 show, there is a significant overlap between states that are represented on the House and Senate appropriations committees, and states where the Corps' most controversial, and possibly most marginal, projects were located.

Table 2.1 Senate Committee on Appropriations membership compared with Corps of Engineers Projects Reviewed or Cut, 1977

Senators from States with Reviewed/Cut Projects	Projects on Review/Cut list in Senator's State
Stennis (MS) Chairman, Public Works S-C	Tennessee Tombigbee Waterway
Hollings (SC)	Richard B. Russell Project
Johnston (LA)	Tensas Basin
	Bayou Bodcau
	Mississippi River, Gulf Outlet
	Red River Waterway
	Atchafalaya-Bayous Beouf, Chene and Block
McClellan (AR), Chairman, Appropriations	Tensas Basin
	Cache Basin
Huddleston (KY)	Dayton
	Yatesville Lake
	Paintsville Lake
Proxmire (WI)	LaFarge Lake
Eagleton (MO)	Meramec Lake
Schweiker (PA)	Tyrone Lake
Bellmon (OK)	Lukfata Lake
Hatfield (OR)	Applegate Lake
TOTAL: 10 out of 25 senators	TOTAL: 17 out of 22 projects

Note: These projects include those that appeared on the original cut list of nineteen projects as well as fourteen additional projects President Carter chose for extensive review in March 1977.

As is evident from the tables, both the Senate and House committees on appropriations and their respective subcommittees on public works were chaired by Southerners during this skirmish with the president— who, ironically, was himself a Southerner. These legislators, made powerful by their seniority, obtained a disproportionate share of the Corps projects (some 9 out of a total of 22) that were considered of questionable merit by President Carter. But it must be kept in mind that the Corps' support comes from all of the members of the appropriations committees, regardless of region. Of the twenty-two Corps projects reviewed or cut by the administration, twenty of them were located in states that had legislators on one of the two appropriations committees. As a region, the South does not receive a disproportionate share of water development projects; but to the Carter administration it did have an overabundance of projects of questionable value. Perhaps this was due to the fact that Carter was a Southerner and therefore especially familiar with the local controversies surrounding the projects.

Table 2.2 House Committee on Appropriations membership Compared with Corps of Engineers Projects Reviewed or Cut, 1977

Congresspersons from Districts with Reviewed/Cut Projects	Projects on Review/Cut List in Congressperson's State
Bevill (AL), Chairman, Public Works S-C	Tennessee Tombigbee Waterway
Edwards (AL)	Tennessee Tombigbee Waterway
Whitten (MS)	Tennessee Tombigbee Waterway
	Tallahala Creek Inlet
Boggs (LA)	Tensas Basin
	Bayou Bodcau
	Mississippi River, Gulf Outlet
	Red River Waterway
	Atchafalaya-Bayous Beouf, Chene and Block
Flynt (GA)	Richard B. Russell Project
Natchee (KY)	Dayton
	Yatesville
	Paintsville
Steed (OK)	Lukfata Lake
Flood (PA)	Tyrone
Murtha (PA)	Tyrone
McDade (PA)	Tyrone
Coughlin (PA)	Tyrone
Shipley (IL)	Fulton
Yates (IL)	Freeport
Michel (IL)	Freeport
O'Brien (IL)	Freeport
Obey (WI)	LaFarge Lake
Burlison (MO)	Meramec Lake
Alexander (AR)	Tensas Basin
	Cache Basin
Duncan (OR)	Applegate Lake
TOTAL: 19 congresspersons out of 55	TOTAL: 19 out of 22 projects

Note: These projects include those that appeared on the original cut list of 19 projects as well as 14 additional projects Pres. Carter chose for extensive review in March 1977.

Carter was not the only person speaking out against pork-barrel politics in the late 1970s, however. For example, the Coalition for Water Project Review was formed by more than twenty environmental groups, all of which opposed the construction programs of the Corps. These groups no longer limited their objections to environmental factors. By 1977 they had adopted a strategy of challenging the projects on the basis of economics. Moreover, the environmentalists were joined in this tactic by such money-conscious groups as the National Taxpayers Union as well as public interest lobbies such as Common Cause and the League of Women Voters.[22] A good illustration of this economic-oriented strategy is found in the lawsuit filed by the Environmental Defense Fund and a railroad company against the Tennessee-Tombigbee Waterway. The suit claimed that the Corps of Engineers' cost-benefit analysis was calculated so as to make it appear that the project would result in a net economic gain. According to the suit, the project would benefit a small group of private barge operators, harm the railroad interests, and would in the process destroy 30,000 acres of forests and 17,000 acres of farmland.[23]

The Carter strategy also placed great emphasis on the economics of water projects, although the administration did not neglect environmental considerations. The president's press release of 18 April 1977 stated that "activities which are wasteful, unsafe, or economically or environmentally unsound simply cannot be pursued. Water resource development programs of the Corps of Engineers, the Bureau of Reclamation, and the Tennessee Valley Authority are a case in point."[24] The press release went on to summarize the costs and benefits of each project, and reached the following conclusions regarding three of the most marginal projects: First, the Meramec Lake project would inundate 12,600 acres in order to provide total flood protection for 11,900 acres and additional recreational benefits for the area—these latter accounting for 25 percent of the project's total benefits. Second, the Atchafalaya Project would benefit two oil rig companies at a cost of $20.3 million and would cause the inundation of 7,500 acres. Third, the Bayou Bodcau project would benefit sixty families at a cost of $240,000 per family.[25]

Much of the criticism directed at the Corps' cost-benefit formula concerned interest rates. The law required that an interest rate of 3.25 percent be applied to any project authorized before 1969, even though funds for the project might not actually be appropriated until a later date when interest rates would be higher. In 1974 the rate was boosted to 6.37 percent. Carter wanted to raise it to 10 percent.[26] His 18 April 1977 press release stated: "Many of the projects I reviewed were authorized at such low rates that even though we are building them today, we are pretending that the cost of capital is still the same as it was many years ago."[27] By changing the interest rate from 3.25% to 6.37% five Corps projects on Carter's cut list lost their favorable cost-benefit ratio.[28]

In addition to revamping cost-benefit formulas, Carter's proposed water policy called for five additional reforms: (1) Greater emphasis on environmental protection; (2) Increased dam safety; (3) More attention paid to water conservation; (4) Increased cost sharing among states and the federal government; and (5) A redirected public works program.[29] The first three reforms posed little threat to the Corps of Engineers. Quite the contrary, the agency readily incorporated all three functions into its expanding repertoire of responsibilities. However, the latter two reforms presented a significant challenge to the Corps' traditional functions.

Carter's cost-sharing provision would require users of water projects to help pay for them. As he said, "I will work with the Congress to develop a system to recoup the costs from the beneficiaries."[30] But much of the agency's strength derived from the fact that it practiced the politics of distribution for most of its two-hundred year history. For example, a dam that directly benefits a specific area is paid for by the nation as a whole. It is precisely this characteristic that makes them so appealing to Congress and to the well-organized recipients of such projects who, in Carter's words, "pay nothing for their construction or maintenance."[31]

The absence of a requirement for payback or cost-sharing was one of the most important factors that, until 1986, distinguished the Corps from the Bureau of Reclamation. A case in point was the Applegate Lake project in Oregon. The dam was to be planned and constructed by the Corps, and the Bureau of Reclamation would then operate the resulting Applegate irrigation system. When President Carter ordered a review of the project, the Corps quickly completed its study, while the Bureau became bogged down in calculating repayment schedules. During appropriations hearings, a Corps spokesman explained why the Bureau of Reclamation was behind schedule:

responsibility for repayment of irrigation costs [i.e., the Bureau of
Reclamation's part of the project] rests with the Department of the Interior
pursuant to Federal laws. ... The project will not be operated for irrigation
purposes until the Secretary of the Interior makes necessary arrangements
with non-Federal interests to recover the costs, in accordance with Federal
reclamation law.[32]

Later, Carter expanded his cost-sharing plan to include state governments. Secretary of the Interior Cecil Andrus predicted that the proposal would be accepted by "those states that do have good projects
and are willing to put their money where their mouth is."[33] It was suggested that the states pay 5% to 10% of project costs. But this modest
proposal, like the idea of user fees, evoked a strong negative response
from Congress. None of the administration's cost-sharing proposals
became law.

Yet another controversial reform proposed by President Carter was
his "redirected public works program." This proposal involved nothing
less than a complete turn-around in the nation's tradition of water
development. Margot Hornblower of *The Washington Post* wrote that:

> The new water policy ... will be an effort to reverse the historic tide of mas-
> sive structural waterworks, providing billions of dollars in federal subsi-
> dies for selected areas and economic interests. ... Such changes would
> amount to a revolution in water policy, challenging the historic American
> faith in technology as the answer to all water problems.[34]

The success or failure of Carter's attempt to "revolutionize" water
policy can be measured by the number of structural projects that continued to be funded in the ensuing years. The public works iron triangle
battled the president at every turn, so that by the fall of 1977 the presidents' reforms were in disarray. In an effort to salvage something out of
his original lofty goals, Carter signed a compromise FY 1978 public
works bill which provided $2.8 billion for the Corps—$150 million over
his earlier request—and a total public works appropriation of $10.9 bil-
lion. In an effort to meet the Congress halfway, Carter agreed to fund
half of the projects that were on the original cut list. The president
called the bill "a precedent-setting first step." Environmentalists called
it a sellout. And the Congress promised to renew the fight to fund the
nine projects that went unfunded, but not de-authorized, in FY 1978.[35]

Over the next three years of his administration, Carter valiantly fought for water policy reform. He was no more successful than he had been in 1977, the first year of his presidency. Through 1978 Carter battled the Congress on two related fronts: Project authorization bills and the annual appropriation bills for the Corps and the Bureau of Reclamation. The House wanted to authorize as many as 125 new projects while the president had his own list of thirty-six new projects that met his new criteria.[36] Ultimately none of the authorization bills became law.[37] Carter also objected to the level of funding proposed by Congress, and vetoed the FY 1979 appropriation bill for public works. But the final compromise bill that Carter signed into law cut little funding from ongoing water projects; the total appropriation was just slightly less than the original House bill. The president did extract one concession, however; the Congress agreed to temporarily delete six of the eight projects that had been deleted the previous year.[38]

In 1979 Carter announced two new proposals aimed directly at reducing the power and independence of the Corps of Engineers. In early February he made public a plan to create a Department of Natural Resources (DNR). The new department would include most of the agencies housed in the Department of the Interior, plus the Corps of Engineers. This reorganization was intended to increase the president's control over that particular agency by reducing its autonomy, and with it attenuate its strong alliance with Congress. The idea of a Natural Resources Department was, of course, nothing new. A generation earlier the Hoover Commission recommended that all agencies involved with public works—including the Corps—should be placed in the Department of the Interior.[39] Former president Richard Nixon also proposed a Department of Natural Resources which would have complete control over planning and policy for civil works.[40] These proposals, and others like them, threatened the status quo; consequently all of them have failed. A Southern senator reportedly told Carter about his prospects of getting a DNR: "You're going to get your nose bloodied on this one—why take on one you're sure to lose?"[41]

The other proposal which presented a significant threat to the Corps of Engineers concerned President Carter's view of an enlarged role for the Water Resources Council. Under his plan, the Council would be the final arbiter in determining which projects would be recommended to Congress for funding. Both houses of Congress wasted no time in voting down the plan.[42]

Carter continued his fight to decrease the public works budget throughout 1979. During congressional hearings Representative Bevill of Alabama provided his critique of the president's proposed budget:

> there is 183 or 184 projects either deleted, or slowed down. To be more specific, 56 ongoing studies deleted, 15 advanced engineering and design projects deleted, 59 studies and advanced engineering and design projects, and 46 construction projects that have been stretched out, and no new starts.[43]

Congress' principal concession to Carter was to defer funding for two projects: The Yatesville Dam, which would have required the relocation of 93 cemeteries, 213 dwellings, 6 churches, and 4 commercial buildings, with a primary benefit of "flatwater recreation"; and Bayou Bodcau, which would have benefitted 60 landowners at a cost of $240,000 each.[44]

After three long years of feuding punctuated by some minor victories, Carter clung tenaciously to his policy reform agenda. During the first month of 1980 the president informed Congress that he wanted 125 projects cut from the 1981 budget.[45] But the $12.1 billion public works he signed later that year restored nearly all of those 125 projects, at an estimated cost of $111 million. For instance, the bill included funding for the controversial Yatesville Dam, and it also appropriated $212 million to continue the construction of the Corps' most ambitious and most expensive project, the Tennessee-Tombigbee Waterway. (Total cost for this one project was estimated at $1.4 billion, with a cost-benefit ratio of .87 calculated at 6 3/8% interest.)

Reviewing Carter's four-year crusade against the Corps of Engineers in particular and public works in general, we found that the agency emerged essentially intact and unreformed. The president was unable to change the cost-sharing provisions that have helped to make the Corps so powerful. He failed to create a Department of Natural Resources. The mandate of the National Water Resources Council was not enlarged. The president also failed to turn America away from the so-called structural approach to solving our water problems, as was evident in more recent budget proposals. His attempt to terminate questionable projects was only temporarily successful as Congress eventually funded most of them, and the savings that Carter managed to eke out of the Congress were only a small percentage of the total expenditures for water projects in these four years. During the Carter presidency, the Corps' budget increased by about $600 million. That is approximately a 24 percent increase in four years.

One quite significant change was wrought by Carter, however. He succeeded in imposing a "no-new-starts" policy on the Corps of Engineers. This worried numerous congressmen who were afraid the Corps would run out of business. But the agency, in a characteristic mode of behavior, appeared calm; it never publicly questioned administration policy, preferring to wait for the political climate to change.[46] To further insure future activity, the Corps budgeted a considerable amount of money in the 1981 budget (with Carter's approval) for thirteen new "preauthorization studies," two new dam safety assurance projects, and five new major rehabilitation projects.[47] This obviously left the door open for a great deal of future work, a "no-new-starts" policy notwithstanding.

The Carter reforms detailed here constituted the most aggressive attempt in forty years to increase presidential control over the Corps of Engineers. In the short run the agency emerged from this confrontation in good shape. Its relationship with Congress and its position in the executive branch were not modified, and its budget was significantly larger in 1980 than in 1976. Moreover, the agency expanded its operations into several new areas. Continuing a long tradition, the Corps managed to convert political challenges into bureaucratic opportunities. There were a number of new responsibilities gained by the Corps during the Carter years. For example, when Carter ordered a review of all federal water projects, the Corps promptly screened all of its 292 projects planned for work in 1978. The agency's review concluded that nineteen of those projects needed further study. The nineteen projects were dubbed a "hit list" when Carter announced he would indeed study them further, and possibly exclude them from the budget. The point is that the president relied on the Corps to do an objective review of its own projects.[48] A month after the first cut list was announced, the Corps made public a list of thirty-eight additional projects to be reviewed. This document was released at the same time that the congressional backlash against the president's proposals was gathering momentum. This newest list further provoked the Hill, but resentment was aimed at Carter rather than the Corps, which was perceived as only doing what the president had ordered it to do.

Agency officials made other astute moves as well. In response to increased public concern about environmental degradation, the Corps established an Environmental Effects Laboratory in the mid-seventies which "gives evidence of changing with the changing times."[49] Other additions to the Corps' responsibilities were actually initiated by President Carter. In 1977, the White House requested that the Corps of Engineers begin a safety inspection program of nonfederal dams. The inspection of 9,000 "high hazard" dams in fifty states ultimately required until 1981 to be completed. The Bureau of Reclamation was not asked to do any of the inspections.[50]

The dam safety program was not the only instance where President Carter expressed a preference for the Corps of Engineers over the Bureau of Reclamation. In his reorganization plan to create a Department of Natural Resources, he recommended the transfer of all Bureau of Reclamation construction and maintenance responsibilities to the Corps.[51] Had this proposal been adopted, it would have meant the demise of the Bureau.

The Corps' budget also received a boost from Mother Nature. In 1980, two natural disasters—the eruption of Mt. St. Helens and Hurricane Allen—resulted in a substantial increase in disaster relief funds. In the case of Mt. St. Helens, the Corps came to the rescue with $172 million for clean-up activity.[52]

The 1982 budget which Carter sent to Congress—his last—proposed a 12 percent increase in the Corps of Engineers' budget, pushing its total outlay to an impressive $3.36 billion. The budget for operations and maintenance alone was $1.085 billion, a 20 percent increase that the Corps considered "austere funding."[53] But the 1982 Carter budget never went beyond congressional hearings. One of newly elected President Reagan's first acts was to throw out the Carter budget and substitute his own, one which was designed to "stretch out" capital investment in the civil works program.

The proposed Reagan budget reduced the Corps' funding increase by $230 million. This amounted to about a 7 percent reduction from the Carter proposal; still, it was a 5 percent increase over the Corps' budget for the previous year. President Reagan thus proposed a budget of

$3.135 billion for the Corps in fiscal year 1982. Ominously, more than two-thirds of the Republican administration's proposed cuts were made in the agency's construction program, with more than two-thirds of the total reduction attributed to three projects—the Red River Waterway, the Big South Fork National River and Recreation Area, and the notorious Yatesville Lake.[54] The first two projects were slated for a gradual phase-out by the administration, and the Yatesville Lake Project, which was on Carter's original cut list as well, was the only project out of 199 that received no funds in the Reagan budget. The agency, however, was reluctant even to give up entirely on the other two projects. As the Director of Civil Works pointed out, these projects were not being terminated or de-authorized; they were only being deferred until some future time when they would be needed.[55] In the end even Yatesville Lake received some funding for "relocating graves."[56] Ultimately Congress approved an appropriation bill of $2.97 billion for the Corps. This was virtually the same level of funding as it had the previous year.

The Corps and its congressional supporters successfully resisted any significant cuts in the agency's budget during the first Reagan administration. It also circumvented many of the cuts which Reagan proposed in personnel. For 1982, the president requested an 8 percent reduction in the agency's full-time permanent positions. These reductions were planned to continue for six years, until they reached a total reduction of 18 percent from the 1982 workforce of 32,173.[57] The Corps, however, had sufficient flexibility in its budget to circumvent personnel ceilings through the mechanism of "contracting out" (i.e., hiring outside personnel to compensate for manpower reductions). Like several other agencies, the Corps made it clear in the appropriations hearings that it would rely heavily on this strategy. In hearings, Congressman Bevill criticized not the Corps but the president by calling this "phony economics"; he wanted the Corps to do *all* of the work in-house.[58]

One area in which President Reagan initially succeeded in changing the Corps' budget priorities for FY 1982 was in its recreation program. However, at least part of this success can be attributed to the Corps' acquiescence.[59] For many years recreation had been a stepchild in the agency: there, but not completely accepted. This status was reaffirmed in 1981 when an agency spokesman defined low priority items as recreation and, surprisingly, flood control projects.[60] As a result, during Reagan's first term the Corps' recreation budget was cut by approximately 30 percent. Most of the personnel cuts sustained by the agency were linked to its recreation functions. Interestingly, these cuts came at a time when there was a move afloat to give back those recreational facilities to the federal government which earlier had been acquired by state and local governments. In times of budgetary retrenchment, it appears that neither the federal government nor state and local governments want to spend scarce resources on outdoor recreation. Finally, the FY 1982 Reagan budget also reduced funds for environmental and water quality studies.[61]

President Reagan, like his Democratic predecessor, attempted to alter the traditional approach to project funding. First, he tried to augment presidential control over project selection by creating an Office of Water Policy to be chaired by the Secretary of the Interior. Congress, however, refused to provide funds for the office's project review functions.[62] Next, the president responded with Executive Order 12322 authorizing the Office of Management and Budget (OMB) to review public works projects, but the Congress stubbornly continued to consider project authorizations that had not been reviewed by OMB.[63] Third, he proposed that the states pay for a substantial portion of project costs. Initially, it looked as though Reagan's cost-sharing proposals might be accepted by the legislative branch, since it too had jumped aboard the "economy in government" bandwagon. But opposition from Westerners and Southerners reduced the possibility of a standardized cost-sharing provision being enacted during Reagan's first term. According to one observer, by 1983 cost-sharing "has become as popular on Capitol Hill and in the ranks of the Reagan administration as an outbreak of mumps."[64]

By the end of Reagan's first term in office the Corps was still a powerhouse in water politics. But the Carter attacks on the Corps' mission, and Reagan's persistence in cutting domestic budgets and downsizing domestic programs, were not isolated incidents. Fundamental changes were occurring in American politics, and these changes were having a real impact on the traditional iron triangle that had long dominated water policy. In the early 1980s there were a number of issues that added up to a demand for basic changes in Corps policy.

One of the issues raised against the Corps for many years was the claim that the Corps had a regional bias. For example, Senator Daniel P. Moynihan of New York claimed in 1979 that there was "an overwhelming regional imbalance in where Corps projects are built."[65] Northern legislators had complained for years that the Corps favored the South. There are a couple of reasons why that was believed to be the case. First, many of the Corps' most controversial projects were in the South, including its biggest project, the Tennessee-Tombigbee Waterway. A second reason for this presumed regional bias has been the considerable visibility and notoriety of Southern legislators who chair important committees. They often irritate their colleagues, and the public, by using their positions to gain a disproportionate number of projects for their districts or states. Senator Robert Byrd of West Virginia is one example of Southern legislators who have done so.

The data presented in table 2.3 show that the impact of these Southern committee chairpersons has been exaggerated. They were able to draw projects to specific areas, but not to the South as a whole. In other words, they were not able to create a regionwide bias in the location of Corps projects. In 1978, only about 16% of the Corps' projects were being constructed in the ten states of the Confederacy (excluding Texas). Twenty years earlier, in 1958, about 14 percent of the Corps' projects were being constructed in the South. Actually, a large percentage of the Corps' projects are in the seventeen Western states in which the Bureau of Reclamation operates (42 percent in 1978). These percentages indicate that the Corps of Engineers was not limited to any particular region of the United States. Its nationwide operation is one of the great advantages that the Corps has over the Bureau of Reclamation, the latter agency having been limited to water development only in the seventeen Western states. However, in politics perception is as important as is reality, so the *perception* of a regional bias helped fuel calls for reforms in the mid-1980s.

A second problem experienced by the Corps in the 1970s and early 1980s was negative publicity. Numerous articles and books attacked the Corps of Engineers. With titles such as *The River Killers*, "Dams and Other Disasters," or "Flooding America in Order to Save It," these writers reflected the growing opposition to massive water projects. Also at this time a Supreme Court justice referred to the Corps as "public enemy number one." Protest went further than just writing, however. Some Corps projects became the sites of demonstrations in which direct action tactics were employed. Even the politically conservative National Taxpayers Union labeled public works projects "fiscally irresponsible."[66]

Table 2.3 *Corps of Engineers Projects by Region*

	South	North	West
1958 Actual Authorized Projects N = 208	30 (14%)	87 (42%)	91 (44%)
1978 Carter Budget Request N = 192	31 (16%)	81 (42%)	80 (42%)
1982 Carter Budget Request N = 186	48 (26%)	67 (36%)	71 (38%)
Proposed Project Deletions, Reagan, 1982-86 N = 5	4	1	0

Source: Corps of Engineers budgets submitted to House Committee on Appropriations, Subcommittee on Public Works.
Notes: South—ten states of the old Confederacy, excluding Texas; West—seventeen states authorized for Bureau of Reclamation projects; North—remaining states in the Northeast and Midwest. Excluded from sample are cross-regional projects, District of Columbia, Puerto Rico, Alaska, and Hawaii.

The opposition also has taken the Corps of Engineers to court. The plaintiffs in these cases are groups such as "Save Our Red River," "Save Our Sound Fisheries," and "League of Kentucky Sportsmen." Not all of the suits are brought by environmentalists. In several instances entire towns banded together to sue the Corps.[67]

Opponents of the Corps pointed to an audit done by the firm of Price, Waterhouse and Company, which concluded that the Corps had not only overbuilt many projects but had understated the costs of those projects. An example was Eufaula Lake in Oklahoma, where only 3 percent of the water was being used, even though the project was completed in 1964.[68] The audit also accused the Corps of establishing artificially low prices for water, which burdens the national taxpayer while encouraging wasteful water use at or near the site. This complaint was endorsed by a number of water experts.[69]

The Corps, as a prominent member of the federal establishment, also faced the conservative, anti-government sentiment that characterized the Reagan administration. For some people, the agency's activities were just another example of a distant federal bureaucracy meddling in local affairs. Much of this opposition came from conservative elements of the population which traditionally were supportive of Corps projects. An example of this public sentiment is found in the appropriations hearings for 1982, where private individuals addressed the subcommittee. The following statement was made by a citizen who was upset by a Corps project next to his home:

> the Corps has been wasteful, unbridled, self-serving, and corrupt. ... Recourse to Corps harassment and other actions is difficult because of the size and complexity of the agency, and its taxpayer-funded legal force. ... The Corps has used its budgetary funds to expand Corps power and influence into the private sector.[70]

In sum, by the mid-1980s the Corps was being criticized by the press, environmental groups, fiscal conservatives, the courts, and even some traditional supporters. And the budget-conscious Reagan administration was resisting most domestic spending programs, including water development. Before the 1984 election the Reagan administration budgets provided a generous increase in the Corps budget, but after winning reelection the president slashed the agency's budget. Congress reacted by reinstating the funds for FY 1986, but it was clear that Congress would have to make some basic changes in federal water policy if it wanted any further projects to be approved by President Reagan. In particular, Reagan insisted that the beneficiaries of projects pay at least part of the cost.

Prior to the election, President Reagan had indicated that his administration would not vigorously pursue project cost-sharing. But after 1984, cost-sharing became the keystone of the administration's effort to reform the way the federal government finances water development. Reagan had numerous allies in Congress, including environmentalists and liberal Democrats who shared his conviction that the long tradition of pork-ladened federal water development projects had to be significantly altered. A coalition for reform took shape soon after Reagan's second inaugural. There was a growing momentum favoring reform, but advocates realized there were still many defenders of the Corps' pork-barrel in Congress. Thus, the best strategy was to produce an omnibus water authorization bill with lots of projects spread all over America, but which contained significant reform provisions as well.

In 1985 the advocates for reform introduced HR 6, a bill that was destined to fundamentally alter the way the Corps operates. The Senate version of the bill contained all of the reforms called for by environmentalists and by the Reagan administration, but the House version quickly became loaded with pet projects, many of which had yet to be approved even by the Corps! Reagan declared he would veto it because "eight percent of the projects are of dubious economic or environmental benefit or have been incompletely studied."[71] Rather than accept the reforms contained in the bill, the House refused to pass HR 6, even though an omnibus authorization bill had not been passed in sixteen years. Jamie Whitten in the House and Robert Byrd in the Senate—legislators well known for their pork-barrel tendencies—led a move to exempt the entire Mississippi River basin (41% of the United States) from the reforms.

The following year the Reagan administration proposed an increase in funding for the Corps, from $2.8 billion to $3.1 billion. This helped buy some support for the president's position on HR 6. The bill included numerous reforms and also authorized 377 new Corps projects with a total price tag of over $16.5 billion.[72] It was made clear to legislators that they would not see any of these new projects unless they also swallowed the reforms. During appropriations hearings that spring, Robert Dawson, Assistant Secretary for Civil Works, testified to the need to pass the reform bill: "I would predict that a year from now when we are here together, we will either be celebrating a new revitalized Army Civil Works program or we will be talking about a project that is withering away … we are looking for an omnibus bill that will give us a new lease on life."[73] Throughout the pivotal year of 1986 the various interests jockeyed for support; clearly a momentous decision was on the table. With only minutes remaining in the 99th Congress, the vote was taken: The bill passed overwhelmingly in both chambers. The strategy of holding new water projects "hostage" until reforms were accepted had worked.

The 1986 Water Resources Development Act (WRDA) was hailed by one senator as "the most significant water resources development bill in over 50 years."[74] The act's most significant changes included:
- Automatically de-authorizing hundreds of unfunded projects.
- Limiting cost overruns, which had been a perennial problem with the Corps and other Defense Department agencies.

- Setting a ceiling on annual construction spending.
- Requiring that fish and wildlife mitigation occur simultaneously with construction, and not simply as an afterthought.
- Eliminating the use of "regional benefits" in the Corps' benefit-cost analyses, which had allowed the agency to grossly inflate project benefits.
- Authorizing a Harbor Maintenance Trust Fund which, with the existing Inland Waterways Trust Fund, permits the Corps to collect user fees to support its work.
- Creating an Office of Environmental Policy in the Civil Works Directorate.
- Establishing an Environmental Mitigation Fund.
- Providing authorization for the Corps to modify existing projects to improve environmental quality.
- And perhaps most important, mandating cost-sharing.

The cost-sharing provision in the bill requires the nonfederal sponsors of a project—usually state or local governments—to pay between 25 and 100 percent of project costs, depending on the purposes of the project. It also requires that the nonfederal money be paid "up-front," that is, at the beginning of the project rather than after the project is finished. Senator Stafford of Vermont claimed that cost-sharing was "the single most important reform ever crafted onto the Nation's water resources development policy,"[75] because it changed the nature of the Corps' political environment. Suddenly local sponsors had a powerful, material incentive to be judicious in their choice of projects. The year after HR 6 became law, General Heiberg of the Corps testified in Congress that "We have lost through this bill the epithet of pork. It has changed the way we do business."[76]

The passage of the 1986 Water Resources Development Act came as a shock to some agency employees. "It was revolutionary," one employee told us. "We in the rank and file did not like it, but now we've gotten used to it." Continuing its long tradition, agency officials thus have attempted to turn adversity into opportunity, for it is now clear that the act was the beginning of what can be called the "modern era" of the Army Corps of Engineers. Although many politicians and bureaucrats initially excoriated the cost-sharing requirement, eventually it became obvious that cost-sharing creates a built-in funding mechanism;

at a time when federal resources have become increasingly scarce, it is a distinct advantage to have institutionalized access to non-federal funding sources.

The modern era of the Corps of Engineers has presented a number of new opportunities which the agency has embraced with vigor. These new assignments certainly are not without controversy or opposition, but they do provide new avenues of agency expansion. As it has done in the past, the agency has striven to embark in new directions while also attempting to maintain its ties with its more traditional supporters. In essence, the Corps follows a strategy well known to countries or regions that in the past produced a single commodity; in the new world order they expand and diversify to protect themselves. The Corps' eggs are now in a number of new baskets.

Four new missions will keep the Corps employed—and politically viable—well into the twenty-first century, we think. They are: the wetlands program; infrastructure development; environmental restoration and protection; and regional water management. In addition, there undoubtedly will be opportunities to satisfy old allies with a modest serving of traditional projects. Each of these missions will be discussed as to its political promise and possible pitfalls.

In 1972 Congress passed the first of several bills that are known as the Clean Water Acts. Section 404 of the 1972 act requires that anyone proposing to deposit "dredged or fill material" into navigable U. S. waters obtain a permit from the Chief of Engineers.[77] The act itself did not specifically mention wetlands, but a 1975 court decision determined that wetlands were indeed bodies of water and therefore were subject to the 404 permitting process.[78]

The 404 wetlands program, which the Corps jointly administers with three other federal agencies, has given it a visible role in protecting America's environment. And, contrary to the predictions of many environmentalists, the Corps has been diligent in its enforcement of the 404 provision. A 1993 GAO review of "takings cases" filed against the United States government, for example, found that the most common complaint was that the Corps refused to grant a permit. The second most common complaint was that either the EPA or the Corps had issued a cease and desist order.[79] This does not mean, however, that the United States has halted the loss of wetlands; the same GAO report notes that, between 1974 and 1983, the country lost an average of 290,000 acres of wetlands every year. But that loss cannot be laid entirely at the Corps of Engineers' doorstep. Other ongoing commercial activities, over which the federal government has little control, are the major cause.

While the 404 permit program has provided the agency with an enhanced stature among some interests, it has proven to be a difficult program to administer. Several attempts to create a biologically valid—and politically acceptable—definition of a wetland indicates how problematic the issue is. In 1987 the Corps developed a working definition of wetlands that many thought was too narrow. So the agency began working with the other agencies that jointly administer the program, and in 1989 they developed a "wetlands manual" that contained a much more expansive concept. This, however, infuriated many developers and their allies in Congress, so it was back to the drawing board. In 1991, it was noted before Congress that "the four agencies that were party to the manual are hard at work on the revisions."[80] Some legislators were so incensed over the issue that they attached a rider to the FY 1992 appropriations bill prohibiting the agencies from using the 1989 manual until they complied with the Administrative Procedures Act and held public hearings to determine what is a wetland. This in turn sparked a defense of the manual. The defense was led by Congressman Wayne Gilchrist, whose district surrounds Chesapeake Bay. He introduced the "Wetlands Improvement Act of 1991," which mandated continued use of the manual.[81] The bill did not become law, but the controversy over the wetlands manual is indicative of the political sensitivity of this issue. Currently the Corps is using its 1987 definition of wetlands until the National Academy of Sciences completes a study on the issue. That report was published in May of 1995.

The Corps' latest effort to refine its wetlands program involves "compensatory mitigation" and "mitigation banking." These techniques would award mitigation credits to permittees for creating or restoring wetlands when their duly permitted activities negatively impacted wetlands. In other words, if the Corps issues a permit to a developer that destroyed some wetlands, the permittee would have to replace the loss with a comparable wetland area elsewhere. This minimizes the adverse economic impact of the 404 program, while still meeting the national goal of "no net loss" of wetlands.[82] The Clinton administration's "Wetland Plan" currently endorses this market-based approach.

A second area of growth for the Corps is infrastructure development. In the past this was simply referred to as "public works," but that term became associated with pork barrel politics, so in the 1980s policymakers began using the antiseptic term *infrastructure*. In the last fifteen years there have been numerous studies documenting the decline and imminent collapse of America's transportation network, including waterways, its water supply systems, and other public structures.[83] The Corps responded to this crisis by developing an impressive infrastructure initiative. In testimony before an appropriations subcommittee, Assistant Secretary for Civil Works Robert Page stated that the agency's budget for fiscal year 1991 "proposes to place new emphasis on improvement of American infrastructure."[84]

Of course, in many ways this is what the Corps has been doing for nearly 200 years. Thus the infrastructure problem presents an opportunity tailor-made for the Corps of Engineers. It is a mission waiting to happen, and the agency is responding well.

Thus far the amount of money in the Corps' budget specifically allocated to the infrastructure line-item is relatively small. For example, the agency requested $21.4 million for FY 1993. However, the potential costs of upgrading the nation's water infrastructure are staggering; the National Infrastructure Advisory Committee's 1984 report stated that "water [development] needs are projected to be nearly $100 billion through the year 2000."[85] More recently the Corps was the lead agency of an interagency task force called the "Federal Infrastructure Strategy Program." The task force compiled a series of reports from 1991 to 1994. These reports document past investments, current and future needs, and formulate a national strategy to meet those needs.[86]

A third major thrust within the contemporary Corps is in the area of environmental mitigation and restoration. The agency may very well spend its second 200 years cleaning up damage from its first 200 years. This mission was recently explained before Congress by a Corps spokesman: "Environmental activities of the Corps have evolved over recent years into a coherent program with a unified philosophy—the restoration and preservation of significant environmental resources consistent with the dual fiscal principles of efficiency and cost sharing."[87]

Perhaps the best example of this activity is the agency's massive effort to restore the Kissimmee River watershed in Florida. In the 1960s the Corps channelized the river, thus destroying its natural flow pattern. This in turn had a devastating impact on the wetlands of southern Florida, including the world-famous Everglades. The Water Resources Development Act of 1988 authorized a Kissimmee River Headwaters Revitalization Project, and a 1992 act authorized the Kissimmee River Restoration Project. Basically, in its effort to put the river back where it was the Corps is engaged in "one of the largest environmental restoration projects ever undertaken."[88] The Kissimmee project can be described as the TVA of the 1990's.

Other restoration and mitigation projects include an effort to restore the anadromous fish runs in the Columbia River Basin, which were dramatically reduced by both Corps and Bureau of Reclamation dams, and a cooperative program with the South Florida Water Management District. In addition, the environmental mission has provided the Corps with a way to spend even more money on what environmentalists call the greatest boondoggle in history, the Tennessee-Tombigbee Waterway. The 1991 appropriations bill included $15 million to restore wildlife habitat along the waterway.

The Corps' environmental projects go beyond just repairing damage done in the past, however. Agency personnel are working with both EPA and the Department of Defense on environmental restoration projects. The agency even has a "Magnetic Levitation Transportation Pilot Program." All of this activity spurred Congressman Pursell to remark in appropriations hearings, "Mr. Secretary [for Civil Works], based on your testimony this year we see a dramatic major sensitivity to the environment."[89] The following year the Corps' budget stressed "the Army's new environmental approaches." All nine of the agency's proposed new reconnaissance studies that year were for environmental restoration.[90]

The Corps' transition to environmental protector has been encouraged by the Clinton administration. However, the Republican-dominated 104th Congress may not be so supportive of the agency moving further in this direction. Once again the Corps may have to adjust its objectives to a swiftly changing political reality.

A final area where the Corps has been investigating new directions for itself relates to the shift from water *development* to water *management*.

The former involves structural solutions such as constructing dams and levees, while the latter relies on nonstructural alternatives such as planning, regulation, price incentives, and efficiency enhancement. Water management also calls for a greater degree of cooperation and joint effort among various agencies of government, among levels of government, and with nongovernmental organizations (ngo's).

Probably the best example of this shift to enhanced water management is the government's response to what came to be termed the Great Flood of '93, which did between $12 and $14 billion in damages, and led to $6 billion in federal aid to flood victims. Shortly after the summer flood ended, President Clinton set up the Interagency Floodplain Management Review Committee, chaired by General Gerald Galloway. Its final report presents a convincing argument that the nation's flood policy should be revised:

> Recognition in the early 1960s of the natural functions and resources of the floodplain—habitat, scenic beauty, water filtration, storm buffer, ground-water recharge, and floodwater storage—caused the nation to reconsider its policy of supporting wholesale conversion of natural areas to other uses. Persistent flood losses during a half century of flood-control programs raise serious questions concerning the long-term efficiency of such programs. A movement to reduce flood damages through nonstructural means, limiting unwise development of the floodplain and evacuating those at most risk, gradually has become a viable alternative to the construction of dams, levees, and floodwalls.[91]

Another area of innovation in water management is occurring at the other hydrological extreme, drought. In 1989, in the midst of a serious drought in the American West, the Corps began a "National Study of Water Management During Drought." This study recommended dramatic changes in how the nation responds to water shortages. In its report to Congress the drought study team succinctly identified the weaknesses of past policy and the promise for improved water management:

> There is broad agreement, if not consensus, among water scholars about what the primary flaws in American water management are: inefficiency and lack of holistic management (rooted in the divisions of water management responsibilities according to political boundaries and agency

missions); the practice of pricing water below its real value; and the failure to involve stakeholders in water management.. .... As the era of dam building draws to a close, performance through sheer abundance of water supply storage must now be assured by more management.[92]

Indeed, more management is what the nation is getting from the Corps. It is not only what it has always been, the "Nation's Builder," but more recently the agency has become a vast repository for research, planning, and innovative water management techniques. A list of its recent studies indicates the diversity of the agency's interests and activities:

- International Joint Commission (U. S.-Canada) Great Lakes Fluctuating Lake Levels Study
- Missouri River Water Control Study
- Columbia River Water Control Study
- Environmental Restoration of the Kissimmee River in Florida
- Florida Everglades Restoration Project
- Upper Mississippi River Flood Plain Management Study
- National Drought Management Study
- Alabama-Coosa-Tallapossa (ACT) and Appalachicola Chattahoochee-Flint (ACF) River Basins Study
- Red River Chloride Control Study (water quality improvement for water supply)
- Water Supply Planning and Conservation for Military Facilities.

Contained in this list is a nationwide network of research, management initiatives, and, in some cases, construction potential. It is a vast expanse of activities befitting a reinvented bureaucratic superstar. Additionally, the Corps still has a solid base of traditional supporters; agency insiders point out that, some day, there will be a need for more of the usual kinds of water development.[93]

In fact, the "some day" is now. Notwithstanding the numerous changes occurring within the agency, described above, many members of Congress continue to practice distributive politics. Although WRDA 1986 was intended to drastically alter water politics, its effects so far have been more modest. Since its passage, cost-sharing on Corps projects has averaged about 25 percent. That is, local sponsors have contributed one-quarter of the project's total costs, while the federal government assumed the remainder. To a vote-seeking legislator, obtaining a 75 percent federal contribution to a local or regional water project is hardly an insignificant accomplishment.

An examination of recent project authorization and appropriations bills makes it clear that Congress has not completely given up on the pork barrel. As their predecessors did, contemporary chief executives from Jimmy Carter to Bill Clinton have proposed funding a small number of new Corps projects; these usually have been scrutinized as to whether they are in the national interest, as opposed to purely local or state interest. Then, the House and Senate toss in a few dozen more projects, which often are in the districts or states of appropriations committee members. Although the president strenuously objects, and may threaten a veto, most projects generally manage to make their way through Congress.

A review of articles from the Congressional Quarterly's *Weekly Report* published between 1988 and 1994 further documents the fact that "old" and "new" water politics coexist today in Washington. For example: "The final [FY 1989 appropriations] bill funded start-up of construction on about 40 new water projects, essentially following the House position. The Reagan Administration had originally requested 13 new starts"; "Water Pork Makes Comeback in FY '90 Spending Bill"; "Super Collider Paves the Way for Members' Pork Projects"; "Chairmen Deftly Divvy up Water Projects [in 1991]"; "The House passed a water projects authorization bill that significantly alters the cost-sharing formula and funds $1 billion worth of projects over the administration's budget ceiling; Bush promises a veto"; "For FY '94 Congress provided $134.6 million for 52 new project starts; Clinton wanted to spend only $30 million. ... Of the 52 new starts, 27 are located in the states of members of the House and Senate Water Appropriations Subcommittees"; and, "For FY '95 the House Appropriations Committee funded 18 new Corps projects that were not requested in the Clinton budget."[94]

It is within this difficult dichotomous political environment—a strong lobby for change and a perhaps equally strong lobby defending the status quo—that the Corps of Engineers must work. Not an easy task. All things considered, the agency has done a respectable job of threading its way through this Scylla and Charybdis of contemporary water politics. However, environmentalists still tend to look with suspicion on Corps' activities, and so agency officials have more work to do in building bridges to reach that community. Moreover, the environmental lobby has been successful in promoting the interests of what it sees as a more environmentally correct agency within the federal establishment. That is the EPA. Thus a real challenge to the Corps as it enters its third century of existence is in convincing policymakers and the general public that it can be both a civil engineering *and* an environmental engineering agency. Its track record to date gives one reason to think that it can accomplish this feat.

THE U.S. FOREST SERVICE

Several agencies came into being around the turn of the century, as the progressive and conservation movements joined forces to produce significant changes in governmental policy. The movements were combined under the presidential leadership of Theodore Roosevelt, who considered his efforts on behalf of a conservation program to be his most important contribution as president.[95]

Three agencies in this study are the products of what Samuel P. Hays termed the "progressive conservation movement": The Bureau of Reclamation, the National Park Service, and the U.S. Forest Service. Of the three, the Forest Service stands out as the most complete representation of the several concerns and issues which fueled the early conservation movement in this country. This achievement is due in no small part to the foresight and vision of the Service's first chief forester, Gifford Pinchot, an individual whose crusade on behalf of conservation values was nearly as important as that of Roosevelt's. In fact, the two men in combination were what gave the movement many of its lasting achievements.

> The Eastern hero of the conservation movement, and by far the most influential figure in the field, was Gifford Pinchot. Born in Connecticut of an old Pennsylvania family and educated at Yale, Pinchot chose forestry as a career because of a youthful inclination, and his wealthy father encouraged him to get training in Europe, where the science was most advanced. ... Pinchot's most important friend was Theodore Roosevelt. ... They were both Ivy Leaguers who had mastered the out-of-doors, both endowed with boundless energy and interested in translating ideas into action.[96]

Though the Forest Service was not officially created until 1905 with Pinchot at its head, the momentum behind its creation had been building for some twenty-five years. What had been occurring in the United States with respect to one of its most valuable natural resources, the forest, was nothing less than a national scandal. Forest practices, if they could be called that, simply amounted to cutting down the most valuable trees, abandoning the cut-over land and then moving on to more lucrative areas. The timber industry moved west with the frontier, and toward the end of the nineteenth century the big timber interests "had been looking forward to cutting a similar path [of destruction] across the public domain."[97] In his valuable autobiography, Pinchot described the prevailing mentality in this manner:

> The lumbermen, whose industry was then the third greatest in this country, regarded forest devastation as normal and second growth as a delusion of fools, whom they cursed on the rare occasions when they happened to think of them. And as for sustained yield, no such idea had ever entered their heads.[98]

Beginning around 1870, a number of bills pertaining to the public timberlands appeared in Congress, but it wasn't until 1891 that "the most important legislation in the history of forestry in America slipped through Congress without question and without debate."[99] The 1891 Act dealt principally with the repeal of the 1878 Timber and Stone Act, but a small unnoticed amendment paved the way for the creation in due time of the national forest system. Section 24 of the 1891 act states:

> That the President of the United States may, from time to time, set apart and reserve, in any State or Territory having public land bearing forests, in any part of the public lands wholly or in part covered with timber or undergrowth, whether of commercial value or not, as public reservations, and the President shall, by public proclamation, declare the establishment of such reservations and the limits thereof.[100]

Presidential initiative in creating forest reserves was quickly forthcoming. By 1897 some 17 1/2 million acres had been withdrawn from the public domain, and in February of 1897 with just ten days left in office President Cleveland signed an executive order (thereby enraging Western representatives and timber interests) to set aside an additional

21 million acres of forest reserves, thus more than doubling the existing forest system.[101]

A good part of the next seven years, from 1898 to 1905, was taken up with the attempt to merge the existing forest reserves—administered by the notoriously corrupt General Land Office in the Interior Department—with the small group of foresters working out of the Agriculture Department. Pinchot was tireless in his efforts to provide a secure organizational base for the fledgling national forest system:

> The Government forests—43,000,000 acres of Forest Reserves, and several times more millions of unreserved public timberland—were all in the charge of the Interior Department, which had not a single forester to look after them.
>
> All the Government foresters, the whole two of them, were in the Department of Agriculture, with not a single acre of Government forest in their charge. Forests and foresters were in completely separate water-tight compartments.
>
> It was a fantastic situation.[102]

In 1905 Pinchot succeeded. That January Congress passed an act authorizing the transfer of the forest reserves from the Interior Department to Agriculture, thereby merging the Forestry Division with the forests and placing Pinchot at the head of government forestry. One of the most powerful agencies of the federal government thus was created.

In recalling the conservation movement of this period, there is a tendency to emphasize only the natural resources aspects of the movement and to ignore the political, economic, and social issues of the day. That is why Hays' term, *progressive conservation*, is more appropriate than simply *conservation*, for it connects what time has tended to disconnect. And it is important to an understanding of the organizational history of the Forest Service to remember that progressivism and conservation were symbiotic concerns. In other words, the development of this agency into a highly professional, dedicated, and powerful organization can be explained only by recalling the philosophy on which it was founded. Perhaps more than any other agency in our sample, the Forest Service owes much of its present strength to its ideological foundation and to its founder. According to Dana and Fairfax, Pinchot's commitment to scientific forestry created the aura of expertise which still surrounds the Forest Service: "Under Pinchot's leadership, the agency began its long history as the epitome of technical competence and scientific management."[103]

Forestry—that is, the scientific and technical management of the timber resource according to the principles of wise use and sustained yield—is the academic discipline upon which Pinchot founded government forestry. This professional base has, as we will point out presently, served the agency well. But coupled with this was a reformist impulse which motivated a generation of conservationists to bring about some basic changes in American society. Toward the end of his autobiography, Pinchot wrote directly and eloquently of his conception of conservation:

> The Conservation policy then has three great purposes.
> First: to wisely use, protect, preserve, and renew the natural sources of the earth.
> Second: to control the use of the natural resources and their products in the common interest, and to secure their distribution to the people at fair and reasonable charges for goods and services.
> Third: to see to it that the rights of the people to govern themselves shall not be controlled by great monopolies through their power over natural resources. Two of the principal ways in which lack of Conservation works out in damage to the general welfare are: (A) By destruction of forests, erosion of soils, injury of waterways, and waste of nonrenewable mineral resources. Here is strong reason for Government control. (B) By monopoly of natural and human resources, their products and application, and of the instruments by which these are made available.
> Monopoly means power—power not only over the supply of natural resources, but also power to fix prices, and to exact unfair profits which lead to higher living costs for the people. It is the very essence of democracy that the greatest advantage of each of us is best reached through common prosperity of all of us. Monopoly is the denial of that great truth.
> Monopoly of resources which prevents, limits, or destroys equality of opportunity is one of the most effective of all ways to control and limit human rights, especially the right of self-government.
> Monopoly on the loose is a source of many of the economic, political, and social evils which afflict the sons of men. Its abolition or regulation is an inseparable part of the Conservation policy.[104]

The agency's commitment to both progressive, public-spirited values and to scientific forestry ultimately contributed to its growth and widespread acceptability. Dana and Fairfax observed that "Forestry was less a movement than a maturing, diversifying profession."[105] This diversification led the Forest Service, in due time, into a number of new areas of activity, and helped create the general perception of the agency as a highly respected source of expertise and information on natural resources issues.

The evolution of the Forest Service bears many resemblances to the history of the Corps. As we show in chapter 5, both agencies weathered the politically difficult decade of the 1980s to remain powerful organizations—although not so powerful as they once were. The Forest Service, like the Corps, has sustained itself over a ninety-year history by its adherence to utilitarian and pragmatic values. That is, the agency has always stood for the use and development of the public forests of the nation, and it has, by and large, administered the national forest system through applying the general principle of "the greatest good for the greatest number, in the long run." How the agency has operationalized this principle is important to understand. It began with the recognition that scientific forest management meant that forests were to be managed with a view toward maximizing all possible uses of the forest resource. A constant and assured supply of timber—what Pinchot referred to as "tree farming"—may have been the primary product of a forest. But foresters were not to lose sight of the forest for the trees: Also of value were, and are, watershed and wildlife management, mineral extraction, grazing of domesticated animals, and outdoor recreation. All potential uses of the forest were to be balanced, somehow, by government foresters who had a sound, practical knowledge of the particular forest in question. This practice of multiple-use management —a concept very similar to the Corps' multipurpose water development philosophy—developed over the years. It was eventually given statutory recognition by Congress in its passage of the Multiple Use-Sustained Yield Act of 1960. The Forest Service called this act "a major milestone in the long history of the National Forest."[106]

The history of the Forest Service, like the Corps, reveals a remarkable ability to sense changing public priorities and to adapt its mission to meet those demands. This organizational flexibility is in part a product of the nature of the agency's mission. Both agencies were given broad mandates to manage, conserve, use, and develop the resources in question. Both the Corps and the Forest Service benefited, up until recently, from less scrutiny on the part of Congress and their departmental superiors than has been the case with several of the other agencies in this study. In other words, the agencies were given considerable leeway in how they attained their objectives, and they used this leeway at least in part to gain further advantages. Congress infrequently challenged the agencies' expertise.

Furthermore, these agencies have benefited from the fact that they are the providers of basic goods and services to a broad-based constituency. The Corps' pork barrel is of course notorious; it is perhaps a lesser known fact that there has existed—since even before the actual creation of the Forest Service—a network of interests and alliances supportive of that agency's mission and programs. Its founder Gifford Pinchot skillfully utilized interest groups such as the American Forestry Association, the National Board of Trade, and the American Forest Congress in his efforts to found the federal agency. Once founded, the Forest Service and the timber industry developed a mutually supportive alliance, which at least one historian of the Progressive Era viewed in harsh terms:

> In practice the Forestry Service [sic] allowed timber operators to overcut, even devastate national forests in many places. The line between a cordial relationship and a corrupt relationship was hard to draw when private operators and a public agency became as close as the Forestry Service and the timber industry did. These problems were poorly understood at the time, as the famous Pinchot-Ballinger affair was to demonstrate.[107]

Another strength is that the Forest Service has always conceived of itself as a multipurpose organization. This was demonstrated early in its history, when in 1918, in an appropriations committee hearing, the agency spoke of four principal activities in which it was then engaged. First, management of the national forest system was discussed as a primary function. This function was further broken down into timber production, forest maintenance, recreation, water and power development, and so on. A second principal activity was land classification and surveying. A third area of concern was fire-fighting. In the years preceding 1918, droughts had resulted in devastating forest fires throughout the country. In response to these fire losses, the agency emphasized the improvement of its fire fighting techniques; the use of airplanes was suggested in the hearings at this time but was then dismissed as too impractical and expensive. The fourth area of activity was research. The agency has always placed a strong emphasis on forest research, and in 1909 "experiment stations" were first established within the agency to do long-range empirical investigations, ranging from studying the results of various cutting techniques to observing the effects on timber growth of different climatic conditions. Over the years, a period of sustained research on a particular subject has generally preceded the introduction of major new activities in the agency's growing repertoire. Hence the agency's research activity has been an especially fertile source of strength.

Following World War I the Forest Service began developing a major new functional activity. It saw a need to extend scientific forestry practices beyond national forest boundaries, and so "cooperative" activities with states and with private forest owners were greatly increased at this time. In 1924 the Clarke-McNary Act was passed which authorized the expenditure of federal funds for federal-state cooperation in tree planting, fire fighting, and forest planning. The Forest Service thus assumed an educator's role with respect to the applied science of forestry. Having had the largest laboratory in the country in which to experiment, it now felt itself ready to, in Pinchot's words, "spread the gospel of practical forestry."[108] In 1980 spreading the good news continued to be important. The Forest Service's 1981 budget request estimated that "research and cooperative forest activities is ... to be almost double the 1977 level."[109]

By 1930, the chief forester stated that "a Federal policy of forestry has been developing for almost 60 years. It has been built up by successive legislative enactments and the resulting activities. It is not a specific and limited program, but rather is the gradual unfolding of a national purpose."[110] This statement summarizes very well the prevailing ideology of successful organizations in our sample. Personnel see their functions as continuous ones, constantly evolving, and intimately linked to the national welfare. This attitude is in marked contrast to the kind of perception informing agency personnel in several of the other agencies in this study. For example, Bureau of Reclamation and Soil Conservation Service officials focus on specific and finite objectives;

often in testimony, there was mention made of a time when their activities would be completed and they would (God forbid!) go out of business. Not so with the Forest Service, however, or with the Corps and the National Park Service. On the whole, they see their missions as being both permanent and vital to the nation's well-being. An evolutionary perspective is built in to these agencies; little fear of extinction is ever expressed.

Agencies like the Forest Service tend to be innovative in their approach to problems, which is not to say that they cannot also, at times, be conservative in their outlook. Rather, they have an expansive tendency. The history of the Forest Service contains numerous examples of such imaginative thinking. For example, one that we like best occurred in the early 1930s when the agency turned its attention to the problems of soil erosion in the Great Plains states. Following a severe drought the agency launched its "Great Plains Shelterbelt Project." The project, enthusiastically supported by President Franklin Roosevelt, envisioned a huge windbreak of trees to be planted in a strip 100 miles wide and extending from Texas to the Canadian border. By 1938 the chief of the agency reported that "since 1935, and despite drought, grasshopper plagues, and dust storms, nearly 7,000 miles of new shelterbelts have been established."[111] In 1942, after the Service had planted over 18,000 miles of shelterbelts, the program was turned over to the Soil Conservation Service, another Agriculture Department agency, to administer.

The agency responded in a similar manner during the 1950s, when outdoor recreation demand sharply rose. It initiated Operation Outdoors, a five-year program of repair and expansion of its recreational facilities. In 1961 it instituted its Visitor Information Service to provide visitor centers, nature trails, and interpretive services for the burgeoning number of visitors to the national forests. In all of this, of course, the Forest Service was engaging in a healthy competition with its principal rival, the National Park Service, with outdoor recreation being the common, programmatic ground between them.

By 1950 the agency had organized itself into three main functional divisions. All of the agency's many programs or activities fell under one of the following three headings:

1. Management, protection and development of the national forest and national rangeland systems—a system encompassing approximately 191 million acres of land in 1994;
2. Cooperation with state and private forest land owners in fire protection and in promoting better timber practices;
3. Forest and range research.

This tripartite division lasted forty years, until the Congress decreed a fourth primary function. Reflecting the public's considerable interest in global issues, in 1991 an International Forestry mission was added to the agency's traditional three-point agenda.

When another wave of environmental concern swept across the country in the late 1960s, the Forest Service was well-equipped to handle the resulting increase in public scrutiny of its programs. To hardcore environmentalists, the Corps was public enemy number one, but the Forest Service also came in for its share of criticism. For example, the Bitterroot National Forest controversy, which concerned the agency's practice of clear-cutting, touched off years of investigation by Congress, and others, concerning not only the practice of clear-cutting but virtually all of the agency's management practices as well as its basic philosophy. The legislative result was the National Forest Management Act of 1976.[112]

But despite considerable criticism from environmentalists, the agency's response to the passage of NEPA in 1969 was similar to that of the Corps of Engineers. It was positive. Neither agency openly criticized the act, nor did their officals dismiss it and/or minimize its significance. In 1970, for example, forest officials gave Congress their reaction to NEPA:

> Since practically all Forest Service management activities relate directly or indirectly to the environment, this Act supplemented and strengthened historic conservation efforts. However, in keeping with intent of the Act, the Forest Service now has focused even more attention on environmental situations and is analyzing and studying the ecological consequences of its various activities more thoroughly.[113]

In 1972 the agency estimated that it spent $13 million in implementing NEPA. By 1974 that figure rose to $28 million. Despite, or perhaps because of, increasing public scrutiny of its programs and practices, the Forest Service committed a great deal of time and energy throughout the 1970s to an examination of its own activities.

In response to these various political pressures and the 1964 Wilderness Act the Forest Service stepped up efforts to inventory its lands for possible inclusion in the National Wilderness System. Through the RARE I and RARE II programs (Roadless Area Review and Evaluation), the Service attempted to categorize land as to its suitability for wilderness designation. This inventory included nearly all of the 190 million acres in the national forest system, and was designed to allow for "massive involvement of the public."[114] Reflecting the Forest Service's commitment to the ideal of multiple use, the RARE II Program was billed as a "quest for balance in public land use."[115] They, like the Corps, launched an extensive public participation program throughout the 1970s in an effort to respond positively to new demands.

The Forest Service also quickly established itself as a leader in the movement toward governmentwide comprehensive planning. Congress mandated extensive planning programs in the Forest Service through passage of the 1974 Forest and Rangeland Renewable Resources Planning Act (RPA for short), which was amended by the 1976 National Forest Management Act.[116] These acts required the Forest Service to formulate resource management plans for all units of the national forest system by 1985. The RPA required a two-stage process consisting of, first, an assessment, that is, an inventory of present and potential future uses of the nation's forests and rangelands, and second, a program stage where various alternative plans were presented and analyzed.[117] While this planning process certainly was not problem-free,[118] the Service used congressionally-mandated planning to expand its budget and justify its many activities. According to Christopher Leman,

> Although the RPA has been given too much credit for the Forest Service's subsequent budgetary windfalls, there is no mistaking that the agency has done very well in appropriations since 1974. For example, for the first year after release of the first RPA report, fiscal year 1977 appropriations for the Forest Service increased 47 percent, more than the total increase in the four years from 1977 to 1980 for the Bureau of Land Management, an agency with functions similar to the Forest Service's, but without a total resource assessment and program development effort.[119]

The Forest Service also actively pursued the requirement for public participation in this process, using to its advantage the requisite public meetings and hearings. The RPA statute proved to be popular with the Forest Service constituency and with its allies in Congress. Thus the agency adroitly cultivated its support through a comprehensive planning process that served for many years as a model for other natural resource managers. As an indication of its importance, until Reaganomics forced a significant change in priorities, research to meet RPA goals had been the fastest-growing component of the Forest Service's budget.[120]

Enter Ronald Reagan, the country's most conservative president since Calvin Coolidge occupied the White House in the 1920s. Upon taking office in 1981, President Reagan vowed to be a "Roosevelt in reverse": He and his administrators would cut and slash a federal bureaucracy that had grown enormously since the New Deal. They would also impose a new set of priorities on what was left. To effect these changes in the Forest Service, an agency with a well-known reputation for independence, the president appointed John Crowell to an assistant secretary's position in the Agriculture Department. Crowell formerly had been an attorney for a large timber company, and in his four years in office overseeing the Forest Service Crowell "tried his darndest," a former employee said, to reform the agency. So did George Dunlop who replaced Crowell in 1985. Dunlop previously had been on the staff of North Carolina's Republican senator, Jesse Helms, and in his capacity as assistant secretary Dunlop behaved "like Attila the Hun," an interviewee in the agency told us.

The 1980s proved to be difficult years for the Forest Service. Not only did its total appropriation remain static during Reagan's first term, but more significantly the administration succeeded in doing what it set out to do when it entered office. That was to change program priorities within the agency. In the process it significantly altered the public's image of the Forest Service. Funds for recreation, planning, research, and technical assistance to state and private forestry were continually targeted for reductions, while appropriations for production-oriented programs, such as energy, minerals, road building, and timber, were increased.

Specifically, in President Reagan's first budget submitted to Congress, that for FY 1982, a total Forest Service appropriation of $2.2 billion was requested. This represented a 20 percent reduction from the previous year. However, almost all of this proposed reduction came from the Administration's ultimately unsuccessful attempt to eliminate the Land and Water Conservation Fund. The LWCF was a federal land acquisition program set up in the 1960s to benefit not only the Forest Service but several other resource-managing agencies.[121] Although the Reagan and Bush regimes continued to push for drastic cuts in the agency's land acquisition budget through 1990, the Congress decided otherwise. In Reagan's proposed budget for FY 1986, for example, the land acquisition program was to drop from $43.6 million to a mere $2.3 million. Instead, Congress authorized a Forest Service land acquisition budget of $49 million for FY 1988. The program increased to $88.7 million in FY 1993, despite President Bush's proposal to cut it to $5.5 million by FY 1990.[122]

We examine in more detail the agency's budget in chapter 5. However, notwithstanding the fact that its appropriation showed an absolute increase during the Reagan-Bush years, much of the increase was tied to the timber production program. In discussing funding increases for wildlife, and for fisheries management and support, at the outset of the Reagan presidency, Chief Max Peterson told Congress:

> That increase is to be used in support of the timber program. You will recall we are going into roadless areas where we have not previously had detailed information on wildlife and fish. We will be doing land-disturbing activities, so we feel we need to increase support as we move into these previously unroaded areas.[123]

The pressures to increase timber production on the national forests had been operating for a long time. Charles Porter, a former congressman from Oregon, wrote in 1992 that the trend toward overcutting in Oregon and Washington began more than thirty years ago. "Out here in the Pacific Northwest federal forest managers in Region 6 ... permitted 10 percent more timber to be cut than was grown in 1952, a percentage that went up to 57 percent in 1987, 25 years later. No one seems to know," he added, "what the accumulated debt is in board feet, but it has to be staggering."[124]

It is evident from the data in table 2.4 that the Forest Service regularly harvested in the neighborhood of 10–12 BBF (billion board feet) since the mid-1960s. Why then, did the agency come in for such a barrage of negative publicity and a bevy of lawsuits beginning in the mid-1980s? Three reasons, we think. First, there is the cumulative effect that high timber harvests had on the national forest system, which Congressman Porter and others pointed out. Second, the harvests were coming from a continually shrinking resource base. In order to comply with environmental objectives, the agency in the 1970s withdrew large tracts of land for wilderness designation and to protect bird and animal habitat. That left less land in which to do as much or more cutting. It gradually became apparent that the level of harvests prior to 1980 could not be sustained. Third, the Forest Service was being told by President Reagan's political appointees to the Agriculture Department that they wanted even higher yields from the national forests. In making that demand, the Reagan administration went overboard.

Table 2.4 Timber Harvests on National Forests, 1950-1995

YEAR	VOLUME IN MILLIONS BOARD FEET
1950	3,501,568
1955	6,877,535
1960	9,366,897
1965	11,243,725
1970	11,526,725
1975	9,173,785
1980	9,178,209
1985	10,941,266
1990	10,500,278
1993	5,916,938
1995*	5,000,000

Source: USDA Forest Service, Timber Management Division, 1994.
*Estimate, Appendix to the Budget of the United States, 1994.

The Forest Service tried to resist those demands. Shortly before he left office in January 1985, Assistant Secretary John Crowell wrote the chief of the agency "another in a series of memos by which I have expressed dissatisfaction to you about the process of formulating the RPA recommended program."[125] Crowell listed nine shortcomings in the agency's long-range plan, as mandated by the Forest and Rangeland Renewable Resources Planning Act of 1974. These included the agency's reluctance to balance receipts and expenditures so as to bring "the National Forest System to a profit-making situation," its hesitancy to impose user fees on the recreating public, and its disregard for "straight-line outputs" at least until FY 1990 in the fish and wildlife, recreation, and research programs.

But the assistant secretary's primary grievance concerned timber yields, and the agency's refusal to embrace the administration's basic principles: That the "national forests are an extremely valuable asset" and that they "need to produce a monetary return more nearly commensurate with the value they represent than has ever been so before. Monetary returns," Crowell wrote, "are particularly important at a time when the national debt exceeds $1.5 trillion, and when annual budget deficits are … $200 million."[126] Crowell gave the chief ten days to submit a plan showing a rise in timber sales that would "reach a 20 billion board foot annual level by 2030."

A frustrated Crowell resigned just after writing this memo, and the Forest Service did not comply with the assistant secretary's demands to completely redo its RPA recommended program. Nevertheless, the pressures to make the forests turn a profit continued through the 1980s. The Timber Supply Relief Act of 1984, which bailed out an ailing timber industry by instructing the Forest Service to buy back what it had previously sold, and then resell it, was symptomatic of presidential and congressional priorities during the decade. Although the act received relatively little attention when it was passed—nothing like the notoriety given to the Chrysler and Lockheed bailouts—it wasn't long before environmental activists began adding things up (or subtracting them as the case may be), and objecting to the bottom line.

With increasing frequency from 1984 to the present, environmentalists trained their sights on the Forest Service. The agency inherited, from the Corps of Engineers, the unflattering distinction of being Public Enemy Number One. The battleground was principally, though hardly exclusively, the Pacific Northwest and Rocky Mountain Regions, where not only established organizations like the Sierra Club and the Audubon Society criticized the agency but a whole new generation of interest groups sprouted up to protect the spotted owl, the grizzly bear, the Pacific salmon, old-growth forests, and the yew tree. These included Americans for the Ancient Forests, Grass Roots, Forest Watch, and even an intraagency organization called Association of Forest Service Employees for Environmental Ethics (AFSEEE). About

1990 AFSEEE began publishing "Inner Voice," a newsletter which tended to be highly critical of the agency.

Although the environmentalists' grievances were diverse, they invariably had a common denominator: Reaganomics was transforming the Forest Service from a multiple-use agency into a single-use one. "Tree farming," Gifford Pinchot had called it in the early twentieth century. But even that utilitarian conception of forestry didn't capture what a Forest Service official in 1990 called the "rape-pillage-and-plunder mentality" that was in the process of destroying a fine organization.[127]

The "John Mumma Affair" symbolized this turbulent and troublesome decade for the Forest Service. The first wildlife biologist ever to be appointed to the position of regional forester, Mumma headed up region one, the northern Rocky Mountains, when the demands for timber production reached a crisis stage. This was during the Bush administration.

He was one of the first to speak out. "I can't do it," he said in a meeting with Chief Dale Robertson and other Forest Service officials. "I can't reach the region's timber harvest targets without breaking the environmental laws of the land."[128] But this was not what officials in the Washington office wanted to hear, so in 1991 regional forester Mumma was reassigned to a staff position at headquarters. He was given, he said, "no options ... , just told it was for the good of the service, a time for a change."[129] Rather than submit to what he considered a demotion and a de facto reprimand, Mumma decided, with great reluctance, to retire from the Forest Service in October of 1991.

John Mumma immediately became a *cause célèbre* among environmentalists. They coined the term "Mummacide" to describe what was occurring within the agency. They also began documenting other cases within not only the Forest Service but in other resource agencies where whistle-blowers were being silenced. One result of the Mumma affair was that another new organization came into being. Calling itself PEER, Public Employees for Environmental Responsibility, this group is a governmentwide version of AFSEEE. Both organizations remain active in attempting to reorient federal resource managing agencies. Although in our interviews top officials of the Forest Service minimized the importance of the AFSEEE and PEER movement, we note that such organizations are unprecedented in the history of the agency.

Their existence speaks to deep philosophical differences within what was once an unusually cohesive agency.

Some of those conflicts were addressed when President Clinton took office in 1993. One of his first acts was to convene a Forest Summit to thrash out the numerous problems plaguing the Pacific Northwest region. The Clinton administration also succeeded in forcing the resignation of Dale Robertson, chief of the agency under Reagan and Bush. He was replaced early in 1994 by Jack Ward Thomas, a forester whose long and distinguished career emphasized wildlife biology. Under the current administration, therefore, the agency appears poised to recapture the stature it lost during the 1980s when the public became convinced that it had mismanaged the nation's forest.

Its adaptive orientation ought to help the agency bounce back. Historically, the Forest Service has responded to criticism and attacks in the same manner as the Corps. Although in some instances the agency initially resisted new policy demands, it eventually finds the wherewithal to incorporate them into an expanding list of responsibilities and functions. This occurred with the Reagan administration's insistence on increasing timber yields (to the ultimate detriment of the agency), and it occurred more recently, and with a more positive outcome, when Congress instructed the Forest Service to develop an international forestry component. Over time, therefore, the agency has adroitly absorbed many of the forces that have threatened its domain or its integrity.

Lending strength to the Forest Service's capacity to absorb new responsibilities has been its professional base.[130] Many scholars have noted the relatively high degree of autonomy accorded this agency within the executive branch structure. Some have linked this phenomenon to its reputation for expertise in a particular discipline. At times, the agency has acted as though it were not a part of the Agriculture Department but instead an independent agency like the Environmental Protection Agency. At other times, however, it has been subjected to substantial presidential direction. But unlike other agencies these instances are the exception rather than the rule. Perhaps the best way to describe the Forest Service, then, is as the outlier within the Agriculture Department.

A measure of its independence is found in the career histories of its chiefs. All of them have been career civil servants and all but one have had advanced degrees in forestry. None has been what is referred to as strictly a political appointee. This contrasts with both the National Park Service and the Bureau of Land Management, agencies whose heads are usually political appointees. However, according to an agency official whom we interviewed in 1994, the present chief forester comes perilously close to that designation. Because of the unprecedented turmoil within the agency during the Reagan-Bush years, the Clinton White House felt it necessary to make a statement when it appointed a new head. One result, according to this employee, is a perception within the agency that "Chief Thomas is half of a political appointee." Although Thomas personally is widely respected within his agency, some people have expressed concern about a trend toward politicizing the chief's job.

The agency has resisted attempts to politicize it. The universal career path within the agency is from the bottom up, and the present chief is no exception in that regard. As Culhane noted, "There is no lateral entry into the service; all line officers work their way up from the bottom, giving them a common background and view."[131] Of course, Herbert Kaufman noted the same phenomenon in his classic *The Forest Ranger*. The prestige associated with the discipline of forestry, or silviculture, and the predominance of this discipline within the agency, has contributed to its power base. At least until recently, the public's image of the agency has been a positive one: As a valuable repository of scientific expertise.

Forestry always has been the dominant profession within the Forest Service. Agency estimates in the early 1980s showed that approximately 16 percent of its total workforce was comprised of foresters. The data compiled by Culhane in his comparative study of the Forest Service and the Bureau of Land Management likewise underscored the dominance of the discipline: About 90 percent of the Forest Service's *professional* staff were trained foresters.[132] Statistics drawn from the Flathead National Forest in Montana profiling its 1992 workforce also show the continued dominance of forestry. Out of approximately 270 permanent employees, 44 were professional foresters, including the Forest Supervisor. That is slightly over 16 percent.[133] For the agency as a whole, figures for 1994 showed that foresters accounted for approximately 15 percent of the total workforce, just a one percent decline from the early 1980s. Foresters thus appear to be holding their own within the Forest Service.

A comparison of the Forest Service with another land manager, the National Park Service, regarding their professional bases yields interesting results. The dominant profession within the Park Service is "park ranger." Data collected in the early 1980s showed that approximately 12 percent of the agency's workforce was composed of rangers, as compared with 16 percent foresters in the Forest Service. By 1994, the percentage of rangers in the Park Service had risen to about 21 percent: Out of 16,000 permanent employees, 3,400 were classified as park rangers.[134]

One might conclude that the Park Service was becoming more professionalized over time, but two qualifications need to be made before reaching that conclusion. The first is that forestry is a more universally recognized discipline than is ranger; rangers can—and do—have degrees in various fields. But the second qualification is even more significant. In the late 1970s the Office of Personnel Management abolished the requirement that park rangers have college degrees at all. This change no doubt accounts for most of the increase in the number of rangers in the agency. Furthermore, it is not always viewed as a step in the right direction. For example, in a 1994 interview with a park superintendent (who had a college degree), he lamented the fact that in the near future "there will be a whole generation of park employees, without college degrees, clogging the system."

We thus conclude that the Forest Service, despite encountering severe problems during the 1980s, still maintains a competitive edge vis-à-vis other land managing agencies. If it can remake its reputation with the general public and with the environmental community, if it can fend off the radical proposal to privatize the national forests, and if it can incorporate "ecosystems management" into its traditional professional base of forestry, then it will continue to be a superstar. We speculate on the likelihood of the agency making these critical moves in chapter 6.

SUMMARY: SYNERGISTIC ORGANIZATIONS

Among our seven-agency sample, two federal organizations—the U.S. Forest Service and the Corps of Engineers—stand out. They have larger workforces and significantly larger budgets than their five cohorts, factors which we compare in detail in chapter 5. They also have reputations as powerful agencies; though controversy surrounds the tasks which they perform for society, even their critics usually accord them grudging respect for their professionalism and for their sense of political acumen. Like a powerful politician, we may not always like what he or she does, but in an achievement-oriented society respect flows from getting things done. And few people have ever accused either agency discussed in this chapter of not getting the job done!

The histories of the Corps and the Forest Service illuminate an interesting and little-discussed characteristic of organizational behavior, and that is that some agencies are able to put together their various resources in such a way as to produce a powerful combination. In the first chapter we discussed several sources of power upon which agencies can draw. If agencies are weak in one area they can perhaps compensate for that deficiency by being stronger in other areas. But some combinations of factors appear to act within an organization in a synergistic manner: The effect of their combination is not simply a sum of parts, but rather their interaction combines to achieve an effect of which each factor individually is incapable of producing. Our finding is that at least certain complex organizations, such as bureaucracies, show evidence of behaving like biological organisms, from which the concept of synergism is drawn.

We thus see bureaucracies as entities, even organisms, that are constantly changing and adapting to their environments, which also are in a state of flux. Some agencies are better equipped to make the necessary changes to secure their continued influence, and even survival, than are others. This former group, those which compete better than the others, is blessed with a potent combination of resources. In the case of the Corps and the Forest Service, these include: a pro-development, multiple-use mission; a pragmatic or utilitarian ideology; a clear beginning (through a direct congressional statement of purpose at the time of its creation, or through the work of a strong founder, or ideally both); a scientific and/or military basis of expertise; internal recruitment to leadership positions; a coherent, well-defined public image; and unusually strong support from Congress (or sometimes from the chief executive) as well as from large, well-organized constituencies outside the formal institutions of government. Both the Corps and the Forest Service have been, of course, constituent parts of what are commonly referred to as iron triangles, whose purpose is to protect and promote the interests so arranged.

In our examination of the histories of these two superstars, we did not find the limiting factors, or weaknesses, that seem to handicap the other agencies that we studied. As we discuss in the next two chapters, the five other agencies have not been the beneficiaries of synergism to nearly the same degree as have these two. Thus a more typical pattern of organizational development is our next subject.

Agencies that Muddle Through:

The National Park Service, the Natural Resources and Conservation Service, and the Fish and Wildlife Service

THE NATIONAL PARK SERVICE

When the pilgrims first landed on the shores of the New World, they considered the American wilderness to be an obstacle in the path of the advancing European civilization. It was not until well into the nineteenth century that some individuals began arguing for the protection of the remaining vestiges of the great American wilderness. These nineteenth century preservationists and leaders of the romantic movement in America were interested in preserving specific wilderness areas principally for their aesthetic value. This brought them into direct conflict not only with the powerful economic interests of the time but also with the less ideological conservationists, like Gifford Pinchot. Although preservationists and conservationists were allied in their opposition to the unchecked exploitation of the public lands, there was much on which they did not see eye to eye. As a group preservationists were devoted to protecting in perpetuity the pristine character of the remaining public lands, while conservationists supported the utilitarian ideal of "wise use." As a result, these two conflicting approaches to the public lands were frequently in direct competition with each other in their efforts to gain control over public lands. The nineteenth century conservation movement was a movement divided.[1]

The first significant victory for the preservationists occurred in 1872 when Congress created a 2.2 million acre preserve in the Yellowstone Valley, to be "withdrawn from settlement, occupancy or sale ... and dedicated and set apart as a public park or pleasuring ground for the benefit and enjoyment of the people."[2] Several other national parks were added in the succeeding twenty-five years and in 1906 Congress passed the Antiquities Act, which empowered the president to establish national monuments by proclamation and without the approval of Congress.[3] By 1916 there were sixteen national parks and twenty-one national monuments in existence. These areas, however, were not the inviolate sanctuaries that the preservationists had envisioned and desired. Due to inadequate funding plus the absence of any federal agency charged with the responsibility of protecting these parks and monuments, they became routinely used for grazing, farming, and lumbering. The parks existed only on paper. Furthermore, the economic exploitation of park lands was often tolerated and even encouraged by local interests who resented federal control—especially if it meant preservation—over the public domain.

The use of park lands for utilitarian purposes reached an apex in 1913 with the bitter struggle over the proposed Hetch Hetchy reservoir project within the boundaries of Yosemite National Park. Developers argued that the reservoir was crucial to the continued growth and economic development of the San Francisco area, and after a protracted conflict they won the right to build a dam within park boundaries.[4] To the preservationists this was indeed a great and painful loss; it also established an important precedent in that it illustrated the political weaknesses inherent in the preservationists' position. As many saw it, their "extremist" position on issues of development would inevitably put them in the minority.

The Hetch Hetchy controversy, however, underscored the need for a new federal agency to manage the recently created park lands. After several years of procrastination and controversy, Congress passed enabling legislation in 1916 establishing a National Park Service with a mandate to do the following:

> regulate the use of ... national parks and monuments...conserve the scenery and the natural and historic objects and the wildlife therein and to provide for the enjoyment of the same in such manner and by such means as will leave them unimpaired for the enjoyment of future generations.[5]

Thus the mission of the new agency was to preserve the parks in a natural state yet also to provide access to these same parks so that they could be enjoyed by the public. An inherent conflict between preservation and public use was written into the original mandate of the new Service. In 1918 the Secretary of the Interior reiterated the need to satisfy both of these goals (without specifying how)in an administrative directive which stated that the parks must be maintained "unimpaired," yet also set aside for the "use and pleasure of the people," including "educational as well as recreational use."[6]

This built-in conflict in the Park Service's mission has repeatedly caused problems for park policymakers. An example of the kind of difficulties created by a dual mission is seen in early Park Service policy in the Yosemite Valley. Many people felt that Yosemite was the star gem of the entire park system, and so Stephen Mather, first director of the Service, strongly encouraged automobile travel to the valley in hopes that the silent beauty and isolation of the park would encourage people to support the fledgling Park Service. The Service even organized auto caravans that toured Valley roads. But within ten years the Valley became clogged with cars, and the qualities which had inspired director Mather to encourage park visitation soon became lost in the effort to use what was also supposed to have been preserved.[7] Some sixty years later, the Park Service continued to grapple with the conflict between use and preservation. One proposal in its mid-1970s Yosemite Park Plan would have visitors tour the park through chartered air service instead of by automobile.

By the time of the Park Service's creation in 1916, the split between conservationists and preservationists had grown into an intense rivalry. Gifford Pinchot stated at the time that the creation of a preserve where timber-cutting was illegal was nothing more than an indefensible attempt to outlaw scientific forestry.[8] The first director of the Park Service, Stephen Mather, was a millionaire businessman who devoted the last two decades of his life to the establishment of the Park Service. But unlike Pinchot, he never developed a close working relationship with prominent political figures. Nor did Mather have the charismatic personality of Pinchot. Although Mather had the support of celebrities like John Muir, the more pragmatic conservationists dominated the centers of power in Washington. As a result, the Park Service was created in the shadow of progressive conservation which was, as we noted in chapter 2, institutionalized in the Forest Service.[9]

Throughout the first thirty years of its official existence, from 1916 to 1946, the Park Service enjoyed one period of impressive growth. This was during FDR's New Deal. With two park lovers at the helm—Franklin Roosevelt in the White House and Harold Ickes running the Interior Department—the agency did well. Military battlefields were transferred from the Department of the Army to the Park Service for administration, the 1934 Historic Sites Act was passed, thus giving the agency another mission, scenic parkways were planned and constructed, and wilderness areas were designated. Agency officials generally were instructed to expand the park system wherever they could, but especially in the eastern third of the nation where most Americans still resided. Under Ickes and FDR, then, the Park Service, like the Forest Service, became a genuinely *national* entity.[10]

However, its budget, even during the heady years of the New Deal, rarely kept abreast of its expanding responsibilities. Park officials continuously complained about their shoestring budget. So did Secretary Ickes before congressional appropriations committees. When World War II forced a major reordering of public priorities, the "expendability" of the service became evident. Its budget was cut from $21 million to $5 million, and its central headquarters were moved to Chicago (Ickes' hometown) to literally make room for more important operations in Washington.[11]

With the end of the war, the parks gained a new and welcomed visibility when postwar prosperity brought record numbers of visitors to the parks. But too many years of fiscal frugality left the Park Service unprepared to deal with the rush of new visitors. To exacerbate the problem, Congress failed to appreciably increase funding for the Park Service even after the end of the war. The resulting financial bind proved to be not only detrimental to the agency but physically damaging to the parks; there was no way the Service could adequately maintain or patrol them on its annual appropriation. In 1949 Director Newton B. Drury issued a report called "The Dilemma of Our Parks." It described the deterioration and destruction of park land and park property caused by so many visitors and so few staff. A similar report was issued twenty-six years later and it reached essentially the same conclusions. This one was titled, "The Degradation of Our National Parks." More negative reports were to follow.

The solution to this problem, as proposed by the Park Service, was to initiate a massive development program to accommodate increased visitation. At this point in the agency's history the preservation aspect of its mandate became secondary. The Park Service, however, overlooked the possibility that such a development program might in the long run exacerbate the very problems it was designed to cure by encouraging even greater visitation than the agency could keep up with. In fact, this spiralling effect, where resources never quite kept up with visitor use, has been a major theme in the history of the Service.

To meet public demand, in 1956 the agency launched its Mission '66 program. This was an ambitious ten-year development program that increased visitor capacity enormously but which "has done comparatively little for the plants and animals" and "nothing at all for the ecological maintenance of a park."[12] Another author observed that "some of the Park Service's problems ... will be traced to its own effort [Mission '66] to attract the public."[13] The funding for Mission '66 finally totalled about a billion dollars; it is virtually the only program in the history of the Park Service that has been generously funded. It is also a good example of the Park Service competing successfully with its principal governmental rival, the Forest Service. Culhane noted that "Since the turn of the century, the two services had battled about jurisdiction over especially scenic areas of public lands. The Forest Service generally came out on the short end of the stick, losing a net 4.5 million acres to the Park Service through 1960. Thus, from the Forest Service's point of view, Mission '66 signaled a reintensification of this long-standing jurisdictional duel. ... "[14]

The agency was successful in this instance primarily because it decided to compromise its preservation goal by opting for more publicly attractive utilitarian goals. Although the Park Service may not have consciously abandoned its preservation mission, the agency did not fully appreciate the extent to which Mission '66 would impact on that primary aspect of park management. In contrasting the operating principles of the Forest Service with those of the Park Service, for example, Darling and Eichhorn stated that the "U.S. Forest Service was much more politically aware of the trend of the times, as the National Park Service was naive. Mission '66, instead of being a far-sighted planning operation to conserve these choice areas, seems to have been conceived to allow more complete infiltration and uncritical use."[15] For park enthusiasts, the Park Service has been unfortunate testimony to the cliché, "Damned if you do and damned if you don't."

By the time the Mission '66 program was well underway, park administrators realized that they desperately needed a consistent and coherent management policy that could solve their historic use-versus-preservation dilemma. Under the leadership of George Hartzog, the Service finally produced a clear administrative policy on this issue; it was officially adopted in a memorandum signed by Secretary of the Interior Stewart Udall in 1964. This policy helped resolve the agency's heretofore schizophrenic management of park lands.

The 1964 management framework divided park lands into three categories: natural, historic, and recreational. In his memorandum, Secretary Udall spelled out the basic problem which had plagued the Park Service for so long:

> A single broad management concept encompassing these three categories of areas within the System is inadequate either for their proper preservation or for realization of their full potential for public use embodied in the expressions of congressional policy. Each of these categories required a separate set of management principles coordinated to form one organic management plan for the entire system.[16]

The official Park Service explanation of the new plan contained the long-awaited realization that:

> Even though all of the parks come under the mandate of the Act of 1916 ... it is clear that the purpose and intent of each is not the same as the others. ... In 1964 we recognized three management categories ... to encompass this diversity ... so that resources may be appropriately identified and managed in terms of their inherent values and appropriate uses.[17]

The tripartite management policy had a significant impact on agency operations. Perhaps most importantly, it allowed the agency to adopt a preservationist orientation in some—not all—park lands. Thus the criterion for increased use and development, which in the past had simply been to expand everywhere and anywhere within park boundaries to meet public demand, now became linked to physical impact, or as the agency put it, to "ecological health or repose."[18] In practice this simply meant that zoning for use would hereafter guide park management, and that some areas would be zoned for heavy recreational use and others for minimal use. The Service also adopted a new restrictive road policy. These attempts to curtail or diminish development in some areas reflected the newly defined purpose of the "natural area" category: "The single abiding purpose of National Parks is to bring man and his environment into closer harmony. It is thus the quality of the park experience—and not the statistics of travel—which must be the primary concern."[19]

This plan was initiated in 1964, and was the first of several innovations introduced by director Hartzog in an effort to improve agency operations and to handle the unprecedented influx of visitors. In 1956 visitation was estimated at 55 million, and the Park Service confidently predicted that it would rise to 80 million in ten years. But by 1966 annual visitation had increased to around 133 million, leaving the Park Service unprepared and unequipped. The Service's budget, for instance, had increased threefold during that ten-year period: from $44.8 million (1956) to $136.4 million (1966). With the close of Mission '66, however, the Service suffered a budget cut of over ten million dollars, which was followed by another budget decrease in 1968. By the late 1960s the impact of expenditures for the war in Vietnam became evident in the Park Service's budget. In the meantime, as could by now be expected, visitation increased by another twelve million.[20]

Director Hartzog's management innovations, including his efforts to establish urban recreation areas, were effective constituency-building devices; they made park lands available to a broader spectrum of people and activities. But they also created management difficulties for Park Service personnel, who were imbued with a traditional concept of parks as natural wonders in a sylvan setting. Urban parks, with their problems of crime and crowding, and recreation areas, some of which permitted motorized recreation, offended the sensibilities of some Park Service personnel. The historic role of the park ranger, which focused on natural and historic interpretive activity, had to be suddenly expanded to encompass law enforcement, traffic control, and crowd management. This created morale problems which continue to affect the agency.

In addition to the new management policies, the Park Service was significantly affected by a number of other developments. Several statutes were enacted in the 1960s and early 1970s, when a new wave of environmental concern took hold, that broadened agency horizons. For instance, the Service stated that:

> The mandate to preserve historic resources ... is contained not only in the National Park Service organic act of 1916, but also in five other legislative enactments:
> • Antiquities Act, 1906
> • Historic Sites Act, 1935
> • National Historic Preservation Act, 1966
> • National Environmental Policy Act, 1969
> • Archeological and Historic Preservation Act, 1974[21]

To this list one should add:

> • Land and Water Conservation Fund Act, 1964
> • Wilderness Act, 1964
> • "Protection and Enhancement of the Cultural Environment," Executive Order 11593, 13 May 1971.[22]

Expansion of the agency's mission during the 1960s is revealed in other ways as well. In just four years, from 1964 to 1968, the number of park areas jumped from 218 to 270.[23] Many of these new areas, as we noted, dramatically changed the original conception of a park that had guided Service activities for over fifty years. For example, the new conception of a park was contained in the authorization that created two urban-oriented park areas (Gateway in New York City and Golden Gate in San Francisco) and two cultural centers (Kennedy Center in Washington, D.C. and Wolf Trap Park in neighboring Virginia). In addition, the Service was given responsibility in the 1970s for orchestrating the American Bicentennial Program.[24]

Yet with these additional responsibilities and enlargements of its original mandate, the Service was unable to secure a commensurate increase in funding. Its budget continued to increase incrementally. It did not reflect the prodigious changes occurring in and to the national park system. Meanwhile, director Hartzog continued to force changes in agency operations in an effort to cope with budgetary constraints through increasing the organization's efficiency. He organized the "Field Operations Study Team" (FOST) to recommend more efficient management and administration strategies.[25] At about the same time

Hartzog abolished the use of fifty-six administrative manuals and handbooks which had accumulated over time as the official Park Service bible of "how to do the job."[26]

Another innovation occurring during Hartzog's tenure was the concept of the Golden Eagle Pass, a discounted season ticket to all national parks. When instituted in 1965, it was expected that over 30 million passes would be sold that year. Actually only a million were bought by the public. The Park Service, together with others who had come up with the idea, failed to realize that the American public did not feel it had to pay to get into its own public parks. The Golden Eagle Pass thus raised an outcry of complaints from park visitors who claimed that they should not have to have a ticket to enter a public place.[27]

The debate over entrance fees continued for two decades. In 1986, the U.S. Congress finally passed legislation mandating fees for most units in the national park system. It also set the price of the Golden Eagle pass at a reasonable $25.00. But if agency officials thought that this would help their chronic funding problems, or contribute to greater agency autonomy, they were wrong. According to research done by William Lowry, revenues generated by user fees came with "strings attached ... Simply put, user fees on public lands stimulate constituent interests and allow electoral opportunities."[28]

The political and organizational significance of the "free use" mentality on agency operations has been considerable. One of the Park Service's two primary constituencies—the summer visitor—is broad, diverse, unorganized, and largely unaware of the political and funding problems facing the Park Service. Most visitors do not know the difference between the Park Service and the Forest Service. The general public demands a great deal from park management, yet it offers very little real constituency support. Environmentalists do, but they are often perceived as "extremists" who support the agency's preservation mandate but not its public use one. Moreover, the Park Service has had to compete for funds with other agencies that have better organized support and which offer traditional pork-barrel programs.

Part of the Park Service's problems can thus be traced to public attitudes and to the lack of an organized constituency to support its mass recreation program. The public considers the parks to be theirs in a rather concrete sense; the Service, therefore, merely regulates the use of this public good. In view of the fact that the parks often have been poorly maintained, understaffed, and overcrowded, it appeared that the Park Service was not an outstanding custodian of this public heritage. To add to the problem, the Service for years did not cultivate the active support of its visitor constituency. The director of the Wilderness Society, for example, in 1970 wrote that for a long time there had been "a communication gap between the agency and the interested public."[29]

Still others considered the Park Service and its programs to be a low-priority item on the federal agenda. One Bureau of the Budget official explained the agency's financial dilemma in 1969 like this:

> The poor Park Service! First, recreation was considered a "frill." Now its programs are considered a "middle-income subsidy."[30]

Thus, unlike its more powerful competitor, the Forest Service, the Park Service had difficulty in tapping into a constituency organized around economic interests. Hence its mission was not regarded as contributing significantly to the economic productivity of the country. Instead, its natural clientele had been composed primarily of conservation groups whose major objective—preservation—was seen by many as restrictive, narrow, or even reactionary. This began to change in the 1980s, however; we discuss the impact of "park-barrel" politics on the agency later in this section.

The combination of modest to low constituency support and a relatively narrow mission created serious political and organizational problems for the Park Service. The political impotence of the Service was perhaps most obvious during the Nixon administration. Soon after Nixon entered the White House, he removed the forceful and independent George Hartzog and replaced him with Ron Walker, a political appointee and aide to the president. Walker had been an insurance salesman before joining Nixon's campaign staff, and served as special assistant to the President before his appointment to the Park Service. He had no professional experience with parks, recreation, or preservation.

During Walker's two-year tenure as director, he managed to implicate the agency in an embarrassing boondoggle (shades of Watergate) concerning the development of a campsite reservation system. By 1970, visitation had outstripped facilities to the point where long queues of campers were lining up at the parks, many of whom eventually had to be turned away. Park Service staff believed that a reservation system was the best solution to this critical problem, and so the decision was made to contract out the responsibility of establishing and operating a nationwide park reservation system. (The decision to contract for services was made because the Park Service felt it did not have the manpower or expertise within the agency to operate a nationwide system.) The first contract was let to American Express to handle reservations for six of the most heavily used parks. This operation worked well for one season, but American Express refused to renew the contract due to cost overruns caused by the unanticipated volume of reservation requests.

In 1974 the Park Service decided to expand the reservation system to include fourteen more parks. It issued a prospectus for an expanded contract, this time anticipating a huge volume of requests.[31] After a brief review, Ticketron, having assets of $877 million and extensive experience in reservations, was bypassed along with another company. The contract was instead given to Public Reservation Systems (PRS), a company formed in order to make a bid for the agency's contract. The financial assets of this new company were unknown, but apparently it was clear to some that it had no experience, expertise, or even adequate equipment to do the job. As was expected, PRS' operation was a complete failure; it was unable to handle more than 5 percent of the calls for reservations. A subsequent investigation by the General Accounting Office and an Interior Department inquiry were followed by congressional oversight hearings, which failed to prove any criminal wrongdoing but which did find that PRS had violated its own contract. The investigations also discovered that Park Service Director Ron Walker was a personal friend of the president of PRS, and that he maintained "social contacts" with him during the period in which bids were being considered.[32]

For an agency that was already weak politically, a scandal of this sort had the potential of undermining what modest support there was. For the many park visitors who were the victims of the reservation fiasco, it undoubtedly damaged their faith in the Service's ability to manage the parks in a competent and professional manner. This, coupled with the deteriorating condition of many of the parks, further damaged the Service's image. This attitude was summed up by one of the agency's most powerful interest groups, the National Parks and Conservation Association, in 1976: "There has been an elementary failure to maintain the public property of the American people in the National Park system."[33]

The causes of this failure have been due in large part to the agency's long-term funding problems, and its inability to effectively cope with spiraling visitor use. It is less a comment on the commitment of agency employees to their mission. For example, a review of the Service's budget from 1966 to 1969 concluded that "it is generally assumed that the Park Service is operating on a rock-bottom budget."[34] Another author wrote in 1976 that "the funding situation is the worst in 25 years."[35] The Park Service also was caught in a personnel squeeze. During the 1970s, when visitation continued to soar, the Office of Management and Budget not only set tough limits on funding but set strict personnel ceilings, thereby forcing in some cases "reductions in force" (RIFs). Thus, many congressionally authorized positions were never filled; a number of parks had to reduce their workforces at the same time visitation was rising. From 1972 to 1975, Congress authorized a seven percent staff increase, but the Park Service was allowed none of this increase.[36] The following year, 1976, the Office of Management and Budget imposed a RIF in the land acquisition program that resulted in 103 congressionally authorized positions going unfilled.[37] What happens to the parks when stringent personnel ceilings are mandated is illustrated by the desperate situation in Colorado's popular Rocky Mountain National Park in the 1970s, where visitation increased 77 percent while permanent staff decreased by 20 percent.[38] In sum, impoundment of agency funds and hiring freezes under the Nixon and Ford administrations once again had deleterious effects on agency operations.

The observable deterioration of park lands was only one result of the agency's inadequate budget. There were others which were equally harmful to the viability of the agency. The Service became more reluctant to establish new parks. In 1973, the Service decided to establish a deadline year for "rounding out the National Park System," and then established more stringent criteria for the acquisition of new parks.[39] With the exception of Alaskan lands, there also developed considerable resistance in Congress during the 1970s to proposals for expansion of the park system.[40] Thus in the face of increased demand for park use, the Service became hesitant to support plans for its own expansion, and in fact de-authorized some areas.[41]

Another result of the Service's budgeting and personnel problems was it inability to adequately meet new statutory demands. Chapter 5 further verifies some of the problems the Service had in meeting the requirements of the National Environmental Policy Act and other, more recent, "unfunded mandates." Yet another indicator of agency stress was found in the fact that the Park Service was unable to complete on time its wilderness reviews, as mandated by the 1964 Wilderness Act.[42]

Related to the problems just discussed has been the limited ability of the Park Service to do research on its own operations. It contrasts sharply with the Forest Service in this regard. In discussing the maze of problems confronting the agency, an assistant director stated that "management has no choice but to concentrate on the effect, whereas the real solution depends upon getting at the cause."[43] In reference to the need for "cost-per-visitor" research, an investigation found that the Service could not do that type of analysis because "they do not have the resources available to them. They are also too occupied with more immediate problems of park operations."[44] Another author even favored giving research funds to the Forest Service rather than the Park Service because "the men who report to the Park Service director have been shockingly weak on research in either natural environments or the sociology of human recreation."[45]

Some of the Park Service's budget and personnel problems can be traced to its rather uneven competition with the Forest Service. While the former had difficulty in meeting its original preservation and use mandate, the latter successfully expanded its original mandate to include preservation as one of its many activities. Indeed, the Forest Service boasted in 1979 of managing over 15 million acres of wilderness set aside in the National Wilderness Preservation System as compared with the Park Service's 3.3 million acres.[46] The Park Service also has had to compete with other federal and state agencies as a provider of recreation facilities. Both the Forest Service and the Corps of Engineers, for example, have well-financed recreation programs, though both programs were attenuated under Reagan. The Park Service's rivalry with the Forest Service in this activity is well known. Everhart wrote:

the most celebrated interbureau rivalry in all government involves the Forest Service and the Park Service. ... The long history of competing and conflicting objectives has developed in each agency a keen but wary respect for the ability of the other to stir up mischief.[47]

Clearly, the Park Service has had its share of problems during its eighty-year history—problems in expanding its mission, in the appropriations process, and in competing with more powerful agencies. Despite these weaknesses, the Park Service has met with qualified success in a number of areas. The strength of the organization undoubtedly lies in the commitment of its personnel. Perhaps due to its unusual mission, Park Service employees have demonstrated a deep faith in the idea of a national park system. This has bound them together with a strong unity of purpose. Their esprit de corps was quite evident in a survey of Park Service employees completed in 1977.[48] For instance, 15 per cent of the respondents "strongly agreed" and 61 percent "agreed" that "there is a strong professional bond among Park Service employees." Also evident in their responses was their commitment to environmental quality. The survey also made clear the fact that Park Service employees did not join the Service for the money: 29 percent and 42 percent rated financial incentives as "poor" or "fair" respectively. Indeed, one respondent penciled in: "I'm sure we're the lowest paid agency in the federal government." Despite financial discincentives, 80 percent felt that the Park Service was effective and was doing a good job; 84 percent were optimistic about the Service's future.

This zealous attitude is evident in a former director's characterization of Park Service employment as "our high calling as trustees for the greater things of America."[49] In a more subdued tone, another author wrote that the Park Service "is given high marks for its dedication and performance, under increasingly trying conditions."[50] There are data to indicate that the public also holds the agency in high esteem, and this despite a reluctance to directly help defray operating expenses through increased users' fees. A 1983 poll of public perceptions of fifteen federal agencies put the Park Service at the top of the list, with a 77 percent "favorable" rating.[51]

Toward the end of the troubling decade of the 1970s, the number of park areas increased dramatically, despite the agency's and the Nixon-Ford administrations' reluctance to take on greater responsibilities. The

National Parks and Recreation Act of 1978 added fifteen new park areas. Public Law 96-487 authorized the establishment of ten new park areas in Alaska and expanded three previously established areas, also in Alaska. This more than doubled the number of acres under Park Service jurisdiction. With these major additions the System included 333 separate areas encompassing 73.7 million acres. Park visitation also continued to increase, totalling more than 238 million in 1981.[52]

This significant expansion of the nation's park system, coupled with President Jimmy Carter's more generalized pro-environment stance, quickly produced a political backlash in the West. It became known as the Sagebrush Rebellion, one element of which was a group formed in 1978 calling itself the National Inholders Association (NIA). The NIA organized to beat back further federal encroachment, which members saw occurring both within national park and national forest boundaries (i.e., inholdings), as well as on property lying adjacent to federal lands.[53]

Sagebrush rebels helped elect Ronald Reagan in the 1980 presidential election. Reagan then appointed one of their own, Wyoming's James Watt, to the position of Secretary of the Interior. Watt, like Assistant Secretary John Crowell in the Agriculture Department, came to office with a definite agenda. With respect to the National Park Service, he was determined to deal with a number of controversial and unresolved issues, including park expansion, park degradation, budget shortfalls, concessioner policy, and urban parks.

One of Secretary Watt's first actions was to issue a moratorium on the acquisition of new park lands. In his view, no new acreage should be added to the system until established parks were adequately equipped and maintained. He said:

> They [the parks] continue to suffer, as they have suffered with the poor stewardship which has been demonstrated in the last years and years and years—when we have been authorizing parks for acquisition, when we can't take care of what we have. ... I don't think that is good stewardship. It is my strong recommendation that we not ask Congress for authority to add new lands to the National Park System. We haven't taken care of what we have.[54]

The Congress had a different view, however. Throughout his three-year tenure as Interior Secretary, Watt fought continually with the legislative branch over the issue of park acquisition. So did his less visible successors, like Donald Hodel. First the Reagan administration tried, unsuccessfully, to abolish the Land and Water Conservation Fund, the primary source of funding for land acquisition for the Park Service and other land-managing agencies. When that bold move failed, the administration attempted to drastically reduce the budget for the fund, but the Congress was persistent in providing monies for land acquisition. For example, the Reagan budget for FY 1982 allocated $55.5 million for park land acquisition, but Congress increased the final appropriation to $112 million.[55]

Buttressing Watt's views on land acquisition versus maintenance and improvement were a number of studies released in the early eighties which concluded that the parks were in dire straits. They were reminiscent of previous reports predicting the collapse of the system. For example, a report by the Office of Science and Technology, titled "State of the Parks 1980," found some 4,345 specific threats to the integrity of the park system, including air and water pollution problems, overuse, overcrowding, and unregulated private development at or near park boundaries.[56] Also, a 1980 GAO investigation examined twelve of the largest and most popular parks, and found that the Park Service had:

> not protected the health and safety of visitors and employees using facilities at national parks. ... Substandard water and sewer systems and hazardous lodges, dormitories, bridges, and tunnels need to be repaired or upgraded or their use should be limited. We estimate that unfunded health and safety projects total $1.6 billion for the National Park Service.[57]

According to the Service's own estimates, there were health and safety problems in 113 separate park areas.[58] President Reagan's Park Service Director, Russell Dickenson, stated that the $1.6 billion needed for health and safety improvements cited by GAO was probably low.[59] Yet in 1981, Congress appropriated only $29.5 million to alleviate these operations and maintenance ("O&M") problems. The Park Service requested that this amount be increased to $121.5 million for FY 1982— a fourfold increase which was not granted. Park acquisition thus became a clear political problem—and dilemma—for the agency during the Reagan years. Congress preferred to liberally fund the more popular activity of new park acquisition and authorization (what congress-person would not want to get credit for the establishment of a new park in his or her jurisdiction?), while Reagan's appointees in the Interior Department doggedly pursued the less rewarding, yet necessary, activities of keeping the parks in decent working order. Agency officials were caught in the middle of these competing priorities.

The Reagan administration's budgetary strategy in this regard was to fund operation and maintenance projects as part of a new line item called "Park Restoration and Improvement." (This category did not exist in previous budgets.) The proposed budget for 1982 called for a total expenditure in this area of $105 million. The monies were to come from funds earmarked for the acquisition-oriented Land and Water Conservation Fund. Health and safety projects, however, comprised only $18 million of the $105 million.[60]

The battle over the Park Service's budget continued. For FY 1982, the administration reluctantly approved a small increase over its initial total request of around $500 million. However, that total was somewhat misleading because it included funds transferred from the Heritage Conservation and Recreation Service, an Interior Department unit which was phased out of existence by Secretarial Order 3060, 19 February 1981. If those transferred funds are excluded, the Park Service's revised budget proposal for 1982 actually represented a decrease of $11.5 million. The decrease showed a reduction in spending for management planning, energy conservation, new area studies, and a 50 percent decrease in the amount allocated to operate the new Alaskan parks. Also, the National Visitor Center in Washington, D.C., was closed.[61]

Secretary Watt's policies led almost immediately to charges that he was attempting to dismantle the nation's park system. Opponents of the Reagan-Watt administration pointed to four specific policies that they felt threatened the parks. First, there were charges that the secretary developed a "hit-list" of parks that he wanted to see de-authorized. (As we discussed in chapter 2, a similar hit list existed for water resources projects during the first years of the Carter administration.) A number of departmental memos apparently discussed the desirability of eliminating certain park areas, but in the 1982 appropriations hearings, Watt stated that the Reagan administration:

> does not now have, nor has it had, a hit list of National Parks or other areas which the Department would request the Congress to de-authorize.

Further, there is no plan at this time to develop a hit list. ... I have in several forums suggested that [de-authorization] is an option that could be considered.[62]

A second point of controversy was over urban parks. Secretary Watt, in his confirmation hearings, stated that a greater emphasis should be placed on urban parks but that they should be operated at the state and municipal levels, and not by the federal government. Later he made this quizzical statement: "I will err on the side of public use versus preservation. I don't believe the National Park System should run urban parks."[63] The secretary subsequently made it clear that the Reagan administration would oppose the establishment of any new urban parks. However, the transferral of federal land in urban areas to state or local governments, as with any park de-authorization, would require an act of Congress. De-authorizations not only were not forthcoming, but throughout the decade Congress moved in precisely the opposite direction. A new policy, labeled "park barrel politics," emerged.

A third policy of Reaganomics, as it applied to the Park Service, and which generated considerable discussion, was about liberalized criteria for mining, timber cutting, and other forms of economic development on federal lands. The following exchange between Congressman Sidney Yates of Illinois, a strong advocate for the agency, and Secretary Watt during appropriations hearings illuminated the controversy:

Secretary Watt: I want to open up the public lands to faster development in an orderly manner, so that we can protect the environmental qualities of that land.

Mr. Yates: May I interrupt for just a moment and ask you to define public lands?

Secretary Watt: Those are the lands owned by the Federal Government, excluding the National Park Service areas.

Mr. Yates: That would include the Fish and Wildlife Service and the Forest Service.

Secretary Watt: It would include all the lands that are open to multiple use. If a refuge or a Park Service area is not open to multiple use, then I am not talking about that. Those lands that are available for use should be used.

Mr. Yates: Some of our National Park Service areas are open for multiple use, such as dumping garbage on them. Does that get your attention?[64]

A fourth policy area that Secretary Watt wanted to change concerned concessions. In his confirmation hearings Watt described an expanded role for the private concessioner:

> we need an aggressive program with the private entrepreneurs who are willing to invest and manage resources in the national parks for people. ... We have tremendous biases. We have a bias for private enterprise. We believe concessioners can do the job.[65]

If Secretary Watt didn't succeed right away in achieving a major reform in the agency's concessions policy, at least he got the debate started. Through the entire decade of the 1980s, and into the 1990s, policy-makers and the public looked closely at the issue. As the debate evolved over amending the 1965 Concessions Act, it focused increasingly on the issue of whether the taxpayers of the country were getting shortchanged. Concessions on public lands generated hundreds of millions of dollars for the private companies holding the leases. Yet they paid back to the government on average less than 3 percent of their profits. This situation, coupled with the prospect that a Japanese firm, Matsushita, would be running the concession at Yosemite National Park, sufficiently jolted Congress, and the Bush and Clinton Administrations, into action. In 1994 the National Park Service Concessions Reform Act passed the Senate by a wide margin. It then went to the House for consideration.

Although Secretary James Watt's agenda for the Park Service contained some eminently sensible ideas, such as taking care of what the agency already had before adding on new units, his aggressive and confrontational style worked against him.[66] Most of Watt's reforms were not implemented. Indeed, through the entire decade of the 1980s, the Congress and the Presidency moved along very different tracks so far as park policy was concerned. The Reagan administration, and to a lesser extent, the Bush administration, persisted in applying the principles of "Reaganomics" to the National Park Service. Members of Congress, however, sniffed out a marvelous new opportunity in the 1980s and 1990s to bring home the bacon. They did so through what is now referred to as "park barrel politics." The phenomenon is evident in the following agency-generated graph, comparing administration requests versus congressional appropriations over the last ten years.

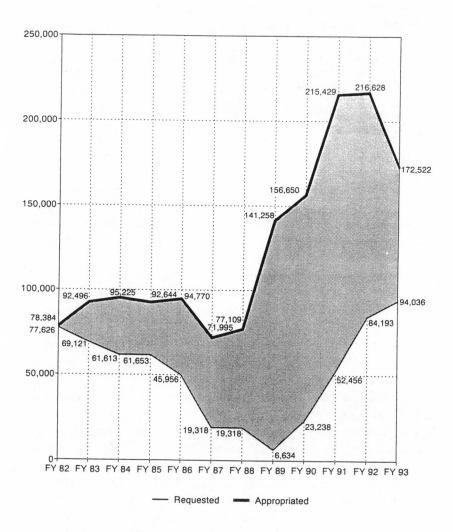

Figure 3.1 NPS Line-Item Construction Funding, $ Requested vs. Appropriated

The Park Service, predictably, found itself caught in the middle of these two conflicting visions of what the organization ought to become. Some agency officials, along with a number of their supporters in environmental organizations, became concerned over what they perceived as a loss of control over their own agenda: Congress, and not the professionals in the agency, was setting the agenda and even micro-managing individual parks. That was the downside to park barrel politics. Other agency officials, though, were more sanguine. One Washington official told us recently that "I am one of the few who happens to think that 'pork' isn't all that bad."

Indeed. The Park Service as a whole has done well during the last ten years. Its budget grew substantially, from about $975 million in 1983 to about $1.5 billion in 1994. Its workforce increased from approximately 15,000 full-time employees in 1983 to 17,700 in 1993. Of the seven agencies discussed in this book, the Park Service arguably made the largest gains during this period. It did so because Congress took a special interest in the agency. With the drying up of the traditional pork barrel—that is, the water development projects of the Corps of Engineers and the Bureau of Reclamation—and with the sea changes occurring in international politics, leading to cuts in defense spending, congresspersons looked for substitutes. They found that parks are popular with their constituents.

What the late Aaron Wildavsky wrote in 1992 about the defense pork barrel applies equally well to the "park barrel":

> Unlike the 1960s, when it could only be acquired by cultivating support of committee members (a lengthy and uncertain process), "pork" has now been democratized. The barrel has been placed out in the street. Now everyone, junior committee members as well as other legislators, has a chance to use defense to benefit their constituents.[67]

The rush to authorize, expand, and fund new parks was a key feature of natural resource policy during the last ten years. From senior legislators who dreamed up the controversial Steamtown National Historic Site in Pennsylvania, through mid-level congressmen who took credit for expanding Saguaro National Monument in southern Arizona, to the most junior senators from California who drafted the massive California Desert Protection Act, adding more acreage and units to the national park system became a widespread activity within Congress. At the same time executive branch officials bemoaned the practice.

Park barrel politics has caused some very real problems for the agency, however. In addition to the above-mentioned one, loss of control, there is a widespread feeling that *existing* parks were damaged by it. Many individuals within the agency feel that the serious problems of maintenance, increased visitor use, understaffing, and a host of external threats that continue to plague most units in the park system went ignored. "The directors of the agency keep telling me I have to do more with less," a former park superintendent of one of the agency's crown jewels told us in 1992. His frustration was palpable when he shot back that "I tell them that I'm going to do less with less." He went on to criticize Congress' pet projects, like the Presidio in San Francisco and the notorious Steamtown, and to heap scorn on "trickle down" economics. "Very little of the sizeable budget increases for the agency," he said, "come down to where the rubber meets the road." Adjusted for inflation, his park had to operate in 1992 with the same budget it had in 1981. And yet he was asked to comply with dozens of new federal mandates. He said that he had no choice but to close down some facilities within the park—an action which naturally raised an outcry from the public, who criticized him for doing a bad job as superintendent. (A year later he made a lateral move within the agency.)

Frustration over such inequities led to what has been described as a "grassroots effort" among Park Service employees to redirect their agency (shades of the Forest Service's AFSEEE movement). Meeting in 1991 in Vail, Colorado, a group of park officials, scholars, and other opinion leaders wrote a report titled, "National Parks for the 21st Century: The Vail Agenda." It has become, in the Clinton administration, the agency's bible on organizational renewal. It is embraced by the present director, Roger Kennedy, by the present Interior Secretary, Bruce Babbitt, and by the White House.

The Vail Agenda is a thoughtful document espousing far-reaching reforms of the agency. Its recommendations are being echoed in several other reports on the Park Service, including the General Accounting Office's 1994 report, "Activities Outside Park Borders Have Caused Damage to Resources and Will Likely Cause More," and *National Geographic's* somber October 1994 article on the state of the parks. It remains to be seen whether much of what these various reports call for actually will be implemented, however. The major obstacle to their implementation is, we think, the new congressional practice known as the park barrel. We doubt whether Congress readily will give up its control of the agency. Thus the Park Service discovered that its recent budgetary success, from increased entrance fees to new park authorizations, did not come without some substantial strings attached. The agency rediscovered its political vulnerability.

THE SOIL CONSERVATION SERVICE/NATURAL RESOURCES AND CONSERVATION SERVICE

By the end of the nineteenth century conservation had become a salient issue and a viable political movement. The early conservationists were primarily concerned with Western natural resources, and for the most part neglected Midwestern and Great Plains soil as a resource in need of attention. It was not until the 1910s that concerned agricultural experts and public officials began the drive for an effective public soil conservation program. Foremost among these men was Hugh Bennett, a government geologist who had done extensive research on erosion in the south. Convinced that soil erosion was destroying American farm productivity, Bennett began what amounted to a one-man crusade against erosion. The first official recognition of his efforts occurred in 1928 when the Department of Agriculture officially endorsed his paper titled, "Soil Erosion, A Natural Menace."[68]

Bennett's drive for a federal soil conservation program was ultimately realized primarily because of two important events, one physical and one political. First, the Dust Bowl of the 1930s provided a visible confirmation of Bennett's predictions. Up until that time, much of the soil erosion that had taken place was of a more subtle form called sheet erosion, a term originally defined by Bennett. Through this slow yet constant process, farmlands gradually lost their topsoil. The Dust Bowl phenomenon, however, was anything but gradual. With its monstrous storms quickly stripping away the fertile topsoil of an entire region, it became obvious that immediate action was needed to control all forms of soil erosion. Second, the election of Franklin Roosevelt provided political support for the institutionalization of the soil conservation cause. Secretary of the Interior Harold Ickes became interested in soil conservation in the early days of the New Deal, and promptly settled on Bennett as the "best expert" for the job.[69]

With strong support from President Roosevelt, Ickes set up the Soil Erosion Service within the Department of the Interior and placed Bennett at its head. The new bureau was to function as a part of the National Industrial Recovery Administration. It would provide assistance to farmers for soil-erosion-control projects and it would create jobs for the unemployed through the Civilian Conservation Corps. At the time of its creation it was estimated that erosion cost the United States about $400 million annually in soil depreciation and reduced yields.[70]

During its first two years of existence, the Soil Erosion Service, under Bennett's and Ickes' leadership, made some headway in conserving topsoil. The Service worked with another Interior Department agency, the Bureau of Indian Affairs, to set up demonstration projects on the vast Indian reservations of the West. The agency also worked extensively in Texas, as a result of the active support of its mission by the influential New Dealer, Congressman James "Buck" Buchanan. Bennett was further aided by the severe dust storms of 1934 and 1935, which brought home his point better than anything else could. The director's political acumen was much in evidence when he scheduled a congressional hearing on a day when "the Capitol building itself was almost blacked out by a dust storm which had originated two thousand miles away."[71]

On 27 April 1935, shortly after Bennett's dust storm appearance before Congress, the Soil Conservation Act was signed by the president after having passed unanimously in both houses. But to Secretary Ickes' chagrin, the act established the Soil Conservation Service within the Department of Agriculture rather than in his Interior Department (Roosevelt was persuaded that it was more properly an agriculture program than an Interior one). The act defined four basic functions for the agency:

1. To conduct surveys, investigations, and research relating to the character of soil erosion and the preventative measures needed, to publish the results of any such surveys, investigations, or research, to disseminate information concerning such methods,

and to conduct demonstrational projects in areas subject to erosion by wind or water;

2. To carry out preventative measures, including, but not limited to, engineering operations, methods of cultivation, the growing of vegetation, and changes in use of land;

3. To cooperate or enter into agreements with, or to furnish financial or other aid to, any agency, governmental or otherwise, or any person, subject to such conditions as he may deem necessary, for the purposes of this Act; and

4. To acquire lands, or rights or interests therein, by purchase, gift, condemnation, or otherwise, whenever necessary for the purposes of this Act.[72]

In order to implement the 1935 mandate, the Soil Conservation Service (SCS) adopted several unique programs and administrative strategies in an effort to circumvent existing political jurisdictions while at the same time to deal effectively with the pervasive problem of erosion.

One of these programs was the establishment of demonstration projects in cooperation with individual farmers. These projects tested different methods of erosion control, demonstrated these methods, and, of course, tried to prevent erosion on the land involved. Following a detailed survey of erosion conditions, specific recommendations for preventative practices were made to the landowners. To participate in a project, a farmer was required to sign a five-year contract obligating him to implement the recommended conservation measures. Although the Service strongly emphasized that soil conservation measures had to be designed specifically to fit a given situation, they typically recommended such practices as contour plowing, strip cropping, planting erosion-resistant crops such as alfalfa and clover, periodic retirement of excessively eroded land from cultivation, shifting from soil depleting crops (e.g., cotton and corn) to soil-conserving noncommercial crops, as well as utilizing small-scale engineering structures such as terraces and dams. By 1936, the Service had established 147 demonstration projects, averaging 25,000 to 30,000 acres each and involving about 50,000 farmers.[73]

Although these demonstration projects were judged to be fairly successful, their impact was limited to a relatively small geographic area; the program was not, therefore, spreading soil conservation principles as quickly as desired. SCS officials thus began looking for other approaches to soil conservation that would provide a more comprehensive method of administration and utilization and which could be developed alongside of the demonstration projects. The solution was to encourage the formation of local administrative units called soil conservation districts. The development of these districts not only helped solve the problem of spreading the word, but it also provided the basis for the formation of an active constituency organized into soil conservation district associations. Thus, the desire on the part of the Service to organize farmers into districts was due to administrative, practical, and political reasons, and was explained as such in 1935 by the secretary of agriculture:

> The problem of preventing soil erosion is a social as well as an individual problem, and the soil conservation district associations rest on this principle. The organized farmers of an entire land-use area make a united attack on a problem which they could not solve individually.[74]

To pave the way for the formation of soil conservation districts, the Department of Agriculture prepared a standardized state conservation-districts law which was submitted by President Roosevelt in February of 1937 to the governors of all of the states, along with his recommendation for its passage.[75] By 1944 only three states (Massachusetts, Connecticut, and New Hampshire) did not have SCD (Soil Conservation District) laws, but in 1946 the spokesman for the Service was "happy to report that all three of those states have now enacted legislation in the interest of conservation."[76]

Once a state law had been passed authorizing the formation of soil conservation districts, specific districts were formed by local referenda. Upon petition of at least twenty-five farmers, a state soil conservation committee would fix boundaries for a proposed district. After public hearings, a referendum was held; no district could be organized without a favorable majority vote. Once organized, districts received annual appropriations from the state as well as technical assistance from both state and federal agencies. Specific land-use regulations were also submitted to the public for approval. If a majority favored enactment, the regulation was mandatory for all agricultural lands within the district.[77] The number of districts grew at a rapid rate; appropriations hearings for the agency reveal that there were 132 districts in 1939, 989 in 1944, 2,074 in 1949, 2,549 in 1953, and about 3,000, covering 99 percent of the farms and ranches in the nation, in 1977. In a 1982 book on the subject, one contributor wrote:

> By 1980, there were about 2,950 conservation districts covering some 2.2 billion acres, 1.0 billion acres in farms. ... In other words, virtually all of the land in the United States was within soil conversation districts, though not all farmers in the districts participated in the program. In 1980, about 46 million acres were protected from soil erosion by soil conservation practice.[78]

Although the soil conservation districts have been a noteworthy success, they have not solved the jurisdictional rivalries that have plagued the Soil Conservation Service since its inception. The 1935 enabling act was designed to establish soil conservation as a distinct program and not simply as an adjunct to other existing agricultural programs. But the mandate inherently conflicted and overlapped with the work of several other federal agencies including its closest competitor, the Agricultural Stabilization and Conservation Service (ASCS). These two agencies have existed side by side for six decades; it frequently was suggested that they be merged.[79] But the Soil Conservation Service has been involved in a series of confrontations with several other federal agencies in addition to the ASCS. These bureaucratic conflicts have been described by investigators as a continuous "state of civil war."[80]

When the Soil Conservation Service was created in 1935, the problem of overlapping jurisdictions wasn't readily apparent. It appeared then as though soil erosion—and the resulting Dust Bowl phenomenon—were problems unaddressed by any existing federal program or agency. To a great extent this was true, but it was the implementation of programs aimed at controlling soil erosion which inexorably led the agency into areas that were heavily populated by other units of the federal bureaucracy. A reading of the preamble of the 1935 enabling act makes this clear:

> it is hereby declared to be the policy of Congress to provide permanently for the control and prevention of soil erosion and thereby to preserve

natural resources, control floods, prevent impairment of reservoirs, and maintain the navigability of rivers and harbors, protect public health, public lands and relieve unemployment.[81]

This list of responsibilities overlaps with the missions of several powerful agencies, including the Forest Service and the Corps of Engineers. To fully understand the problems inherent in such a situation, it is necessary to review some of the instances where the Soil Conservation Service was awarded new responsibilities, only to have them later transferred to other agencies. As one author notes, "From 1937 on, SCS was in and out of a number of water supply programs."[82]

In 1938 the Secretary of Agriculture gave the Soil Conservation Service four new programs to administer. First, the land-utilization program authorized by the Bankhead-Jones Farm Tenant Act was transferred to the Service from the Bureau of Agricultural Economics. This program involved purchase and redevelopment of submarginal lands. All of these lands were acquired by the government because they were extensively damaged or otherwise not suitable for cultivation; so in order to prevent further damage, to bring about proper use of the land and to improve the agricultural economy of nearby communities they were transferred to federal control. The purpose of this program was to restore the land to productive use consistent with its capacities. But in 1954, control of the land-utilization program was transferred to the Forest Service.

Second, the Service was assigned drainage and irrigation investigations formerly conducted by the Bureau of Agricultural Engineering. The Soil Conservation Service also received control of certain phases of the farm forestry program authorized by the Norris-Doxey Act of 1937. These responsibilities were expanded in 1942 to include the Prairie States forestry project, but in 1945 the Forest Service took control of the farm forestry program.[83]

In 1938, the Service began work on a water-facilities program authorized by the Pope-Jones Act of 1937. Under this program the Service, in cooperation with two other Agriculture Department agencies, developed small irrigation facilities for farmers and ranchers that were beyond the scope of the large irrigation projects in which the Bureau of Reclamation was operating. This program also involved water projects other than irrigation, such as the construction of stock ponds. In 1942, however, activities under this program were transferred to the Farm Security Administration.[84]

Another program, transferred to the Service from the Farm Security Administration, was of similarly short duration as an SCS program. In 1945, the Soil Conservation Service began work on water conservation and utilization programs authorized by the Case-Wheeler Act of 1939. The water conservation and utilization program was administered cooperatively with the Bureau of Reclamation, the agency responsible for constructing the water-supply features of the program. The Service was responsible for "developing efficient irrigation farming units for qualified farm families."[85] In practice this involved acquiring the land necessary to establish an operating unit, developing that land for efficient use of water (surveys, levelling, and constructing some water-control structures), selling or leasing developed farm units to qualified farm families, and then providing technical guidance in irrigation farming and soil conservation. By 1949 work had begun on fifteen projects in nine Western states, but appropriations hearings held in 1954 report that only four of these projects were still active; two of these four were scheduled for completion by the end of that year.[86]

Its original mandate to control erosion also brought the Soil Conservation Service into the field of flood control, since water is a primary cause of erosion. As early as 1936, the agency was given responsibilities for water management:

> USDA and SCS responsibilities for water began in 1936 with passage of the Omnibus Flood Control Act. In this legislation Congress recognized for the first time the importance of providing upstream watershed protection to compliment the downstream flood control work by the Army Corps of Engineers.[87]

This new mission not only intensified the ongoing rivalry between the Departments of the Interior and Agriculture, but it also precipitated a clash with the Corps of Engineers. The Flood Control Acts of 1936 and 1944 authorized the Service to study and carry out watershed protection and flood protection programs. The agency was drawn further into water development with the passage of the Watershed Protection and Flood Protection Act of 1954. Although effective erosion control would be impossible without water runoff control, the Service was in a poor position to confront the powerful Corps of Engineers. As a result, the Soil Conservation Service limited its water control programs to small upstream projects, which was essentially all that was left after the Corps had claimed the large, expensive, downstream projects. Underscoring the interagency rivalry that was developing, and which became obvious with the 1954 legislation that gave SCS a small watershed program, was the Corps' position on the bill:

> The Army Corps of Engineers, as the principal flood control and dam-building agency of the federal government, opposed the Act. It questioned the need for upstream flood prevention work and the competence of SCS engineers to make flood surveys and design the dams required.[88]

Further indication of the Service's subordinate position vis-à-vis other agencies was the reorganization of the Soil Conservation Service during the Second World War. In 1942 the Service was consolidated with other agencies to form the new Agricultural Conservation and Adjustment Administration. Less than a year later it was transferred to the Food Production Administration where it remained for just four months, then it was transferred to the War Food Administration. At the end of the war the Soil Conservation Service was again placed under the direct control of the secretary of agriculture.[89]

Clearly the competition between the Service and more powerful agencies has been uneven. Although many new programs have been assigned to the Service over its sixty-year existence due to the attractiveness of the soil conservation ideal, actual implementation of these programs has inevitably tread on the toes of the bureaucratic giants. Most recently, the SCS has found itself competing with the influential EPA in the area of wetlands protection. The Corps also is involved in this program. This has not only stifled expansion of the agency's role, but has caused chronic funding difficulties for the programs that have remained within the Service. As early as 1955, budget cuts were causing real problems for recruiting new employees, especially engineers, at levels above GS-11. Salaries were not high enough to be competitive. In addition, personnel reductions were resulting in increased workloads which inevitably raised questions of whether the quality and availability of assistance to soil conservation districts would suffer.[90]

The Service has been forced to operate within the narrow parameters imposed upon it by a crowded bureaucratic environment. Many of the programs dealing with land use and development that were once administered by the Service have been transferred to other agencies. In the area of water development, the large basinwide projects have been built and managed by either the Corps of Engineers, the Bureau of Reclamation, or the Tennessee Valley Authority. This has left the small localized water projects to the Soil Conservation Service, and it is in this area that the Service has been able to operate with relative autonomy. In addition to the flood control acts cited above, there have been a number of statutes and orders from the secretary of agriculture that have created new responsibilities in this area for the Service.

In 1953, the secretary of agriculture placed the Soil Conservation Service in charge of administering all departmental flood prevention and river basin investigations. In the same year, the Service was given responsibility for selecting sites for pilot watershed-protection projects and providing assistance to local groups. Work was quickly begun on sixty projects. The purpose of this program was "to test the practicability of complete watershed protection as a means of conserving soil and water; of alleviating damages from floods, silting of reservoirs, and impairment of stream channels."[91]

The culmination of previous flood control programs came with the enactment of the Watershed Protection and Flood Protection Act in 1954. The Service was given primary responsibility within the Agriculture Department for providing technical and financial assistance to local groups in relation to upstream watershed conservation and flood prevention programs. These local groups agreed to carry out and share the costs of these projects. In subsequent years the authority of this act was amended to include municipal and industrial water-supply development (1956), fish and wildlife development (1958), and water-based public recreation (1962) as purposes eligible for federal cost-sharing with local groups. Small watershed projects thus have been a major focus of the Soil Conservation Service activity over the years. From 1954 to 1972, an estimated 1,235 projects were completed.[92]

The Soil Conservation Service has not limited its activities to water projects, however. There have been a number of programs which include a wide array of erosion prevention techniques. One such program is the Great Plains Conservation Project, authorized by Congress in 1956. This program was aimed at the ten Great Plains states which were most susceptible to wind erosion. Under this voluntary program, assistance is provided to ranchers and farmers in developing operational plans and practices which would minimize the adverse effects of the climate (high winds and recurring droughts), conserve water, and protect against erosion. After a master plan had been developed for a farm or ranch, the Service and the producer would then enter into a long-term cost-sharing contract. As long as the producer accomplished the requirements of his operating plan on schedule, he would receive cost-sharing payments which, by law, could not exceed 80 percent of the cost of installing each eligible practice. Practices eligible for cost-sharing included windbreaks, terrace systems, dams, and irrigation works. By 1959, there were 1,337 long-range cost-sharing contracts in force.[93] By the end of 1975, a total of 49,626 such contracts had been signed.[94] Although the program survived the difficult decade of the 1980s, it is targeted for elimination in the agency's FY 1995 budget.

Another addition to the Service's activities is its resource conservation and development program, which was mandated in the Food and Agriculture Act of 1962. The Soil Conservation Service has administrative leadership for this program within the Agriculture Department and works with four other departmental agencies. Like the Fish and Wildlife Service, the agency's mission has evolved into one with a heavy emphasis on interagency coordination. The program is designed to expand "economic opportunity" in an area by helping local organizations devise plans for the development, conservation, and utilization of natural resources and to provide new employment opportunities to local residents. The pattern of providing technical and financial assistance to local project sponsors is, of course, a standard activity for the agency; the resource conservation and development program differs from past programs by its emphasis on improving the overall economy and living conditions in rural areas as well as the wide range of measures undertaken (including recreational developments, rural sewer systems, and municipal water systems in addition to more traditional soil conservation measures). Ten pilot projects were begun in 1964.[95] As of 1973, 123 projects had been authorized.[96]

With the exception of the program just mentioned, virtually all of the programs administered by the Soil Conservation Service emphasize small, local, relatively isolated projects. This has had an important impact on the development of constituency support for the agency.

Early in its history it became evident that in order to survive the Service had to cultivate strong support among small farmers and rural residents. The primary organizational conduit for this support became the soil conservation districts. Over the years the Soil Conservation Service has grown very dependent on this constituency (it is very much like the Fish and Wildlife Service in this regard), and has made assiduous efforts to maintain its support. In a curious way, the relationship has both helped and hindered the agency. It has helped in that the iron triangle—Congressional committees, pressure groups (especially the Soil and Water Conservation Association and the National Association of Conservation Districts), and the SCS—has insured the survival of the agency in the face of attempts to merge it with other federal bureaus. On the other hand, the close alliance between the agency and a small specialized constituency has not been conducive to agency growth. As one scholar on the subject put it,

> Many other federal programs are subject to pressures of this type, but the pressures seem to have more severely compromised the objectives of the soil conservation programs because the lobby for soil conservation itself is so weak.[97]

The agency's emphasis on local, geographically dispersed projects is also a result of statutory requirements, such as the 1954 Watershed Protection and Flood Prevention Act which was described above. Due to the requirement that every project have "local sponsoring organizations,"[98] the Service developed an even closer relationship with a narrow, specialized clientele. As part of its small watersheds program, the Service began to emphasize structural solutions such as stream channelization. This approach was quite popular with agricultural producers since it tended to subsidize production. But by the 1970s, environmental groups began to protest the long-term impact of stream channelization. A representative of the National Audubon Society explained their view of the practice:

> The channelization emphasis in the Public Law 566 program has to be changed because it leads to the same basic blunders and environmental damages that have resulted from similar projects carried out by the Corps of Engineers and the Bureau of Reclamation.[99]

The Soil Conservation Service could ill afford the wrath of environ-mentalists since this damaged its image as a "conservation" organization. At the same time, the Service did not appear to have the organizational capacity to turn to other kinds of projects, especially those referred to as non-structural alternatives.[100] The agency's inability to diversify was due to statutory restrictions as well as to the fear of alienating traditional sources of constituency support.

As a result of the Service's cautious attitude toward change and its continued dependence on a small and specialized constituency, the agency encountered considerable difficulty in meeting the requirements of the 1969 National Environmental Policy Act. Rather than view the act as an opportunity to expand its mission, as did the Forest Service and the Corps of Engineers, the Soil Conservation Service approached the environmental impact statement process as merely an opportunity to reiterate past policy. Service officials did not request any budgetary or personnel increases in order to meet the new mandate. Richard Andrews observed that:

> SCS policies concerning implementation of N.E.P.A. reflected that agency's traditionally client-centered, negotiative patterns of decision-making. ... In short, SCS policies and public statements during 1970 and 1971 suggested an official willingness to listen to the comments of other agencies and indi-viduals, but no inclination to change priorities or projects as a result unless its own staff and local sponsors wished to do so.[101]

By the mid-1970s, traditional sources of support, its traditional solutions, and the Service's traditional niche in the federal bureaucracy began to show signs of erosion. The Service was being forced to adapt to change by outside forces or face extinction. The number of farmers in American society continued to decrease over the years (at the same time as production increased), while the number of environmentally-conscious city-dwellers increased. Helen Ingram summarized the agency's dilemma:

> The traditional agricultural support of agencies such as the Bureau of Reclamation and the Soil Conservation Service has ebbed. In place of support, these agencies have faced increasing objections from urban interests who balk at paying the bills for projects not obviously serving their needs.[102]

In response to profound demographic changes in America and a new wave of environmental concern, the Service searched for new priorities. By 1975 land conservation had become an important federal program, primarily in the form of technical assistance. Also changed was the Service's performance relative to NEPA's environmental impact statement requirement. The Council of Environmental Quality had rated the agency's performance as "seriously deficient" in 1970; but by 1974 the Service's impact statements were described as among "the most improved."[103] Perhaps this was because they had a long way to go.

Efforts to conform to these changing political realities introduced new problems for the Service, however. Congressional spokesmen for the traditional structural approach to soil conservation began to criticize the newer programs. The old programs were perceived by some as being sacrificed to make way for new ones. During the appropriations hearings of 1975, Representative Andrews of North Dakota accused the Soil Conservation Service of leaving its "wife of many years" in order to pursue the "new blonde down the block."[104] Unfortunately for the SCS, it looked as if there was a double standard at work here. When a large agency, like the Corps, moves into new areas it is greeted with praise by legislators; when a small agency acts similarly, it receives criticism of this nature.

An important piece of legislation passed Congress in 1977, the Soil and Water Resource Conservation Act (RCA). This statute, like a number of others that followed in the wake of NEPA, and which affected other agencies, instructed the SCS to embark upon a comprehensive inventory and evaluation of the nation's natural resource base. It also encouraged the agency to rethink its mission. According to one scholar, the results of the four-year planning effort were meager. Leman wrote that the agency generated volumes of data but ignored real program evaluation, such as the Forest Service was doing under the National Forest Management Act. He concluded: "As a whole, RCA did not work well in my view." [105]

The RCA planning process may not have generated immediate, observable changes in the agency, but according to another analyst it produced longer range dividends. First, the agency "concentrated on [the difficult task of] quantifying soil erosion." This effort ought to be viewed positively. Second, the process begun in the late seventies was part of a continuing effort within the Soil Conservation Service to respond to the "new environmentalism" of the era. This scholar observed: "In retrospect, the RCA seems to have become one of the instrumental factors in passage of the conservation provisions of the 1985 farm bill."[106]

When Ronald Reagan entered office in 1981, the Soil Conservation Service was in a precarious organizational position. Its traditional constituency was growing smaller, it hadn't yet forged a new alliance with environmentalists, the Reagan philosophy frowned on government subsidies, *even* to farmers, and scholars were criticizing the agency for its inability to change with changing times. It looked as though the Service was about to bite the dust.

Consequently during President Reagan's first term, the SCS, like most other domestic agencies, experienced belt-tightening. Its 1981 budget of $588 million declined to $577 million in 1982.[107] An agency spokesman explained the reductions in a 1982 appropriations committee hearing:

> Both the fiscal 1981 and 1982 estimates have incorporated into them a series of reductions reflecting the current administration's efforts to reduce federal travel, procurement, use of consulting services and employment levels. Total reductions of $6.3 million in fiscal year 1981 and $2.7 million in fiscal 1982 have been made to reflect these savings.[108]

Moreover, in its initial year in office the Republican Administration succeeded in making a significant change in the nature of the Service's leadership: It replaced a careerist with a political appointee. Peter Myers, a Missouri farmer, became the first chief of the Soil Conservation Service not to have risen through the professional ranks. Although Myers generally was acknowledged to have been a talented and intelligent executive, as evidenced by the fact that he quickly moved up to the position of Assistant Secretary of Agriculture, it nevertheless marked a new era in the history of the agency. Every chief since Myers has been a political appointee.

Of course, the politicization of the federal bureaucracy during the Reagan years was not confined to the SCS. It was a governmentwide strategy aimed at achieving more centralized control over the executive branch. But some agencies, including some covered in this study, successfully resisted the trend. The SCS could not.

However, the passage of new legislation during the 1980s and 1990s rivalled in significance the change from a career chief to a political appointee. The Food Security Act of 1985, the Clean Water Act of 1987, and the Food, Agriculture, Conservation, and Trade Act of 1990 all affected the SCS. In various ways the three statutes opened a window of opportunity for the agency to broaden its mission and to connect with the environmental community. Several provisions in these congressional acts gave the Service, for instance, a role to play in wetlands conservation, they established the Conservation Reserve Program (CRP), they authorized the agency to monitor and control nonpoint source water pollution (farm runoff), and they provided the authority for an environmental easement program for rural America. Thus the message from Congress to the agency was clear: Become more environmentally conscious, or else.

But at the same time as the Congress was nudging the agency in this direction, the White House, under President Reagan, considered abolishing the agency. The decade of the eighties was an anxiety-ridden one for SCS employees. One official in Washington told us that nearly every year a new organization chart for the Agriculture Department appeared. They would be read with trepidation by SCS staff. In fact, he said, "The OMB's budget proposal for FY '86 almost zeroed out the Soil Conservation Service!" Only an intense lobbying effort on the part of Secretary John Block spared the agency from the budget-cutters' axe.

The reorganization proposed under President Bush was a kinder and gentler one; it would have subsumed the SCS into a large entity called the "Farm Services Agency." But while reorganization of the Agriculture Department was long overdue, little occurred during the Bush presidency. It wasn't until Clinton was elected in 1992 that governmental reorganization got off the drawing boards.

President Clinton made it clear that he was serious about this issue when he appointed Michael Espy, an Afro-American, to the position of Secretary of Agriculture. Espy's mission was to reinvent the department. Early in 1994 Clinton made another significant appointment, that of Paul Johnson, an Iowa farmer and a former state legislator who had distinguished himself as an architect of environmental legislation. He was made chief of the SCS. At the same time Pearlie Reed, an Afro-

American who had been with the agency for twenty-five years, was appointed to associate chief. Reed thus became the second-in-command, and the highest-ranking careerist, in the agency. With this leadership in place, and pushing for it, reorganization of the Agriculture Department finally passed Congress. It was signed by the president in October of 1994.

What our research discovered as the principal organizational problem plaguing the Soil Conservation Service throughout its sixty-year existence appears to have been, at long last, ameliorated. The "crowded bureaucratic niche" in which the agency operated finally has become a little less crowded. Under the reorganization act, the entire SCS, along with parts of the ASCS, is now a "new" agency. It is called the Natural Resources and Conservation Service (NRCS). In addition to all of the SCS' ongoing programs, the NRCS will have authority for the following: Wetlands Reserve Program, Waterbank Program, Colorado River Salinity Program, Forestry Incentives Program, and Farms for the Future.

When we recently suggested to a high-ranking official of the agency that it looked like the SCS was getting "a new lease on life," he replied that he would put it this way: "The reorganization represents an enhancement of the agency's ability to meet the conservation and natural resources needs of the country."

In other words, the SCS/NRCS is a classic example of an agency that muddled through a difficult period. It managed to survive presidential attempts to abolish it entirely, it has moved towards incorporating environmentalists among its clientele, and it appears to have made some progress in diversifying its workforce to meet the needs of the next century. Probably the new agency's greatest internal challenge, like that of the Forest Service, is in recruiting what an official described as an "interdisciplinary, technical workforce" that can operationalize ecosystems management in America's agricultural sector. It is a sector which continues to shrink. For the first time since 1850, it was reported recently that the number of farms in the United States has fallen to below 2 million.[109] The agency, therefore, must redesign its professional workforce at the same time as it is being required, by both the White House and Congress, to downsize and decentralize in response to these demographic changes. These are not insurmountable problems, but they do require ingenuity, strong leadership, and considerable esprit de corps. The recently accomplished reorganization may provide the impetus that is needed to realize these goals within the new Natural Resources and Conservation Service.

THE U.S. FISH AND WILDLIFE SERVICE

Of the seven agencies examined in this study, the Fish and Wildlife Service has the dubious honor of having the most chaotic organizational history. Tracking the agency's evolution is no small task in itself, for it has undergone, from its inception in 1871 to its most recent reorganization in 1970, numerous and frequent permutations. The contemporary agency is thus descended from what Richard Cooley described as a roving parentage. This condition of its history is both cause and effect of its present weak position in the federal bureaucracy, and it serves to underscore the importance of an organization's history to its ability to function effectively at any given time.

The genesis of the Fish and Wildlife Service can be traced to an 1871 resolution of Congress, wherein concern over the possible deterioration of the fishery resource was voiced. Congress resolved

> That the President be ... authorized and required to appoint, by and with the advice and consent of the Senate, from among the civil officers or employees of the government, one person of proved scientific and practical acquaintance with the fishes of the coast, to be commissioner of fish and fisheries, to serve without additional salary.
>
> And be it further resolved, that it shall be the duty of said commissioner to prosecute investigations and inquiries on the subject, with the view of ascertaining whether any and what diminution in the number of food fishes of the coasts and lakes of the United States has taken place; and if so, to what causes the same is due; and also whether any and what protective, prohibitory, or precautionary measures should be adopted in the premises; and to report upon the same to Congress.[110]

By 1892 the Fish Commissioner together with an assistant inspector were given the chore of enforcing a legislative prohibition against barricading streams to capture salmon. The government's interest in overseeing the Alaskan salmon industry became evident at this time, and the early history of the U.S. Fish Commission became inextricably intertwined with this one industry.

A pattern of agency dependence upon the largesse of the fishing industry began at this time. The fish inspectors were not provided with a governmental means of transportation so they frequently were obliged to rely upon the boats of salmon packers to get from one cannery to another.[111] Related to this was the action taken by Congress in 1903 to create a new agency, the Bureau of Fisheries, and to house it in the then Department of Commerce and Labor. The U.S. Fish Commission in the Treasury Department was assimilated into the Bureau. According to Cooley this transfer was the first step taken to insure that the regulator was controlled by the regulated, since the orientation of the Commerce Department was both positive toward and supportive of the commercial fishing industry.[112] Given a dual mandate from Congress, to conserve and protect while at the same time to promote the fishery resource, the Bureau understandably was beset with difficulties in distinguishing between its two primary, and often conflicting, functions. Like the National Park Service, the Fish and Wildlife Service originally was told to pursue two quite opposed functions, and each agency's history records the numerous problems arising out of an original dichotomous mission. As we will see, the Fish and Wildlife Service was never able to resolve the contradiction to its advantage.

Not only was the Bureau of Fisheries plagued with problems related to its mission, but in its formative years the agency also became identified with a particular geographic region and a particular industry—Alaska and the salmon business. From its inception in 1903 until passage of the White Act in 1924, the Bureau was utterly unsuccessful at regulating the salmon industry. According to Cooley, it not only lacked the necessary expertise, but also the will. Congress, moreover, was for a long time reluctant to act on the issue of regulating the fishing industry:

> Bills continued to be introduced in each session of Congress "for the protection and conservation of the Alaska fisheries," but for one reason or another they drew sufficient opposition from the interest groups to prevent their passage. As prices of canned salmon soared during the war, the intensity of fishing and canning operators rose to new heights with little interference from the federal government. The factor most responsible for causing a break in the legislative stalemate was the collapse of the markets for canned salmon immediately following World War I.[113]

Passage of the White Act in 1924 temporarily improved the Bureau's situation, for the legislation contained specific and enforceable provisions to regulate the fishing industry in order to guarantee future supplies. As Cooley notes, however, the impetus for the legislation did not arise from a commitment to conservation values but rather from the desire to guarantee continual pecuniary enrichment to the industry.[114] Enacted when the industry was in an economic slump, the Bureau of Fisheries became a convenient scapegoat and was criticized from all sides for not having effectively regulated the industry in the past! Thus while conservation and regulation were temporarily in vogue, with a change in the economic conditions surrounding the fishing industry, the Bureau lapsed back into its ineffectual role. For example, in reviewing the agency's mid-century accomplishments, Senator Ernest Gruening of Alaska said:

> It is, in fact, the story of a colossal failure, the failure of a United States government agency entrusted with the high responsibility of conserving this great national heritage to perform its function. The fact is that during the years of their trusteeship the federal regulatory agencies—since 1940 the Fish and Wildlife Service—instead of regulating the industry were regulated and controlled by it. The twenty years of Fish and Wildlife control, from 1940 until statehood in 1959, were the most disastrous of all. These were the years of the decline and near-extinction of the Pacific Salmon in Alaska.[115]

The contemporary agency to which Gruening refers is the result of a 1940 executive reorganization which combined the hapless Bureau of Fisheries with the somewhat more successful Bureau of Biological Survey. This union came a year after a previous reorganization was ordered by President Franklin Roosevelt that transferred the Bureau of Fisheries from the Commerce Department to the Department of the Interior. That reorganization also brought the Agriculture Department's Biological Survey into Interior. (To this extent, Secretary of the Interior Ickes' raid on other departments was successful, although it is worth noting that he was not able to extend his influence over two of the most powerful resource agencies, the Forest Service and the Corps of Engineers. They remained in the Departments of Agriculture and War respectively.) As was the case with the 1946 merger which produced the Bureau of Land Management, the U.S.

Fish and Wildlife Service was the product of hybrid thinking with the object being the creation of an offspring that hopefully combined the strongest elements of its parentage.

An important result of this merger was the transformation of a dominant-use agency into a rather more diversified organization. The Bureau of Biological Survey brought to the new Fish and Wildlife Service a federal concern for the conservation and protection of wildlife. In 1900 Congress passed the Lacey Act, which enjoined the secretary of agriculture to prohibit the interstate commerce of game killed in violation of local laws. With a clear conservationist intent, the act reads in part:

> That the duties and powers of the Department of Agriculture are hereby enlarged so as to include the preservation, distribution, introduction, and restoration of game birds and other wild birds. ... The object and purpose of this Act is to aid in the restoration of such birds in those parts of the United States adapted thereto where the same have become scarce or extinct, and also to regulate the introduction of American or foreign birds or animals in localities where they have not heretofore existed.[116]

Three more legislative actions enlarged the responsibilities of the Department of Agriculture and its Bureau of Biological Survey before the 1939 reorganization. In 1918 Congress passed the Migratory Bird Treaty Act, signed with Great Britain (for the commonwealth of Canada). This act, as modified by a 1934 statute commonly referred to as the "Duck Stamp Act," comprise the statutory authority for the creation of a national wildlife refuge system. The 1934 act provides "funds for the acquisition of areas for use as migratory bird sanctuaries, refuges, and breeding grounds," and "for developing and administering such areas."[117]

Also in that year the Fish and Wildlife Coordination Act was passed. Transferred to the Fish and Wildlife Service in 1940, this authority may well epitomize the kind of problems subsequently encountered by the Service. The act contains a general statement concerning the importance of preserving the nation's fish and wildlife resources, and implies that any federal project which might affect these resources is to be carefully reviewed and evaluated. It was not clear, however, what projects and which federal agencies were covered by the legislation (or so some reasoned), and thus many powerful agencies simply exempted themselves from the Service's scrutiny. For example, the Atomic Energy Commission created in 1946 insisted for some time that it was not affected by the legislation and therefore did not have to consider the Fish and Wildlife Service's recommendations. The major limitations of the 1934 act were thus its discretionary nature and the lack of any enforcement provisions. "Coordination" was simply not a sufficiently strong concept to force federal agencies at the time—or perhaps at any time—to take an unbiased look at the possible adverse environmental effects of their activities. Thus the effectiveness of the act, as is the case with much of what the Service did and does, depended more on the voluntary compliance of others as it did on the actions of Fish and Wildlife coordinators. In the eyes of many, the Service has been perceived as not much more than an organizational nuisance.

By the time the Fish and Wildlife Service was established in 1940, its environment, functions, and problems were fairly well defined. Since there was no legislative action on this executive reorganization until 1956, the Fish and Wildlife Service existed for some sixteen years without an organic act. This of course did not help the agency to rapidly develop into an influential protector of the nation's fish and wildlife resources. Moreover, the Service's political development was hampered by problems that it inherited from agencies which it replaced. The Bureau of Biological Survey, previously a unit in the Department of Agriculture, had been for years the locus for an intense battle between wildlife preservationists and sportsmen. The former pushed for the creation of inviolate wildlife refuges which would protect rare and/or endangered forms of animal life; but the latter wanted a refuge system that would insure a continued supply of wildlife for consumptive or recreational use. A third group—ranchers—pressured the Bureau in the direction of predator control. When the Fish and Wildlife Service was formed in 1940, it fell heir to much of this political conflict that previously had plagued the Bureau of Biological Survey. The new agency also inherited the political instability of the Bureau of Fisheries, which had been transferred from Commerce to the Interior Department just two years before it became absorbed in the "new" Fish and Wildlife Service.

The history of the Service from 1940 to 1969 is the description of an agency gradually expanding its services within a clearly circumscribed range. That is, the agency did not actively seek out any new functions, and in fact lost an important commercial function in 1956 due to its inability to reconcile the two missions. Budgetary limitations coupled with a relatively obscure mission go a long way toward accounting for the Service's low profile.

Like the Bureau of Reclamation, the Fish and Wildlife Service's budgetary base for years was derived primarily from earmarked monies. Beginning in 1934, the federal government began collecting a tax on migratory bird hunting licenses (the Duck Stamp). These revenues were earmarked: ninety percent of it was authorized to go toward the federal acquisition of wetlands and other bird and waterfowl habitats. The remaining ten percent was to be spent on managing the refuges. Yearly fluctuations in the fund provided an unstable budgetary base for the Service and consequently hindered the agency's activities. Service personnel found it particularly difficult to operate and maintain a wildlife refuge system on an uncertain ten percent of stamp receipts, and Congress often was reluctant to give the agency an additional appropriation. The appropriations hearings for this period contain frequent references—accusations about and apologies for—the deteriorating condition of the refuges. Finally in 1960, however, the Duck Stamp Act was amended to give the agency a more favorable financial environment.

Congress' stinginess toward the Service was in part a reflection of the agency's narrow mission as well as the lack of strong, broad-based clientele support. Most of the activities engaged in by the Service have little impact on the general public or on any large segment thereof. While the Service has contributed significantly to the protection and preservation of several species of wildlife, the problem is that these benefits are not experienced or even much appreciated by the mass public. For example, most waterfowl are not shot on the refuges and the only encounters that the average duck hunter may have with the Fish and Wildlife Service is when he buys a duck stamp at the postal service or at other locations. Similarly, the Service has been of importance in the maintenance of many species of fish in the United States, through both its own research and operation of fish hatcheries as well as through its assistance to state fish programs. Unfortunately, the fish nurtured by the Service can be caught nearly anywhere, and so the agency does not always get the credit—and political support—it deserves.

Consequently, of the two primary conservation activities engaged in by the agency, neither one is notable for an impressive growth rate. When the Service was established in 1940, there existed ninety federal fish hatcheries. Twenty-five years later, in 1965, there were eighty-nine. Ten years later, in 1975, the Service had increased its hatcheries to a total of ninety. Then the Reagan administration reduced the number of hatcheries to 69, and currently there are only 71. The number and size of national wildlife refuges did undergo some growth but not, according to agency personnel, fast enough to keep up with the public demand that burgeoned in the 1950s. In 1941, the Service managed 267 refuges, totalling 13.8 million acres. By 1967, the number was up to 307, covering some 28.8 million acres. However, with the additions of new Alaskan lands, the acreage contained in the refuge and wildlife system skyrocketed to 88 million; the number of separate refuges climbed to 413. Today the agency manages a total of 786 refuges, hatcheries, and other units encompassing 90.5 million acres.

But despite this rather dramatic increase in both units and acres, there has not been a concomitant rise in recognition or political "credit." The Service seems to be perennially overshadowed by better known agencies. For example, by 1970, the Fish and Wildlife Service managed more land than did the National Park Service,[118] yet the latter agency enjoyed considerably more public recognition than did its lesser-known counterpart. In addition to its having an obscure mission the Fish and Wildlife Service has been a distinctly regional agency: 86 percent of its total land holdings are contained in three Alaskan refuges, and nearly all other refuges are located in a few Western states where population has been sparse until recently. Undoubtedly this regionalism accounts in large part for the agency's lack of national visibility.

By 1956, considerable interest on the part of Washington policy-makers had developed in restructuring the Fish and Wildlife Service—in particular, in depriving it of a primary part of its duties. With the 1940 reorganization the Service began to view itself principally as a research and refuge-managing agency with a pronounced conservation-oriented mission. Consequently, the commercial fisheries section of the agency received short shrift. Pressure from the fishing industry thus induced the government to reorganize the Service, and after lengthy debates between the two houses of Congress and with the executive branch, a compromise measure was reached. The legislative result was enactment of the Fish and Wildlife Act of 1956. This statute gave the agency its long-awaited organic act but it also laid out a rather elaborate reorganization that effectively bifurcated the Service. The legislation created the position of Assistant Secretary, within the Interior Department, for Fish and Wildlife, plus the position of Commissioner of Fish and Wildlife. Beneath these positions there was created a U.S. Fish and Wildlife Service, but "consisting of two separate agencies,"[119] each of which would have the status of a federal bureau. Thus came into existence the Bureau of Commercial Fisheries and the Bureau of Sports Fisheries and Wildlife, plus a kind of phantom agency called the U.S. Fish and Wildlife Service which existed at the assistant secretariat level.

While on an organization chart the reorganization may have looked like the Service was at long last getting the recognition it deserved, this was clearly not the case. The Assistant Secretary for Fish and Wildlife soon became the Assistant Secretary for Fish, Wildlife, and Parks, and by 1976 the Bureau of Outdoor Recreation also came under his or her direction. During the reorganization hearings a departmental official had characterized the Service as "merely a little branch buried in the Department of the Interior."[120] The 1956 reorganization did little if anything to change that condition, and indeed the division of the Service into two distinct bureaus presaged future trouble. In 1970, the Bureau of Commercial Fisheries was returned to its original home in the Commerce Department to be merged with the newly created National Oceanographic and Atmospheric Administration. The Bureau of Sports Fisheries and Wildlife, which was what remained of the original agency after it succumbed to the powerful centrifugal forces that operate in many natural resources agencies,[121] became—again—the U.S. Fish and Wildlife Service.

The recent history of the agency, from its 1970 reorganization to the present, shows a familiar pattern of behavior. A major problem of the Service has to do with its organizational character—that is, its outlook and orientation to public policy. The agency is perhaps best characterized as a secondary service organization. It has not been able to break out of this conservative orientation. The attitude of agency personnel is basically that of being enthusiastic, behind-the-scenes helpers. Rather than its becoming a leader in the environmental movement which developed during the 1960s, the Service maintained its traditional low profile and was frequently criticized for its timidity. A Department of the Interior spokesman commented on this in 1972:

> When I came to Washington to assume jurisdiction over the Bureau of Sports Fisheries and Wildlife just 9 months ago, I expected to find a small, hard-hitting, nationally influential protector of fish and wildlife. ... One element of my image of the Bureau proved accurate—it was small. Other than that, it was not exaggerating to characterize the organization as a paper tiger. ... Here we had, then, a group of highly motivated, well trained professionals who were frustrated and somewhat demoralized in achieving their mission.[122]

In 1973, the Secretary of the Interior admonished the agency for still not having become the biological arm of the department. The apparent reluctance of the agency to take on new responsibilities may be a result of the Service's failures in the past to hold on to existing programs. After the 1956 reorganization, for example, the Service sustained yet another blow to its mission. As described earlier, the agency had supervision over the game and fish laws for the territory of Alaska, and it shared with other Interior Department agencies the general responsibility for the federal administration of Alaska throughout half of the twentieth century. However, when Alaska became a state in 1959 much of this authority was turned over to the state. The Service retained control only over those same duties that it had in the other states—the administration of its federal refuges and fish hatcheries, which admittedly are large, and also a limited supervision of wildlife programs on the other federal lands in the state.

Throughout the 1960s the agency followed behind the growing environmental movement in this country. An irony of the Fish and Wildlife Service's position with respect to the environmental issue is found in its commitment to a rodent and pest control program at this time. In a study commissioned by the Secretary of the Interior, the Service was criticized for its zeal in pursuing this one particular activity, and was in effect told that it had gone far beyond the bounds of necessity in implementing a minor program. At the same time, the Service, which had long had the authority to review the use of pesticides for their effect on fish and wildlife, did little to further the movement to regulate pesticide use. It supported such actions, but again it did so in its traditional, supportive role. Taking the lead in any activity or issue was an alien role for the agency.

The environmental movement and the ensuing legislation passed by Congress dealing with environmental quality issues had a major impact on the Fish and Wildlife Service in the decade of the 1970s. Organizationally, the agency was quite unprepared to deal with the overwhelming increase in its workload resulting from the new legislation and new programs. The 1969 National Environmental Policy Act, the planning and construction of the Trans-Alaska pipeline, the stringent Endangered Species Act of 1973, plus the several air and water quality acts virtually overwhelmed the small agency. The Service was well aware of the potential for its own aggrandizement contained in these acts, but since it had never developed a strong organizational infrastructure it was ill-equipped to take advantage of the moment.

Consequently, the word *overcommitment* runs like a red thread through congressional oversight and appropriations hearings beginning in the early 1970s. It may provide the most accurate assessment of the Service in this period. Within its established programs, the Service tried to put the greatest emphasis on its refuge program, yet the consistent conclusion of agency officials and others was that the refuges were understaffed and in a process of disintegration. Agency figures for 1973, for example, show an average of three administrative personnel per refuge. One member of Congress complained about the poor condition of the refuges, stating, "I don't think there is a single member of this Congress who is not besieged by mail to upgrade refuge facilities."[123]

The workload, and resulting paper work that soon became the most obvious result of a national concern with environmental quality, proved to be an enormous burden on the small agency. In 1971, the Service anticipated having to do the following "coordination" work: reconnaissance and feasibility studies for 50 Bureau of Reclamation projects, 140 Corps of Engineers projects, and 410 other federal water projects; the review of 6,000 Department of the Army permit applications for work on navigable waterways, leading to the preparation of 400 reports; 130 nonfederal applications for the Federal Power Commission, 50 for the Atomic Energy Commission, and 16 for the Forest Service and the Bureau of Land Management.

In addition, the Service expected to review at least 1,200 environmental impact statements during the last half of fiscal year 1971. Understandably, the Service felt itself inundated. An agency official complained in 1972 to the appropriations committee: "our management resources include 30 million acres of habitat, 629 field stations, personnel of 3,958 ... there is a situation of imbalance, this is imbalance of programs to our capability which does result in an overcommitment."[124] There was simply no way that the agency could effectively deal with the staggering increase in its duties that resulted from this latest concern for the environment.

The Service's problems in meeting the mandate of the National Environmental Policy Act were exacerbated by what has been called a "brain drain" from the agency. With the passage of NEPA, federal agencies were suddenly in need of biologists and related professionals who could prepare impact statements for agency activities. The Fish and Wildlife Service, which had such people, began losing its personnel to higher-paying agencies. Thus NEPA, which was highly congruent with the agency's environment-oriented mission, could have been expected to contribute substantially to the Service's growth and visibility. Instead, it caused innumerable problems for an agency quite unprepared for new mandates and for the predatory activity of other federal agencies.

Funding for the Fish and Wildlife Service in recent years has likewise taken a cautious, incremental path. From 1975 to 1980, the Service received a moderate increase in funding, culminating in a 1980 budget of $433 million.[125] But the agency's budget came under attack by the Reagan administration. Secretary of the Interior James Watt voiced considerable criticism of the Service in the 1982 appropriations hearings, and promised to revamp the agency's priorities:

> there will be major—and I want to underline the word "major"— there will be major changes in the management of the Fish and Wildlife Service. ... It [the Service] need not stop economic activity, economic growth and job opportunities. In too many instances I believe that it has. ... With the changes in budgetary requirements that I am requesting, we will get the attention of the management of the Fish and Wildlife System and new ways and new techniques will be installed throughout that service. I mean throughout, not just in Washington.[126]

The 1982 proposed budget for the Fish and Wildlife Service underwent a curious series of revisions, primarily because of the conflicting demands generated by Secretary Watt on the one hand and an enormous increase in responsibilities on the other. As mentioned earlier, the 1980 Alaska National Interest Lands Conservation Act (ANILCA) established nine new units of the National Wildlife Refuge System, and enlarged and consolidated several existing units. As a result, the total acreage of National Wildlife Refuge lands administered by the Fish and Wildlife Service in Alaska jumped from 22 million to 76 million.[127] In spite of these increases, the Reagan administration cut the agency's budget. The Department of the Interior originally intended to increase the agency's budget, with OMB's agreement, and so $5 million was added for resource management. In a subsequent round of budget decisions, however, the agency's funds for this particular item were reduced by $42.6 million. In fact, during a recess in the appropriations hearings, several cuts were made by the administration which necessitated a repeat discussion of items already reviewed by the subcommittee because, in the space of a few days, the totals had changed significantly.[128] The acting director of the Service described his agency's budget *before* these reductions were made as "a bare-bones budget" which does not provide sufficient funds "to carry out all the responsibilities which Congress has given us."[129]

With the resignation of James Watt as interior secretary, the fortunes of the Fish and Wildlife Service improved marginally. But the agency still faced a series of budget cuts at a time when its duties were expanding exponentially. Throughout Reagan's eight years in office the agency found its only friends in the Democrat-controlled Congress; as one Fish and Wildlife Service employee put it, "Congress saved the Service" during that difficult time. The Bush administration was somewhat more supportive, but the agency had to deal with an interior secretary, Manuel Lujan, who was antagonistic to many of the agency's goals. Thus, throughout the eighties the agency fought a defensive strategy to avoid being overwhelmed by both its critics and its workload. Two issues in particular have caused problems for the agency: wetlands protection and the Endangered Species Act.

The Fish and Wildlife Service, along with the Corps and two other agencies, administers the "404" wetlands program (see also the earlier discussion of the Corps of Engineers' role in chapter 2). But unlike the

Corps, this task is directly related to the basic mission of the agency. Because of that, it has created political problems for the Service. During the Reagan years, for instance, the opposition to wetlands protection came directly from the White House. President Bush was more supportive of the wetlands program, promising a "no net loss" policy, but then the issue became mired in the debate over the definition of a wetland. Nevertheless, between 1989 and 1992 the agency's wetlands budget increased 156 percent. The agency's director noted in hearings that "for 1991, this agency was able to enhance, restore, or protect some 542,000 acres of wetlands"[130] The Clinton administration has continued the policy of no-net-loss, but the question of what constitutes an appropriate definition of a wetland has yet to be resolved.

A second and more problematic challenge for the Fish and Wildlife Service is the administration of the 1973 Endangered Species Act (the ESA). This act created two "listings" of animals and plants: the "endangered" list which includes species at risk of extinction throughout a significant portion of their habitat; and the "threatened" list which includes those species that are not yet at risk, but are likely to become so in the foreseeable future. The act requires the Fish and Wildlife Service to designate "critical habitat" for all listed species. In addition, it sets up a specific time-table for the listing process. Any person or party can petition to list a species. The agency then has ninety days to determine if the petition is scientifically credible. Then, within a year the agency must complete an extensive research process to determine whether the species should be listed and, if so, to issue a "recovery plan" to aid the species' survival. The Fish and Wildlife Service must also review all listings every five years to see whether the status of any species should be changed.[131]

In short, the Endangered Species Act created a huge new administrative burden for the understaffed agency. The act's power was not fully realized, however, until it was used in an attempt to stop the construction of the Tellico Dam in Tennessee. That effort ultimately failed, but environmental groups and wildlife activists realized the act was a potent weapon in their fight to protect natural habitat. As a result, by the 1980s the Fish and Wildlife Service was inundated with petitions for listings. As of January 1995, 944 species in the United States were listed; but only 415 recovery plans have been completed for these species. The agency also has listed 532 foreign species, but recovery plans for these are not required. Another 4,100 candidate species are waiting to be reviewed.

Despite this enormous backlog, the Fish and Wildlife Service spends much of its funding on a few high-profile species. A recent analysis of spending patterns for recovery plans found that fifty species received 85.5 percent of the funding; 229 listed species received no funding whatsoever.[132] For example, in FY 1991 the government spent $24.6 million on the bald eagle, but only $3.50 on the sperm whale.[133] This is despite the fact that the bald eagle is "making a remarkable comeback."[134] And, of course, the high-profile conflict over the spotted owl consumes tremendous resources, but no one in the Fish and Wildlife Service could tell us how much has been spent in the effort to protect the owl.

The Reagan administration dealt with conflicts over endangered species by trying to hamstring the agency through budget cuts. But the Bush administration realized that cutting the agency's funding just slowed the listing process, and consequently the agency's budget for endangered species doubled during Bush's tenure in office. The Clinton administration has continued this policy. In budget hearings Secretary of the Interior Bruce Babbitt said that the fiscal year 1994 budget "includes substantial increases in all facets of the endangered species program from prelisting activities through the implementation of recovery actions."[135]

But funding for the endangered species program faces a very uncertain future in the 104th Congress. The act is due for reauthorization, and it must contend with a number of critical and powerful legislators. Don Young of Alaska, the new chairman of the House Natural Resources Committee, is overtly hostile to the act. In the Senate, Frank Murkowski, also an avowed opponent of the Endangered Species Act, is now chair of the Energy and Natural Resources Committee.

Much of the opposition to the Endangered Species Act concerns two related issues: private property rights and economic impact. Opponents of the ESA claim it gives the agency too much control over private property. The act prohibits the "taking" of an endangered or threatened species wherever it is located. The next question is: Does the destruction of that species' habitat constitute a taking? The Fish and Wildlife Service has argued that it does. So have some federal courts. This gives the agency a considerable amount of control over private lands that contain critical habitat. But property rights advocates counter that any federal regulation of private property which in effect reduces the economic potential of the property is a taking under the Fifth Amendment of the Constitution, and thus warrants just compensation.

A frank discussion of the impact of the act on private lands occurred in House appropriations hearings in 1990 at the height of the fight over the spotted owl's habitat in old-growth forests. The following exchange is between Congressman Les AuCoin of Oregon, former Fish and Wildlife Service Director John Turner, and one of the agency's regional directors:

> MR. LAMBERTSON: The legal standard is "take," but there could be habitat disruption activities that would result in a take.
>
> MR. AuCOIN: I understand. This raises an interesting question. If all of that is true, then, could the range-wide recovery plan then include guidelines, frameworks, prescriptions, and proscriptions on both public and private lands for the recovery plan itself?
>
> MR. TURNER: Yes.
>
> MR. AuCOIN: It could?
>
> MR. TURNER: We have worked out what I think are some innovative solutions to these tough questions on what constitutes "takes." We are allowing development and commodity use to continue on private lands and so forth, by setting up these conservation areas.[136]

In other words, the Bush administration tried mightily to minimize the impact of the act on private property, but it nevertheless recognized that the Fish and Wildlife Service does indeed have the authority to regulate private landowners. This attempt to find a political middle ground ultimately failed. The issue of private property put the Fish and Wildlife Service squarely in the sights of the vociferous property rights movement, and environmentalists have vowed to resist any significant alteration of the Endangered Species Act. Once again the Service is caught in the political crossfire.

The other, related issue that has provoked opposition concerns the economic impact the Endangered Species Act has on both public and private lands. The act stipulates that only biological factors can be taken into account when the agency reviews petitions for listing; such decisions must be based on "the best scientific and commercial data available." However, when determining critical habitat, the agency may use scientific data only after "taking into consideration the economic impact" of the designation.[137]

Proponents of the ESA say it has had a negligible impact on economic development. In 1991 the agency completed 2,000 formal consultations (discussions with other federal agencies regarding a protective strategy for a listed species) and 15,000 informal consultations; only twenty-three of these resulted in a finding of "no reasonable alternative" which stopped development.[138] Also, the General Accounting Office found that the agency *had* considered economic impact in the listing process, despite the law.[139]

On the other hand, in those cases where development has been stopped, the economic impact has sometimes been significant. In the case of the spotted owl, timber companies claim that it will eliminate thousands of jobs. Environmentalists dispute that claim, but nevertheless the act has the potential to have a direct and significant economic impact on whoever happens to be working or living in a critical habitat. The Republican majority in the 104th Congress has vowed to amend the Endangered Species Act to permit economic variables to be considered equally with biological considerations when a listing decision is made.

What does all this mean for an agency that is muddling through? In the case of Fish and Wildlife, it means that "overcommitted" is no longer a suffiiciently strong term. Today, two terms better describe the agency: overwhelmed and besieged.

The Fish and Wildlife Service is *overwhelmed* by inadequate resources, bitter controversies, and difficult if not impossible assignments. Evidence of this can be found throughout the agency's recent history. For example, in its fiscal year 1989 budget proposal, the Fish and Wildlife Service's budget was $41 million below the previous year's budget, even though eleven new wildlife refuges had been added to the system. That same year the agency employed just 202 law enforcement agents to patrol 90.5 million acres.

In appropriations hearings in 1991 Secretary Lujan explained that his budget focused on the agency's backlog: "We have proposed to do some catch-up on our refuges ... . We have had 54 new refuges added in the last seven years. We simply have not been able to keep up operationally."[140] In the same hearing, Director John Turner defended his agency's slow response in the spotted owl case: "[Our] workload ...

has been overwhelming." He added that the agency simply lacked "the resources" to respond in a timely manner.[141]

The following year Congressman Sidney Yates had this exchange with Director Turner regarding the agency's workload:

> *CHAIRMAN YATES:* By the end of 1991, you had 472 national wildlife refuges and you're projecting an addition of 14 more in 1992, 5 more in 1993, bringing the total to 491 national wildlife refuges. How are you going to pay for the new refuges and take care of your old ones? Are you going to let your old ones suffer?
> *DIRECTOR TURNER:* It's a balancing question. ... We're trying to hold the line and pick up critical pieces and yet take good care of the 91 million acres that we now have.[142]

We note that not all of the new additions to the wildlife refuge system are due to the Service's desire to "pick up critical pieces." Like the "park barrel" phenomenon that has afflicted the National Park Service, congresspersons sometimes find it in their best political interest to give their constituents a new refuge. This creates yet another major task for the Service; 35 million people visited the agency's refuges in 1994.[143] Thus new burdens are routinely imposed on the Fish and Wildlife Service with little consideration as to their implementation.

If all this expansion of mission and responsibilities were adequately funded and widely supported, it would be in the agency's long-term interest to encourage more refuges, more visitors, and more endangered species petitions. But of course such conditions are not the case. Instead the agency is *besieged* by critics. In the spotted owl case the agency was successfully sued by environmental groups. The judge's scathing opinion read in part: "nowhere in the proposed or final rules did the Service state what efforts had been made to determine critical habitat. Nowhere did the Service specify what additional biological or economic information was necessary to complete this designation. Nowhere did the Service explain why critical habitat was not determinable."[144] An angry Congressman AuCoin told Director Turner that the agency's behavior on this issue made him "do a slow burn."[145] The Forest Products Association also sued the Service on the spotted owl issue.[146] Recently the court approved President Clinton's proposed compromise on the spotted owl, the so-called Option 9, but *both* environmentalists and the timber companies are opposed to it. The Fish and Wildlife Service simply can't win.

The spotted owl is not the only issue where the Service is besieged by an army of critics. In the Colorado River Basin, environmental groups successfully sued the agency to force it to list four native fish species. As a result, the Service determined that the Animas–La Plata Project in Colorado represented a threat to these species, and halted it before construction began. This project was the keystone to the 1988 Colorado Ute Water Settlement, so the Service's action infuriated the two Colorado Ute tribes. The agency also has managed to anger the Navajo nation by placing limits on tribal water and land development.[147]

In sum, the agency faces opposition from environmental groups, extractive industries, developers, Indian tribes, and a coterie of legislators who have assumed powerful positions in the House and Senate. It has few constituencies on which it can depend for support. What does this portend for the agency's future? The answer may lie in the saga of the National Biological Service. In 1993 Secretary of the Interior Bruce Babbitt created a new agency that would perform a nation-wide assessment of the country's biological resources, in much the same manner that the United States Geological Survey mapped the country in the last century. His purpose was to generate sufficient data so that unpleasant surprises concerning the condition of species could be avoided. Thus the new agency would "provide an anticipatory, objective biological science program that will contribute to the development of comprehensive ecosystem management strategies, thus avoiding costs and conflicts such as those involved in several past Endangered Species Act crises."[148]

As in so many other political situations, the Fish and Wildlife Service took the greatest hit: 90 percent of the new agency's budget, and 80 percent of its employees, came from the Fish and Wildlife Service. Virtually its entire research arm was transferred. And, like other Clinton environmental initiatives, this proposal immediately ran into a torrent of opposition. Secretary Babbitt created the agency within Interior by secretarial order, but he wanted a formal congressional authorization to give the agency a solid organic foundation. He probably will not get it. The National Biological Service is opposed by property rights advocates; their spokesman in the Senate is Frank Murkowski, new chair of the Committee on Energy and Natural

Resources. In a recent speech Murkowski hinted darkly that, if any federal biologists came on *his* property without permission, they would never leave. In the House the National Biological Service has been added to a list of agencies proposed for termination.

Despite numerous political controversies, organizational vagaries, and budget cuts, the Service has taken a lead role in developing and implementing "ecosystems management," a concept that has become virtually a mantra among federal resource managers. The agency's current director, Mollie Beattie, is attempting to reorganize the Service's budget into an ecosystems format. To perform this make-over the Service had a 1994 budget of $1.2 billion (which reflects the loss of funding to the National Biological Service), and a total full-time workforce of 7,363.

Thus, the Fish and Wildlife Service grimly marches on. If grizzly bears and bald eagles voted, then the agency's problems would be over. However, the reality is that people want wildlife protection, but they also want many other things that are inherently inimical to habitat preservation. The Fish and Wildlife Service must live with this contradiction. Considering the conditions under which it exists, the Service has done a heroic job. But anything more than a slow muddling through is simply beyond the agency's capacity. In our concluding chapter we offer an organizational alternative for this agency, and for the two agencies suffering from the shooting star syndrome. We will argue that it is time for another reorganization of the Fish and Wildlife Service.

SUMMARY: AN INCREMENTAL MODEL OF DEVELOPMENT

Both the circumstances and the behavior of the three agencies discussed here contrast sharply with the two largest resource managers, the Corps and the Forest Service. These smaller organizations are by no means failures, if one is judging failure by evaluating their respective records of accomplishment; yet one gets the strong impression that they have not developed to their fullest potential, either. Certain limiting factors have produced a history and a pattern of behavior that we think is aptly described as incremental. And, just as Lindblom by no means meant to disparage the bureaucratic behavior that he characterized as "muddling through," we intend no necessarily invidious comparison when we point out, for example, that the National Park Service is not the U.S. Forest Service, despite a long history of competition between them.

The conditions that circumscribe the behavior of these agencies include the following: the nature of the mission; the professional base of the organization; and the nature of their constituencies. In all three histories of the Park Service, Soil Conservation Service, and Fish and Wildlife Service, one can see the circumstances that produce a "typical" federal agency. The Park and Fish and Wildlife Services both had to wrestle with an original, dichotomous mission. Both were given at the time of their creation two independent and essentially conflicting goals—to preserve on the one hand and to use on the other. As we pointed out, this led to some schizophrenic behavior on the part of the agencies' staff in trying to reconcile that which isn't very reconcilable. It also led to considerable criticism. In one case, Congress eventually took away entirely the development function from the agency; in the other case, zoning for dominant use (or nonuse) seems to have settled the issue there. But in both cases the agencies' early development was hurt by the existence of contradictory, ambiguous goals. These divided the organization and its constituency in a way that seemed to produce, to the outside observer, excessively vacillating behavior.

The Soil Conservation Service, now reorganized into the Natural Resources and Conservation Service, did not have a contradictory mission with which to wrestle, but it did have a relatively narrow one. In a 1982 book on the subject, one scholar suggests that the agency had not significantly grown because public attitudes about soil conservation have remained static. In looking at data on federal funding for soil conservation from 1950 to 1980, Easter and Cotner found:

> Over the 30-year period, the expenditure in deflated dollars per year has remained in the $700 million to $750 million range. Therefore, public expenditures to support conservation programs have not increased. This implies that society, through its governmental processes, has assigned about the same level of priority to conservation investment now as it did 40 years ago. In fact, the implication may be a lower priority because total public expenditures have increased rapidly during this period.[149]

This is another way in which organizations get boxed in: Either their functions or their constituencies (or both) are originally limited, and so the agency finds itself competing with other, more flexible organizations. The Park Service's attentive public has been the environmentalists, and they are perceived by many as "far out." The Fish and Wildlife Service had for a time both the Alaskan salmon industry and the sportsmen as its attentive publics; it was accused of becoming a captured agency until Congress, in the 1950s, reorganized it into two separate bureaus. Now the Service has mainly the sportsmen and conservationists as its major clientele groups, and both of these operate somewhat on the fringes of the mainstream of American society. They provide the agency with no more than average group support.

Finally, the Soil Conservation Service came on the scene in the mid-1930s, only to find that there were several other federal agencies already in existence and already doing some of the activities the Service was mandated to do. Competition with agencies like the Corps, the Forest Service, the Bureau of Reclamation, and more recently the Environmental Protection Agency, ultimately left the agency with little room to grow; and so the Service found a secure, though limited, niche in providing small-scale services for farmers living primarily in the heartland of America. As we noted, the Service became relegated to providing the little projects after the bigger agencies got the cream of the crop.

Professional forestry is at the foundation of the Forest Service; civil engineering is the area of expertise for the Corps. The three agencies discussed here are more amalgams of several professions and so do not enjoy the predominance of a single profession. They are, in other words, more interdisciplinary. This characteristic appears not to appreciably help a federal agency develop political influence, although there are signs that this may be changing with the advent of "ecosystems management." The control of information is of course a major source of power for a bureaucracy, and if it can convince those outside the organization that it is one of the few possessors of a certain body of information, then it has an advantage vis-à-vis those that cannot. Both the Corps and the Forest Service convinced many people, over many years, that they were the experts at doing certain things; but this was less true for interdisciplinary organizations like the three described in this chapter. Time and again, for example, the Fish and Wildlife Service has been criticized for not being the biological experts which policy-makers think they should be. The creation in 1993 of a National Biological Service by Interior Secretary Babbitt is but the latest vote of "no confidence" in the agency.

It would take a much larger sample than the one we have to state with certainty that the incremental model is the most typical development pattern in the executive establishment. We suspect, however, that there are relatively few superstars in this population (we have not heard of many if there are), and not a great number of what we call shooting stars either. Furthermore, observing ordinary human behavior prompts us to conclude that most organizations, like most humans, have certain "extenuating circumstances" which cause them to move along at a more or less steady pace rather than to soar. Based on our research, this may be an appropriate redefinition of the term *pathos of bureaucracy.*

Organizational Shooting Stars:

The Bureau of Reclamation and the Bureau of Land Management

THE BUREAU OF RECLAMATION

The Bureau of Reclamation, created by the Reclamation Act of 1902, was an organizational expression of America's westward movement. The act was an imaginative attempt to resolve certain dilemmas posed by our expansion into regions and territories very unlike the lush eastern half of the United States. The historian Bernard DeVoto gave what still is the most succinct and accurate definition of the American West: It is where average annual rainfall measures less than twenty inches.[1] This simple climatic reality is the key to understanding much of the history and development of the western half of the United States.

The reality of the arid West was for most of the nineteenth century ignored, despite mounting evidence to the contrary. Of the westward march, one author wrote:

From the Mississippi River westward, events unfolded like a bad joke. Early reports of a "great American desert" were simply ignored as inconceivable, impossible. But eventually the accumulation of evidence, including rainfall records, established beyond a doubt that west of the vicinity of the hundredth meridian—a line approximately bisecting the Dakotas and extending south to Laredo, Texas—nearly all the land below 8,000 feet ... was too dry for unirrigated agriculture. And west of the Rockies it deteriorated to a lot of inhospitable desert.

> When ignoring the situation didn't make it go away, we tried to drive
> it away with myth and fantasy. Rain would follow the plow (because of
> the increased evaporation from washed soil); rain would follow the train
> (because of smoke particles for drops to form around); rain would follow
> the telegraph (because of electricity in the air). ... There were even those
> who came right out and said what everyone else was more or less hinting
> at: rain will follow settlement for no reason other than the presence of
> good people with a destiny to fulfill.[2]

The government, of course, greatly assisted and encouraged
attempts at settling the West. Throughout the nineteenth century vast
pieces of the public domain were given to various commercial interests,
in particular to the railroads, for the purpose of developing the western
half of the continent. An important bill passed Congress in 1862 (while
representatives from the states of the Confederacy were conveniently
absent), which for the first time made public land available to all
prospective settlers regardless of race. The Homestead Act of 1862
allowed heads of families to acquire up to 160 acres of surveyed public
domain (i.e., western land) for a small fee.[3] The Timber Culture Act of
1873 and the Desert Land Act of 1877 had similar intentions.

Despite these governmental actions to assist not only the
corporations but ordinary settlers as well, one overriding reality
remained: Land in the West was virtually useless without water. A
settler had nothing if he did not also have some water, "and before the
West was going to be settled it was going to have to be irrigated."[4]
Major John Wesley Powell, a government scientist and explorer, was
the first to propose a solution to this troubling dilemma. In an 1877
governmental report, Powell outlined a settlement proposal of the west
by irrigation districts. Though specific features of Powell's report were
not implemented, his realization of the paramount importance of water
to Western development was acted upon. The idea was codified in the
1902 Reclamation Act.

The Reclamation Service was organized within the U.S. Geological
Survey to administer the act; five years later, in 1907, the Service was
removed from the Geological Survey and established under a director.
In 1923 another organizational change was effected; the secretary of the
interior created the position of Commissioner of Reclamation and
renamed the Service the Bureau of Reclamation. It remained the

Bureau of Reclamation until 1979, when the interior secretary announced another name change, together with a change in direction and some change in functions. The Bureau was called briefly the Water and Power Resources Service; the name change reflected an attempt to come to terms with the fact that the Bureau had outlived its original mission and was actively seeking out new ones. Under the Reagan administration, however, its name went back to the original one.

The 1902 Reclamation Act provided that monies from the sale and disposal of public lands in the sixteen Western states (Texas was added to the list in 1906) would go into a special fund in the U.S. Treasury known as the reclamation fund. This fund would then be used

in the examination and survey for and the construction and maintenance of irrigation works for the storage, diversion, and development of waters for the reclamation of arid and semiarid lands in the said States and Territories.[5]

Thus the original mission of the Bureau was a lofty and even romantic one: It envisioned nothing less than the transformation of the West " from a land of sprawling cow towns and crude mining settlements in the midst of barren desert waste into prosperous modern communities supported by lush farmland."[6] That such transformations did in fact occur—metropolises such as Los Angeles, San Diego, and Phoenix were made possible by engineering the movement of water from its natural courses—is testimonial to the fact that the Bureau, for a time, accomplished extraordinary feats that combined sophisticated technology with imaginative goals.

The Bureau, however, was beset with problems almost from the start of its existence. The financial arrangements contained in the 1902 Act for financing these reclamation projects were novel, at least when they were compared with the financing of projects by the government's other water resource developer, the Corps. First, the Bureau's surveys and investigations of potential projects—and these were limited to the seventeen Western states named in the Act unless Congress specifically authorized it to act in other areas (a rare occurrence since the Corps was already ably servicing the rest of the country)—were to be financed by earmarked monies, that is, the reclamation fund. At least in theory, then, this limited the agency's funds to what came in to the

U.S. Treasury from sales of public land. The financing of the Corps' initial surveys was never circumscribed in this manner. Second, once a Congressionally authorized project was underway, the estimated costs of construction provided the basis for calculating the charges, per acre, which water users would be required to pay back to the government:

> The said charges shall be determined with a view of returning to the reclamation fund the estimated cost of construction of the project, and shall be apportioned equitably: Provided, that in all construction work eight hours shall constitute a day's work, and no Mongolian labor shall be employed thereon.[7]

Further, the act specified that repayment by water beneficiaries of the construction costs was not to exceed ten annual payments.

The reclamation fund thus was envisioned as a revolving, "pay as you go" plan which would refinance itself approximately every ten years in order to underwrite a continuing program of reclamation in the West. The original intent was that of a low-cost, partially federally financed, loan program wherein the actual users of the reclaimed water would repay the federal government in ten installments.

This financial arrangement contained a quite different philosophy from that pertaining to the Bureau's major competitor, the Corps, and it caused serious problems for the agency. While "cost-sharing" became a major feature of some Corps projects (with the ratio varying according to the nature of the project, but with the federal government totally financing some projects), this cost-sharing was of a different kind from actual monetary repayments. Beneficiaries of Corps projects —principally local and state governments, but sometimes private water development associations—were to contribute to Corps projects by defraying certain planning and construction costs. For example, local interests were to provide rights-of-way, easements, the condemnation of land necessary to the project, and the like. Costs to the local beneficiaries were thus payments in kind and in services rather than outright cash transactions. This cost-sharing mechanism had the added bonus of virtually assuring Congress and the Corps that there was substantial local and regional support for federal projects. In other words, a Corps project would rarely get underway unless local assurances of the nature mentioned above were forthcoming. This scheme helped defray costs to the federal government but of equal importance it assured the agency of minimal local opposition to its projects. Thus the Corps had not only a hundred-year headstart on the Bureau in the water resources field, but it also has operated in a more liberal financial environment, at least until the passage of the 1986 cost-sharing reforms.

The early history of the Bureau highlights some of its problems. For the first three years of its existence most of the work of the Reclamation Service focused on general surveys and the preparation of construction plans. By 1906, plans were approved for some twenty irrigation projects, which exhausted nearly all of the reclamation fund money. Hearings before the House Committee on Irrigation of Arid Lands in 1906 revealed that the agency had no problem in finding takers for its irrigated land; many of these initial water users were home-steaders since the bulk of the land irrigated by early projects was public domain.

By 1914 the Bureau's problems became more apparent. In subcommittee hearings in that year, spokesmen for the Service were asked about rumors that their agency had begun to stagnate. Agency officials responded by discussing certain technical and financial problems they had encountered in their first twelve years of existence: The construction of a reservoir that leaked; large cost overruns that were due to admittedly inadequate planning; and some unexpected effects caused by irrigation in arid environments. In some areas, it turned out, irrigation caused the water table to rise to such an extent that farms were turned into virtual swamps—a situation as unproductive as the original desert. This problem could of course be alleviated by drainage of the land, but this would increase project costs. Drainage, however, turned out to be essential in many areas due to the natural salinity of the desert land.

In addition to these technical, trial-and-error problems, the reclamation fund was running into difficulty. Income from the sale of public lands was insufficient to cover the costs of projects. Increasingly, water beneficiaries were unable to repay the government in ten years; so the time period of repayment was extended to twenty years. Also, the revolving fund was not turning over as rapidly as anticipated, and this put severe restrictions on new project planning. All in all, the reclamation fund, envisioned as a sort of perpetual motion machine, was seen to need considerable human intervention after all.

An example of the Bureau's problems with regard to its financing formula is seen in the plans, and end result, of the Uncompahgre project in Colorado. It was initially estimated to cost one million dollars and put approximately 140,000 acres under cultivation. The project actually cost three times as much and benefitted only half as much land. In effect, the Bureau had made a major miscalculation which would raise the necessary charges per acre sixfold. In this case, as in others, Congress unilaterally reduced the amount to be repaid by water users. By 1939 some $17,000,000 had been written off in this way. Congress also acted frequently to defer payments on specific projects for a number of years. The agency's accounting procedures to keep track of deferrals and cancellations were clearly bewildering to many Congressional members, not to mention the general public. Even few experts in the Bureau could keep up with the increasingly byzantine budgetary process.

Matters did not substantially improve overnight. In the 1923 appropriations hearings the Service discussed some twenty-six projects, but money was still a big problem. A large backlog of uncompleted projects led the Director of the Service to admit: "In the present state of the fund it is not advisable to take up new work for some years to come."[8]

By 1939, however, the Bureau was recharged with energy. FDR's New Deal, and some spectacular engineering feats such as the Boulder Dam (renamed the Hoover Dam in 1947, after Roosevelt's death),[9] gave the agency a new lease on life. In discussing its past, Bureau officials in 1939 noted: "These mistakes were not engineering mistakes, but rather were the result of pioneering in a new field."[10] Moreover, the reclamation fund, always short of money, had been refinanced. Repayment periods were extended to forty years, and this allowed the Bureau to claim that payments were coming in on schedule. More importantly, however, the fund had been augmented in several ways: Since 1921 part of the oil, potash, and potassium royalties derived from the public lands were to go into the reclamation fund, along with royalties and revenues from some other federal undertakings.

Also by 1939 the Bureau was able to effectively capitalize on the power-generating aspects of its irrigation projects. Power was not mentioned as an objective in the 1902 statute, but by 1939 hydroelectric power had become an important ingredient in water resources development. The Bureau could proudly point to some engineering masterpieces in that regard. The revenue derived from power sales also helped to defray construction costs and to lower rates to water users to an economically manageable level.

According to one case study of the Bureau, the agency began to show signs of an organizational decline from a high point in 1950.[11] By this time the Bureau had skimmed off the cream of the most economically attractive reclamation projects. Good dam sites and potentially rich farm lands became increasingly scarce, and the Bureau was able to pursue its mission only by granting longer repayment periods at low interest rates.

Stratton and Sirotkin state, which our more recent data support, the contention that in the period from 1950 to 1955 the appropriations to the Bureau of Reclamation fell from approximately $364 million to about $156 million. While in 1950 Bureau employees comprised about 61 percent of the entire Interior Department workforce, five years later they accounted for only 38 percent.

Beyond budget and personnel declines the impoverishment of the Bureau of Reclamation can be monitored by the number of political defeats it suffered. First, it lost an important claim to hegemony over water development west of the hundredth meridian. As multipurpose rather than single-purpose water projects came into fashion during the 1940s, a fierce competition developed between the Bureau and the powerful Army Corps of Engineers. In a study of the Kings Rivers project in California, Arthur Maass describes how even the support of such a powerful president as Franklin Roosevelt was not sufficient to wrench control away from the Army Corps.[12] In the Corps' eventual victory on this project, however, the attitude of local residents must also be ranked high. Testimony in March of 1945 by Representative A. J. Elliott of California before a subcommittee of the House Appropriations Committee states flatly that

> local interests are so strongly in opposition to a project built under reclamation law that they have stated that rather than have the project built by the Bureau of Reclamation they prefer no Federal project at all.[13]

The Bureau also began to suffer some embarrassing setbacks to its development mission at the hands of conservationists and the National Park Service—organizations that rarely have been a potent political force. As good dam sites became increasingly scarce the agency began to scan the environs of national parks, national monuments, and wilderness areas for possible project sites. In the Echo Park controversy of the 1950s, conservation forces defeated an attempt by the Bureau to invade Dinosaur National Monument with a man-made reservoir.[14] The most definitive defeat, however, came in the Colorado River Basin Bill of 1968 when conservation groups turned back a Bureau proposal to authorize the construction of two dams in the Grand Canyon of the Colorado River.

In its heyday the Bureau of Reclamation enjoyed a great deal of professional *esprit de corps*. During the 1930s when jobs were scarce, the best engineering students from Western universities were recruited into the Bureau. Reclamation engineers took great pride in the construction of their monumental arched gravity structures such as the Glen Canyon Dam. Traditionally, Bureau of Reclamation engineers proudly compared their skills with those of the Corps, who preferred "easier," earth-filled dams. Nevertheless, from about 1950 on, the agency was finding its role increasingly threatened by the existence of a more powerful competitor in the water resources field and also by its own reclamation laws.

In the face of a threat to its continued existence, the Bureau tried to diversify and broaden its mission, but too often these attempts were thwarted. For instance, by 1950 the agency had begun doing hydroelectric power investigations in Alaska, but this once again brought it into direct competition with the Corps. In the 1954 House Appropriations Committee hearings, questions were raised about a potential duplication of effort. It soon became clear that the Bureau would come out on the short end of the stick, for the Corps claimed that it was operating in Alaska under legislative authority contained in the 1948 Flood Control Act, whereas Bureau operations were based on the generality that they had requested appropriations for investigations of this type in the past and had received them. Once Congress remembered that the Bureau's mission was limited to the seventeen Western states, excluding Alaska, the agency was told to get new legislative authority for its investigations.

Legislative authority for an expanded Bureau role, although frequently mentioned, never materialized.

During the 1950s the Bureau latched on to the then popular recreation boom, and in its 1961 appropriations hearing recreation was frequently mentioned as a benefit deriving from reclamation projects. But while important, recreation benefits could hardly sustain a public works agency for very long. Once public and governmental attention waned, so did the Bureau's recreation program.

By the mid-1960s, competition with the Corps had become increasingly bitter; the Bureau could make few inroads to the Corps' growing monopoly. Secretary of the Interior Stewart Udall, testifying in 1965 before Congress, summed up the Bureau's dilemmas by noting that agency activities were hampered by closer congressional scrutiny of individual projects as well as by its historic repayment requirement. Simply put, he commented that "we have to run through a higher hoop."[15] By this time the Corps was doing more planning and construction than the Bureau even in the Bureau's "own" original territory (the Pacific Northwest in fact turned out to be the Corps' most fertile area for water resources development).

The 1970s were difficult years for the Bureau of Reclamation. Problems arose in a number of areas. For example, nearly all of the prime sites for reclamation projects had been developed. It appeared that the Bureau's principal mission was close to completion. In the 1975 appropriations hearings, agency officers admitted that "the original objective [of the Bureau] has been met. ... The West is now developed."[16]

The Bureau was also a conspicuous target for environmentalists, whose political strength had grown remarkably by the middle of the decade. The Ralph Nader–inspired book, *Damning the West*,[17] was typical of the environmentalists' literature condemning the agency. Environmental impact statements, as mandated by 1969 legislation, also caused problems for the Bureau throughout the 1970s. It experienced considerable difficulty in meeting the extensive requirements for environmental review and for the planning of non-structural alternatives.

In the midst of a trying decade, the Bureau felt itself victimized by Mother Nature when, on 5 June 1976, its Teton Dam failed. This earth-filled dam disintegrated through a combination of seismic activity and erosion, with the result to society of extensive loss of life and property. Damage claims were expected to exceed $400 million.[18] The disaster shook public confidence in the Bureau.

At the same time that the Bureau was attempting to recover from the Teton Dam disaster, Jimmy Carter was campaigning for the presidency on a platform—now familiar—that emphasized environmental protection, government reorganization, and the elimination of waste in federal government expenditures. After his election he ordered his transition team to investigate possible cuts in public works projects. As we also discussed in chapter 2, only a month after assuming office he initiated a review of nineteen marginal projects, eight of which were under construction by the Bureau of Reclamation. In April of 1977, the results of the presidential review were announced, with these recommendations for Bureau projects:

- Fruitland Mesa, Colorado; delete funding and de-authorize project.
- Savory Pot Hook, Colorado; delete funding and de-authorize project.
- Narrows Unit, Colorado; delete funding pending project reevaluation.
- Auburn Dam, California; delete funding until seismic safety studies are done.
- Oahe Unit, South Dakota; delete funding and modify in accordance with local demands.
- Garrison Diversion Project; eliminate certain aspects of the project.
- Bonneville Unit, Central Utah Project; eliminate certain aspects of the project.
- Central Arizona Project; eliminate certain aspects of the project.

Due to these suggested reductions, the budget proposed by Carter for the Bureau's FY 1978 appropriation was $609.6 million, significantly less than the $840.4 million budget proposed by ex-president Ford the month before.[19] The Senate responded by passing a bill that required the president to spend the funds necessary to continue the projects.[20]

Although Western politicians predictably resisted the cuts in water projects, some of them were quite candid about the limited prospects for massive western water projects in the future. Governor Richard Lamm of Colorado, who fiercely resisted the project cuts—three of which were in his state—nevertheless admitted that:

> The days of large-scale Western water projects are coming to an end. Grandiose schemes about making deserts bloom? Some of us have more modest goals and expectations now. I very strongly believe there is a limit to the carrying capacity of the West.[21]

But Lamm also echoed the sentiments of his colleagues in stating that projects should not be deleted once they had been started. Westerners were particularly disturbed that four of the five largest Western water projects were on the Carter list. Interest groups such as the Western States Water Council and the National Water Resources Association—the traditional clientele of the Bureau—joined forces with congressional allies in an effort to preserve continued funding for these ongoing projects. The six Western Senators on the Senate Appropriations Committee and the fifteen Western Congresspersons on the House Appropriations Committee led the fight to fund all of the projects. Ultimately, the Congress agreed to a compromise bill which stopped work on Auburn Dam until safety studies could be completed, and which deleted funds for the Bureau's Fruitland Mesa, Narrows Unit, Oahe, and Savory Pot Hook projects. The Congress also reduced funds for the Central Arizona Project.[22] The House, which was a reluctant partner in the compromises made in the final appropriations bill, noted in the conference report that "the Congress retains the right to select water resource projects for funding," and promised to renew the fight for the projects the following year.[23]

The final budget compromise was due in part to the efforts of several Northern legislators who were opposed to big Western water projects. Another reason why the Congress agreed to delete funds for at least two Bureau projects was because of local opposition from the alleged recipients of the project. Senator James Abourezk of South Dakota, who is remembered as a particularly principled politician, proposed an amendment to the appropriations bill that deleted funds for the Oahe Diversion Project in his state because farmers and ranchers—those who were listed as project beneficiaries—opposed the Bureau's project.[24] The Narrows Unit in Colorado was also deleted because of local opposition. Even the Central Arizona Project, which was popular among most of the state's residents, faced opposition from a local group called Citizens Concerned About the Project (CCAP).

The FY 1978 budget described above went into effect on 1 October 1977, the same day that the new Department of Energy came into existence. In another effort to reduce the operations of the Bureau of Reclamation, Carter transferred the agency's responsibilities for marketing power to the new department. With the continuing diminution of prime project sites and the rising political momentum of budget-cutters and environmentalists, the loss of this function was a notable setback for the Bureau at a time when it could ill-afford it.

As promised, the debate over the water projects continued throughout 1978. The administration once again attempted to stop the Garrison Diversion Project, which was bogged down in a lawsuit brought by the Audubon Society. It was also the subject of a controversy with Canada over the potential impact of the project on international waters. The Bonneville Unit of the Central Utah Project was also targeted for deletion. In June, Carter submitted a list of twenty-six projects— nine of which were being constructed by the Bureau—that he wanted to have deleted or modified. Included on this list was the $55 million Oroville-Tonasket Unit of the Chief Joseph Dam in the state of Washington.[25] The proposed Carter budget for the Bureau was $618 million, a reduction of $63 million from its appropriations for FY 1978. Carter again imposed a no-new-starts policy for FY 1979.[26]

At the same time that the struggle over the budget was taking place, the Bureau lost an important Supreme Court case. In *California et al. v. United States*,[27] the California State Water Resources Control Board argued that the Reclamation Act required the Bureau of Reclamation to satisfy state-mandated water quality controls. The Bureau in turn argued that federal water projects were exempt from state controls. *Amici curiae* briefs were filed against the Bureau by every Western state except Utah. In a reversal of past opinion, the Court narrowly construed the federal government's powers and ruled against the Bureau:

> From the legislative history of the Reclamation Act of 1902, it is clear that state law was expected to control in two important respects. First, and of controlling importance in this case, the Secretary would have to appropriate, purchase, or condemn necessary water rights in strict conformity with

state law. ... Second, once the waters were released from the dam, their distribution to individual landowners would again be controlled by state law.[28]

This case is another example of a limiting provision of the law which affects the Bureau of Reclamation but not the Corps of Engineers; the Court's decision is based on section eight of the Reclamation Act. The Corps is not limited by such legislation.

New challenges faced the Bureau in 1979. In January, Carter issued an executive order which required federal water projects to meet new criteria. Specifically, Carter ordered the Water Resources Council to establish a new set of standards and principles for project planning and to complete an "impartial technical review" on all preauthorization studies. The Council also was charged with developing a new planning manual for calculating costs and benefits and for applying them in a consistent manner.[29]

Carter also proposed a far-reaching reorganization plan that would formally transfer all of the planning and analysis functions from both the Corps and the Bureau to the Water Resources Council. The plan further called for the transfer of all of the Bureau's design and construction functions to the Corps. Obviously, this would leave the Bureau of Reclamation with little to do. Although the plan was never approved by Congress, it illustrates the former president's attitude toward this agency. Even the Corps was preferred over the Bureau by President Carter.[30]

Another indicator of its precarious situation is the fact that the Bureau underwent a name change at this time. Although the agency wanted to keep the word "Bureau" in its new title, Secretary Andrus forced the agency to adopt the term "Service," thereby erasing any reference to the former title. The name change of course had symbolic significance, illustrating that in politics a rose is not a rose by any other name. It signified for many that the Bureau's traditional role as a builder of massive reclamation projects in the West was about to expire. Commissioner Higginson euphemistically explained that the "initial purpose of reclaiming arid western lands has expanded to a much broader responsibility for water and power resource management."[31] A more realistic explanation was provided by Secretary Andrus, which stressed the administration's desire to stringently limit future construction activity by the agency: "National needs now call for greater efficiency in the operation of *existing* structures and their integration in new programs for renewable resources and alternative energy."[32]

The Bureau's "broader responsibility" included some new programs such as wind energy research and investigations into cloud seeding. But these new responsibilities did not rescue the Bureau from a steadily shrinking budget. The agency's total appropriation for FY 1980 was $356 million less than its 1977 appropriation,[33] with the administration requesting that no funds be appropriated for the Garrison Diversion Project or the Oahe Pumping Plant. The former was still in trouble with environmentalists and the Canadian government, and the latter was voted down by the board of directors of the local conservancy subdistrict. Also, the Auburn Dam was delayed pending a safety study.[34]

In late 1979, in a speech entitled "The Bureau of Reclamation Faces the 1980s," Commissioner Higginson assured the National Water Resources Association that:

> The Water and Power Project construction program is still strong. But it is changing. It is responding to new political criteria, economic pressures, present and future water and energy shortages and environmental concerns, but it is a going program.[35]

Commissioner Higginson cited several examples of new programs recently initiated by the Bureau, including the Public Involvement and Environmental Education programs. These are notable because they appeared several years after other natural resource agencies developed such programs.

Commissioner Higginson also cited "Indian water resource development" as a Bureau activity, but this would more appropriately be described as a major problem area for the Bureau rather than a new program. The Bureau has long been at odds with Indian reservations due to conflicting water rights. The western United States developed a doctrine of water rights which is quite distinct from the riparian doctrine used in the East. Due to the scarcity of water in the American West, the riparian doctrine was unsuited to that environment, so the Western states adopted an entirely new approach known as the prior appropriation doctrine. The 1902 Reclamation Act requires the Bureau to allocate water according to state law, or, in other words, to abide by the prior appropriation doctrine, since it is used by nearly all of the states within the Bureau's jurisdiction. But Indian tribes are not subject to state law—they have an exclusive relationship with the federal government—so the federal courts have developed a separate water law doctrine for Indian reservations and other federal lands. This reserved rights doctrine (or Winters doctrine as it is also called) directly conflicts with state water law; hence there has been considerable conflict between the Bureau and Western Indian reservations. The Corps of Engineers, which builds only about a third of its projects where a conflict exists between state and federal water doctrines, is less affected by this problem than is the Bureau of Reclamation.

The Bureau's conflict with Indian tribes has a long history, beginning with the agency's first project in Nevada. Recently, Indian tribes have become more politically sophisticated and therefore they present a significant challenge to the Bureau's traditional *modus operandi*. A case in point concerns Orme Dam, which was proposed as a component of the Central Arizona Project. The CAP, as it has come to be known, is one of the Bureau's largest projects. According to the agency's original plan, the dam would have inundated 70 percent of the Ft. McDowell Indian Reservation, home of the Yavapai Indians. The Indians battled the dam for thirteen years, claiming that the Bureau was insensitive to cultural values and minority interests. The protest against the dam culminated in a 30-mile march called "The Trail of Tears." Finally, under intense pressure from Indians from all over the West, and their environmental allies, the Congress voted to abandon the Orme Dam in November of 1981.[36]

Notwithstanding these major setbacks, many hoped that the Bureau's lot would improve after the 1980 presidential election because of the simple fact that Jimmy Carter would no longer be in the White House. During his tenure as president, he reduced the Bureau's budget by 37 percent (while the Corps of Engineers' budget increased by 24 percent). He attempted to transfer the agency's planning functions to the Water Resources Council and its construction and design functions to the Corps of Engineers. Carter also imposed a new set of criteria on the agency which stressed environmental values and nonstructural alternatives, two policies which the Bureau had fiercely resisted. There were "no new starts" during the Carter Administration, either.

The Reagan administration promised a new beginning in Western water development, and Secretary of the Interior James Watt assured Western governors that the "War on the West" waged by Carter was over.[37] But the new administration also was committed to substantially cutting the federal budget, much of which is uncontrollable. However, Interior's budget was vulnerable. As Leman noted, "the proportion of controllable funds in the 1979 budget for the U.S. Department of Health and Human Services was less than 3 percent, while in the U.S. Department of the Interior, it was 63 percent."[38] Secretary Watt therefore was forced to explain that, at least initially, he would concentrate on reducing the budget of the Department of the Interior rather than embark on an ambitious water development program. Although the Reagan administration allowed a $171 million increase in the Bureau's budget in 1981, its 1982 budget was a big disappointment to the agency. In hearings before the subcommittee on energy and water development Secretary Watt explained his attitude toward the Bureau of Reclamation:

> I had hoped, Congressmen, that we would have a new start in the Reagan 1982 budget for the Bureau of Reclamation. The planning has been so depleted—and the intentions of the past management—not to have such things, means that there wasn't one that I could pull out and put in the Reagan budget. I am sorry about that. We wanted to ... send a signal to the west that the war on the west is over. The best way we knew how to do that was to say we will have a new reclamation start in 1982 for Reagan's budget, but the depletion, the denigration of the planning process over the past years is such that there was not one I could identify to put in our 1982 budget.[39]

As a result, the Bureau's budget was cut once again, with a proposed $62 million reduction in the total budget. This included a 5 percent cut in the construction program, thus delaying construction on eight projects.[40]

In the same subcommittee hearings, Representative Virginia Smith from Nebraska offered the observation that the Bureau was facing the end of an era—the era of big reclamation projects: "A professional in the WPRS says in his opinion two major projects in my district are probably the last irrigation projects that will be built in the United States."[41] One of these projects, the North Loup Diversion, was among the eight chosen by the Reagan administration for reduced funding. The other one, the O'Neill Unit, was halted by a court order that barred further construction until the Bureau of Reclamation prepared an adequate environmental impact statement.[42] It would appear that Representative Smith's suspicions regarding the agency's future were well founded.

But, in keeping with the agency's cyclical pattern of development, the Bureau received increasing support from the Reagan administration. Beginning with the FY 1983 budget, the Bureau's fortunes began to improve. The traditional clientele of the Bureau—western agriculture, ranchers, and associated businesses—strongly supported Ronald Reagan in the 1980 presidential election. Sensitive to this source of political support, the president began to heed their demands for continued water development in the West; and Washington insiders took note: "there are signs that water projects soon may begin to move again under President Reagan, who is more sympathetic than Carter—at least rhetorically—to the dependence of western states on federal water projects."[43]

The Reagan administration's commitment to reclamation projects proved to be more than just rhetoric; for FY 1983 the administration requested a 21 percent increase in the Bureau's budget. The request for FY 1984 called for another substantial budget increase.

The Reagan administration also provided critical support for the Bureau and its constituency in the long struggle with Congress to revise the 1902 Reclamation Act. In 1982 Secretary Watt testified in favor or raising the acreage limitation from 160 to 960 acres, a reform that had long been sought by the large corporate recipients of project water. Ultimately, the 960-acre proposal became law.

The good fortune which the agency enjoyed under Reagan, however, was tempered by harsh criticism emanating from a variety of sources. First, pressure was placed on the Bureau to change the way it financed projects. Originally, reclamation projects were to be funded through a strict repayment plan, but this requirement had been liberalized to the point where projects became viewed by some as excessively generous subsidies to the West. A study by the General Accounting Office, for example, concluded that the Bureau's repayment plan only covered 10 percent of actual project cost.[44] The Bureau's statistics contradicted this estimate, and placed the figure at an 84 percent rate of return.[45]

Nevertheless, there was a growing recognition that reclamation water was considerably underpriced. The Reagan administration and environmental groups both pushed for increased user charges, which would reduce the cost of the program to the federal government and encourage water conservation efforts.

The Bureau was also criticized for managerial problems. Two years after the 1979 reorganization of the Bureau, a GAO investigation found that the agency experienced a decrease in efficiency and an increase in costs as a result of the reorganization.[46] An internal audit of the agency by the Department of the Interior in 1982 revealed numerous management problems.[47] Such problems—in addition to the many other factors we have discussed—may explain why the Corps of Engineers generally fared better during the Reagan years.

The complex budget battles of the Reagan era were just the beginning of another period of conflict and adjustment for the Bureau. In the fifteen years since Reagan first was elected, the agency has faced a series of crises and a rising chorus of criticism. There are four basic problems that have plagued the Bureau in recent years.

First, the Bureau, like most federal agencies, has faced the specter of significant budget cuts. During the Reagan years the agency's budget was static; when he took office it totaled nearly $1 billion, two-thirds of which was for construction. Eight years later the budget was virtually unchanged, with no increases added for inflation. However, the Bush and Clinton administrations have been even less supportive of the agency. By the time Clinton took office the Bureau's construction budget had decreased by another $100 million, and while its total budget is still just under $1 billion, the construction budget is now a little more than half of what it was in 1980.

However, these budget cuts did not prevent legislators from continuing to use Bureau projects as pork barrel. Throughout the 1980s and 1990s Congress repeatedly added new project starts to the president's budget request, most of them in the districts and states of appropriations committee members. And the Bureau, like the Corps, benefited when Congress cut a deal with President Bush; Congress supported his beloved Texas supercollider in return for his support for more spending on water projects.[48]

A second problem for the Bureau concerns its biggest construction projects. In the past, the big projects were the agency's pride and joy;

recently they have become a political morass. Four of them in particular have experienced serious difficulties: the Central Arizona Project, the Central Utah Project, the Animas-La Plata Project, and the Garrison Diversion Unit. The Central Arizona Project (CAP) was originally built to deliver irrigation water to the farms around Phoenix. But the economics of the project have proven unrealistic and unworkable; farmers cannot afford the water for which they fought so long. This problem was predicted two decades ago by some courageous economists at the University of Arizona; enraged farmers nearly drove them out of the state for voicing such heresy. CAP began delivering water in 1985, but in 1991 demand for CAP water began to decline; deliveries dropped from 745,000 acre-feet in 1990 to 420,000 acre-feet one year later. The Central Arizona Water Conservancy District was unable to begin payments on schedule in 1993, and the Bureau granted a post-ponement. At that point things went from bad to worse; two of the biggest recipients of CAP agricultural water declared bankruptcy because they could not pay their CAP water bills.[49] Arizona water officials are presently trying to identify alternative customers for the water, such as municipalities and Indian reservations. They are even thinking the unthinkable: lease their water to rival California!

The Bureau's Central Utah Project (CUP) also has experienced problems. By 1987 the project had overspent its authorization; the Bureau asked Congress for a significant increase in funding. Project proponents wrote a single-paragraph bill asking for the authorization. What they got instead was a four-year battle over the way such projects are funded. Led by George Miller in the House and Bill Bradley in the Senate, an unprecedented number of legislators began to question the legitimacy of the CUP and other big Bureau projects.[50] After several years of acrimonious debate, and considerable political compromise, a much revised CUP was reauthorized by Congress. But, in a move with significant ramifications, the Bureau was replaced by the Central Utah Water Conservancy District as the project's builder. This was done because the Bureau was viewed by both Congress and project supporters as inefficient, slow, and unresponsive.[51] The CUP still is experiencing funding problems, and many observers believe the irrigation component of the project never will be built.

Another Bureau project in trouble is the $563 million Animas–La Plata Project (A-LP) in Southwestern Colorado. Originally authorized in 1968 as part of Congressman Wayne Aspinall's logroll (he got five water projects for his district in exchange for his support of Arizona's CAP), the A-LP was never funded because of its highly questionable economic value and negative environmental impact. But the project received a new lease on life when it became part of the 1988 Colorado Ute Indian Water Settlement; Congress reauthorized the A-LP to provide water to two Indian tribes without having to reduce water deliveries to local non-Indians. Thus the project was recast as an "Indian project" rather than just another big give-away to irrigation farmers, even though the latter will receive most of the project water.

But the reincarnated project immediately ran into problems. Environmental groups such as the Sierra Club, a local group called Taxpayers for the Animas River, and some elements from the Indian reservations formed a coalition to fight the project. Their cause received a considerable boost in 1990 when the U. S. Fish and Wildlife Service issued a jeopardy opinion pursuant to the Endangered Species Act. The Service concluded that construction of the project threatened the continued survival of several fish species in the San Juan River. After more than a year of negotiations a recovery plan for the fish was developed, and the project was once again on track.

Before construction could begin, however, the coalition against the project filed suit, alleging that the Bureau had failed to comply with the National Environmental Policy Act, the Clean Water Act, and the Endangered Species Act. The district court ruled against the Bureau, stalling the project again.[52] Then the EPA listed its own objections to the project.[53] At about the same time, the Navajo nation went public with its objections to the project. Then, in 1994, the Department of the Interior's inspector General issued an audit of the project that concluded neither A-LP nor the nearby Dolores Project (also built by the Bureau) was "economically justified."[54] As of the fall of 1995, construction on the project has not begun. However, in FY 1994 the Bureau's budget contained funding to "continue preconstruction activities including NEPA work and the seven-year research effort on endangered fish habitat."[55]

Finally, the Bureau's Garrison Diversion Unit has experienced serious problems. This massive project was authorized in 1944 and again in 1965 to provide irrigation water to one million acres in North Dakota. But the project immediately ran into opposition from Canada, environmental groups, and Indian tribes.[56] In the mid-1980s the project underwent a complete review by a commission appointed by Congress. David Feldman succinctly identified the nature of the conflict: "The issues generating contention in the Garrison dispute revolve around regional equity, intergenerational justice, equal treatment of disadvantaged groups, and the balance between economic and noneconomic values."[57] In short, just about everything. After extensive hearings, the Garrison Diversion Unit Commission recommended that the project be scaled back dramatically. Congress then reauthorized a much smaller and much revised project in 1986.

In sum, four of the Bureau of Reclamation's biggest projects have encountered persistent and widespread opposition. In the past, such big projects were the bread-and-butter of the agency; now they often create problems, conflict, and occasionally embarrassment. The Bureau has been forced to adjust its objectives to meet the exigencies of contemporary water politics.

A third source of problems for the Bureau concerns a barrage of criticism over subsidies, below-cost pricing, and economic inefficiencies.[58] Criticism of the economics of Bureau projects has played a growing role in the debate over water projects. At a time when the federal government is strapped for cash, questionable financing raises many eyebrows. In recent years the debate over water development economics has focused on three forms of subsidies: interest and pricing subsidies, the practice of double subsidies (naturally called double-dipping), and circumventions of the 960-acre limitation.

A wide-ranging group of economists, fiscal conservatives, and environmentalists have become vocal critics of the Bureau's long tradition of interest and pricing subsidies. Richard Wahl made this point in his 1989 critique of the Bureau:

> What began as a proposal for modest federal assistance in settling the arid West, providing a revolving fund to which costs would be repaid within ten years, evolved into a program that provided major subsidies to irrigation water users—sometimes more than 90 percent of construction costs.[59]

One element of this subsidy is the interest subsidy.[60] In 1987 Congressman George Miller forced the Bureau to calculate the interest subsidy on its irrigation projects. The Bureau determined that the interest subsidy alone averaged $114 million per year since 1903; it had risen to over $500 million per year by the 1980s.[61]

Another form is the price subsidy, which refers to the practice of setting the price of water far below the market price. For example, the General Accounting Office calculated that Central Valley Project (CVP) water users pay between $2 and $17 per acre-foot for water that costs between $42 and $72 on the open market. CAP water users pay $40 to $50 for water that is valued at $250. Price subsidies such as these have been a big issue in recent debates over project authorizations. In the 1988 debate over the reauthorization of the CUP, Senator Bill Bradley opened the hearings with this statement:

> As now formulated, nearly two-thirds of the water supplied by the CUP will irrigate 25,000 acres of new land and provide supplemental irrigation water to 220,000 acres. The cost of the supply systems for irrigation is now estimated at one billion dollars, or $5,000 per acre-foot of water supplied. Each acre of newly irrigated lands will demand some 2 to 4 acre-feet of water annually, for a capital investment of $12,000 to $24,000 per irrigated acre. ...Lands to be served are worth $700 to $800/acre ... . The farmers' ability to pay is $9.40.[62]

A third form of subsidy is the double subsidy. This describes the practice among some irrigators of receiving water subsidies from the Bureau while at the same time accepting surplus crop subsidies from the Agriculture Department. One congressional critic complained:

> As the National Taxpayers Union has repeatedly noted, it is "a national disgrace" to have the Bureau of Reclamation provide over $800 million per year of irrigation water subsidies so that farmers can grow surplus crops, which the U. S. Department of Agriculture then provides over $300 million in commodity subsidies for many of these same farmers not to grow these surplus crops on other parts of their land.[63]

In 1990 an audit by the Department of the Interior's inspector general found that just two large farms in the CVP collected $5.5 million in combined crop and water subsidies from 1986 through 1988.[64] In 1991 Congress requested the General Accounting Office to investigate double-dipping. The GAO found that 38 percent of the Bureau's water subsidies were associated with the production of subsidized surplus crops. The total amount of money at stake was impressive: "the Bureau of Reclamation estimated that annual irrigation subsidies totaled $2.2 billion in 1986, of which $830 million was associated with the production of subsidized crops."[65]

Another subsidy issue concerns the Bureau's administration of the 1982 Reclamation Reform Act, which raised the acreage limitation of subsidized farms from 160 acres to 960 acres. Some large farms have been able to circumvent the limitation by setting up dummy partnerships and land trusts. A series of investigations by the General Accounting Office revealed that a number of agribusinesses in California's central valley received millions in subsidized CVP water, but far exceeded the 960-acre limitation.

For example, the J. G. Boswell Company set up the Westhaven Trust to make it appear that its 23,238-acre farm was actually a set of individual farms not exceeding 960 acres. The GAO investigated Boswell along with five other cases and found that the newly organized trusts and cooperatives were merely ruses set up to circumvent the acreage limitation: "the small landholdings created by the reorganizations continued to be operated collectively as single large farms, much as they were before being reorganized."[66] The 960-acre circumventions, and the double-dipping issue, divided the California congressional delegation and became an important element in the effort to pass a western water policy reform bill in 1992, which we discuss below.

Finally, there is some irony in another set of problems facing the Bureau. Like the Corps, the Bureau has created numerous environmental problems over the years, and now agency officials envision an entirely new mission cleaning up these problems—as well as some environmental problems created by other federal agencies.

One of the best-known environmental horror stories about Bureau projects is California's Kesterson National Wildlife Refuge. This refuge is located in the drainage area of the CVP and is a part of the Pacific Coast flyway. In 1984 toxic levels of selenium in the water of Kesterson Refuge were traced to the Westlands Water District, which is part of the Bureau's CVP. In its own study of wildlife refuges in the CVP service area, the Bureau concluded there was insufficient quality and quantity of water for the refuges because of irrigation diversions.[67] The Bureau then began work on "Kesterson Reservoir on-site disposal cleanup."[68]

At the same time that Kesterson was making national headlines, the Bureau ran into another environmental controversy: Studies done in the 1980s indicated that Glen Canyon Dam was having negative environmental impacts along the Colorado River corridor in the Grand Canyon. In 1989 Interior Secretary Manuel Lujan ordered the department to prepare an environmental impact statement for the operation of Glen Canyon Dam, focusing on its release flow regime. The Bureau was named the lead agency of a team of cooperating agencies that was asked to write the EIS. The work of the team was authorized by Congress when it passed the Grand Canyon Protection Act of 1992.[69] Late in 1994 they produced a draft EIS, which was a result of a long political process that involved all of the factions in contemporary water politics: water users, hydropower interests, anglers, rafters, wildlife supporters, hikers, park proponents, Indian tribes, and state and local governments. All argued, of course, for the preferred alternative that best met their needs. The EIS team received 33,000 written comments on the draft EIS, most of which were form letters and preprinted cards prepared by interest groups.[70] The final EIS came out in 1995. One Bureau employee described the agency's work on the Glen Canyon Dam EIS as "the best example of the new Bureau of Reclamation; it is a landmark."[71] (One might ask, "A landmark to what?")

The Bureau has definitely responded to the environmental challenge, although perhaps the agency is two decades late. The agency's annual budget request now routinely includes environmental work, which includes emissions controls at the Navajo Generating Station, a belated effort to help rescue the Salmon run on the Sacramento River,[72] and grants to help clean up superfund sites.[73] The Bureau also has a "conservation center" in every regional office.

In sum, the Bureau faced an unprecedented series of challenges in the last fifteen years. At times there was a serious question as to whether the Bureau would survive. During appropriations hearings in 1987 Congresswoman Smith became frustrated that the Garrison Diversion Unit (which is in her district) and other Bureau projects were unable to attract sufficient funding: "You know, if we don't have a study of what we do about flood control and municipal and industrial water and irrigation and recreation, pretty soon we will have no Bureau."[74]

But the Bureau refused to die. There have been two responses to the identity crisis faced by the agency. The first came from Congress in the form of a comprehensive reform bill. The debate over the bill included the entire panoply of interests, viewpoints, and conflicts that characterize the chaotic nature of contemporary water policy. The politics of passing the bill was similar to HR 6, the reform bill for the Corps, in that proponents of reform tied their new initiatives to a bill that also authorized hundreds of water projects scattered throughout many states and congressional districts. They bought reform, in other words.

Early formulations of the reform bill included Congressman Miller's bill to stop circumventions of the 960-acre limitation, Congressman Gejdenson's bill to prevent double subsidies, and a bill introduced by Senator Bradley to dramatically change the cost and water allocations of the CVP. These measures were tied to further reforms in specific projects such as the CUP, and a host of other measures.

The outcome of the four-year battle to pass this bill revealed some basic features of contemporary water politics. First, it demonstrated that traditional beneficiaries of federal water policy still have a great deal of influence. Despite overwhelming support for the prohibitions against double subsidies and the 960-acre circumventions, agribusiness interests managed to have those sections of the bill deleted. A Bureau official told us, "The beneficiaries still have a lot of influence. The reformers only had so much political capital to expend, and they chose to expend it on CVP reform rather than the double subsidy and 960-acre issues."

The project beneficiaries' champion in the Senate was John Seymour of California, who collected $563,976 in campaign donations from California agribusiness. Even though the California Business Roundtable supported the reforms, this small but very wealthy and powerful special interest was able to stop legislation that would have reduced the millions of dollars in subsidies they receive each year. These interests also forced the reformers to compromise on several other issues, such as the amount of water set aside for fish and wildlife.[75]

Another characteristic of the debate over the reform bill was the clout of environmentalists, recreationists, and urbanites—the new constituency of the Bureau. Thus, the Bureau has not abandoned its old friends; rather, Congress has forced it, as it forced the Soil Conservation Service, to accept many new ones. The fifty titles in the 1992 act read like a list of Who's Who in water politics. There is money for: numerous irrigation projects, Indian water settlements, wastewater and groundwater studies, several "protection" projects, suburban and urban water, fish and wildlife, wetlands preservation, conservation, salinity control, a variety of research, planning and demonstration projects, rural water systems, and even some money for a veterans' cemetery.[76]

This leads to another characteristic of the politics of the 1992 reform bill: pork barrel. Despite all the talk of a new era of water policy, it is clear that many legislators still think of water projects as a way of bringing home the bacon. Although cost sharing is now a part of most Bureau projects, the federal government still pays about 75 percent of the bills, and that is an attractive inducement to a legislator facing reelection. Congresspersons still like to authorize projects that specifically benefit their constituents, especially if they can take personal credit for them. As we discussed previously, the same holds true for the Corps of Engineers.

The pork barrel tendency was much in evidence during the debate on the 1992 reform bill. The harder the reformers pushed, the more home-state projects their colleagues added to the bill. After the bill had been kicked around for two years, CQ Weekly Report noted that it had "attracted pork, and the bill has now bloated to 40 titles."[77] By the time it passed it had bloated to fifty.

The effort to reform the Bureau via national legislation illustrates the current political environment of the agency. Old allies still retain a great deal of influence, a variety of new interests are vying for control over the Bureau's direction, and in an attempt to please all of them Congress still distributes water projects in a politically efficacious manner. As a result, the 1992 reform bill contained a lot of "green pork" alongside traditional water subsidies.

The other response to the Bureau's identity crisis can be seen in a nearly continuous effort to redefine the agency's mission. In the 1980s, under intense pressure, the Bureau began developing a new direction. Its "Assessment '87" was intended to reorient the agency. According to Dale Duvall, then commissioner of reclamation, Assessment '87 would "expand [the Bureau's] primary focus from large scale, federally sup-ported construction to include comprehensive resources manage-ment."[78] As part of this change the Bureau went through a massive reorganization.

But Assessment '87 proved to be an incomplete transition. There was considerable resistance to this new direction from both within the agency and among the Bureau's congressional supporters. But the Bureau's political leadership persisted; the Reagan appointees who ran the agency began using some of the benefit/cost formulas and project calculations that the Corps used. This infuriated Congressperson Smith: "It appears to me that the Administration is trying to apply Army Corps of Engineers law to Bureau projects ... , which is not authorized by any law, any regulation or any policy on Bureau projects."[79] Technically she was correct, but Bureau leaders knew that failure to apply more stringent project criteria could spell doom for any project under current budgetary constraints.

Early in his tenure as secretary of the interior, Manuel Lujan made another attempt to reorient the Bureau. He began a program called the "Legacy '99 Initiative." In budget hearings Lujan claimed that the Initiative represented a "new direction, which involves shifting its focus from water project construction to innovative and efficient water resources management." This program resulted in a greater emphasis on operations and maintenance. By 1991 the agency had a maintenance backlog of $195 million, and Legacy '99 was designed to reduce that.

Assessment '87 and Legacy '99 were the first steps in a lengthy process of mission adjustment. After several years of soul-searching, and considerable internal conflict, the agency produced another new mission statement in its 1992 Strategic Plan. In unequivocal terms, this document specified a new direction: "The mission: To manage, devel-op, and protect water and related resources in an environmentally and economically sound manner in the interest of the American public."[80] The plan was announced on the 90th anniversary of the signing of the 1902 Reclamation Act.

The ink was barely dry on the Strategic Plan when Daniel Beard was confirmed in 1993 as President Clinton's commissioner of reclamation. He had previously worked for the Bureau's most strident critic in Congress, California's George Miller. (Miller once said that he wouldn't allow the Bureau to build a doghouse in his backyard.) Beard took very seriously the effort spearheaded by Vice-President Gore to reinvent government. Beard's Bureau was one of the first federal agencies to follow through on the reinventing effort, creating yet another revamping of the Bureau. For his efforts Commissioner Beard received the "Golden Hammer Award" from the Vice-President in 1994.

Commissioner Beard's "Blueprint for Reform" was a complete reversal of the Bureau's traditions. It reorganized the agency from the ground up, eliminating the two deputy commissioners and all five assistant commissioners, and it decentralized authority "to the lowest practical level."[81] Even more important, it contained an explicit break with the Bureau's past: "Federally funded irrigation water supply projects will not be initiated in the future." Instead, the agency will "facilitate change from current to new uses of water," and recognize "new constituent groups."[82] In a statement supporting the Blueprint, Interior Secretary Bruce Babbitt said it committed them to "the transforming of the Bureau of Reclamation from a civil works agency into a preeminent water management agency that is cost effective in serving its customers."[83]

What, then, does the future hold for the Bureau? In a starkly realistic assessment, the new regional director for the Upper Colorado River Region explained it like this: "Our future is to serve the public in the 17 western states effectively and efficiently. If we can't do that we should pass from existence."

For a time, the Bureau succeeded in capturing the imagination and aspirations of the American West, but once that mission was accomplished the agency found itself too hemmed in by competing organizations and its own restrictive laws to make a major breakthrough. It appears that the agency finally is carving out a new niche for itself, but it seems very unlikely that it will achieve the kind of eminence it once had when its engineering expertise was combined with the lofty ambition of "making the deserts bloom." If the Bureau does make a resurgence, it will probably be due to long-term demographic changes that show a continuing shift in population to the West and Sunbelt states. But the Bureau will have to fully develop its new service-oriented mission in order to reap any organizational benefits from a more populated West. Whether it can do so even in its reinvented mode is questionable.

THE BUREAU OF LAND MANAGEMENT

In terms of sheer acreage, the Bureau of Land Management (BLM) is the federal government's largest land manager. Its employees are responsible for the administration of 270 million acres of public land. They also supervise mineral leasing and operations on an additional 300 million acres (mostly subsurface) of federal mineral estate. Virtually all of the land under BLM's jurisdiction is located in Alaska and the eleven most western states of the nation (excluding Hawaii). Most of Nevada's land mass, for instance, is managed by the Bureau. If an agency's power were measured solely in terms of real estate, then surely the Bureau would be a powerful organization. But this is not the case. The Bureau of Land Management is a politically weak organization that survived initially because nobody knew what to do with the land that it managed.[84] Today, there are many people who know what to do with these 270 million acres, but they don't have the political power to alter the status quo.

The Bureau is an old-new organization. It came into existence in its present organizational form through a 1946 executive reorganization which combined two weak agencies in the Department of the Interior with the hope that they might lend strength to one another. The Bureau is thus the direct descendant of the Grazing Service, established under the 1934 Taylor Grazing Act, and the rather infamous General Land Office which had been in existence since 1812 and whose history was intimately bound up with the history of the public domain.

What in essence the Bureau fell heir to was a set of problems and issues, never adequately resolved, having to do with grazing on the old public domain lands. Throughout much of the nineteenth century the General Land Office (GLO) was given the next-to-impossible charge of administering the public domain. Adding insult to injury, however, it discharged its duties so as to benefit the vested interests of the time at the expense of the individual homesteader:

> In 1874, an Oregon correspondent for the *New York Sun* questioned the justice of a system which permitted "the local offices to receive applications for homestead and preemption rights and to encourage settlements and improvements on the public domain, only to" receive "instructions from the General Land Office in Washington to drive the settlers away and turn

their improved property over to some railroad corporation." The main trouble, insisted the correspondent, was that the Interior Department was conducted almost entirely in the interests of land grabbers and monopolists, that it paid little or no attention to local laws or customs.[85]

The conservation movement of the late nineteenth century was directed at reforming this scandalous misuse of the public lands. Thus from about 1870 on, large tracts of the best land were withdrawn from the public domain to be set aside for particular uses. Even so, this left a lot of unappropriated acreage under the Land Office's management, land which was best suited for cattle and sheep grazing but upon which homesteading also was attempted. The closing decades of the nineteenth century saw the public range rapidly deteriorating through a large-scale application of the individualistic principles that give rise to "the tragedy of the commons." The historian Samuel Hays described in a vivid manner the conditions then prevailing:

> Much of the Western livestock industry depended for its forage upon the "open" range, owned by the federal government, but free for anyone to use. Moving their livestock from the higher alpine ranges during the summer to the lower grazing lands in the winter, cattle and sheepmen could operate profitably with little capital and no privately owned land. Chaos and anarchy, however, predominated on the open range. Congress had never provided legislation regulating grazing or permitting stockmen to acquire range lands. Cattle and sheepmen roamed the public domain, grabbing choice grazing areas for their exclusive use, but competitors cut the wire. Resorting to force and violence, sheepherders and cowboys "solved" their disputes over grazing lands by slaughtering rival livestock and murdering rival stockmen. Armed bands raided competing herds and flocks and patrolled choice areas to oust interlopers. Absence of the most elementary institutions of property law created confusion, bitterness, and destruction.[86]

These real and often bitter conflicts over public land use remained unresolved for a long time. In trying to find a solution, President Theodore Roosevelt found himself caught between the livestock industry on the one side and western farmers and homesteaders on the other. Despite attempts by his administration to force the issue and to obtain a leasing measure from Congress, none was forthcoming. A leasing proposition for the public domain was not approved until 1934.[87]

The deterioration of the public domain that already was evident in the latter part of the nineteenth century continued unabated. According to the historian Roy Robbins the end of the First World War witnessed the beginning of a severe agricultural depression in the country. This again raised the question of what to do with about 160 million acres of unreserved federal lands:

> The submarginal wheat frontier came to an end. In the twenties, the High Plains of America presented a gloomy spectacle: abandoned homesteads everywhere; grazing lands in very poor condition, some beyond rehabilitation; and more significant still, the big stockmen gradually extending their influence as well as their fences over the public domain.[88]

President Herbert Hoover, who favored ceding the remaining public lands to the states, in 1929 appointed a commission to study the transfer plan and to come up with recommendations for its implementation. A year later the Garfield Commission published its report and, not surprisingly, unanimously supported the president's proposal of turning the public domain over to the states.[89] However, there developed much public criticism of the report. One commentator said that "the plan, in essence, is one of monopoly and eviction, antisocial, undemocratic." Another concluded his analysis of the report by urging congressional action: "When Congress comes to consider the commission's proposals, its duty is clear. It should shelve the report."[90]

That is what Congress did. In the 1930 Congressional elections the Democrats gained control of the House, and when the bill containing the commission's proposals was introduced it was found severely lacking in support. Not only did Eastern congressmen oppose it, as was expected, but rather surprisingly, so did much of the West, including the powerful livestock association interests. Robbins concluded: "Thus ended the dramatic attempt to turn over to the states the remaining public domain."[91]

Nevertheless, reform on the range was essential, not to mention long overdue. Franklin Roosevelt, together with the tough-minded and staunch conservationist Harold Ickes, formulated a new deal with regard to the conservation movement in the United States. Working with Congressman Edward Taylor of Colorado, and others, Secretary of the Interior Ickes combined the immediate and pressing needs for depression relief with conservation objectives to come up with a comprehensive natural resources program. This program included action on the public domain issue:

> Lastly, the Secretary dealt with the great unsolved problem of the remaining public domain—some 173,000,000 acres, mostly grazing lands. Scorning the Republican proposal of ceding these lands to the western states, the Secretary boldly declared that these lands should become, like the national forests, a part of the permanent national domain, with grazing use and rehabilitation governed by means of leasing. This plan would insure not only law and order, but also intelligent use and preservation of these grazing resources for years to come.[92]

The legislative result of these actions was the passage of the Taylor Grazing Act in 1934, "perhaps the greatest contribution of the New Deal administration to the history of the old public domain."[93] According to Culhane, it was no mean feat to secure the passage of this controversial legislation from a reluctant Congress:

> Supported by the Department of Agriculture and the president, Ickes waged one of his famous campaigns, testifying aggressively for the bill, threatening to withhold Civilian Conservation Corps ... camps from the public domain without the bill, and finally (having dredged up a few obscure legal authorities) threatening to withdraw the whole public domain on his own authority. The Taylor Grazing Act was passed June 28, 1934, as a result of Ickes' pressure, Taylor's legislative skill, and the considerable influence of the dust storms of that year.[94]

Though the act had its shortcomings, and these became increasingly evident in the ensuing decade, nevertheless the statute firmly established the federal interest in controlling the public domain. Of this significant act, Robbins wrote:

> For over forty years historians had been heralding the passing of the frontier; without a doubt the old frontier had now passed. ... Thus ends an era. The land of opportunity—opportunity measured in terms of free land—had officially closed its doors. America had come of age.[95]

The resolution of the public domain question proved to be an intractable one, however. Political controversies during and after

World War II engulfed the Grazing Service, leading ultimately to President's Truman's 1946 executive reorganization. The ostensible issue during these years was one of money—that is, grazing fees—but the underlying issue, according to Culhane and other scholars, was one of control of the Grazing Service. Nevada's influential Senator, Pat McCarran, who was chairman of the committee on public lands and champion of the grazing interests, led the attack against a federal fee increase in the 1940s. A vivid description of the conflict is provided by Culhane:

> The fiscal year 1947 compromise appropriation—which slashed the Grazing Service budget to 53 percent of its 1945 level, thus reducing personnel by 66 percent, barely enough to maintain a skeleton staff—was the principal victory in McCarran's crusade to reduce the Grazing Service to dependence on range users. Local stockmen's advisory boards contributed $200,000 ... to the 1947 appropriations of $550,000 to help pay the salaries of local grazers. Grazing Service officials were thus literally paid by the users they were supposed to regulate. Thoroughly cowed, the Grazing Service was led behind the barn and put out of its misery; President Truman's Reorganization Plan Number 2 of 1946 consolidated the Grazing Service and the old GLO to form the Bureau of Land Management.[96]

However, the president's action occurred without authorizing legislation by Congress, so the new agency, the Bureau of Land Management, survived some three decades without a statutory base. From 1946 to 1976, the Bureau was an organization without a clear mission. As was often the case with the public domain lands, the administering agency—this time the Bureau—acted as a holding company awaiting clear statutory direction.

The primary reason for the agency's institutional insecurity is due to the residual nature of the public domain lands. Until 1976, the GLO/Grazing Service/Bureau of Land Management managed land which no one wanted when it was literally free for the taking. Even in 1930 when President Hoover and his hand-picked commission proposed transferring this land to state ownership, many in the West were uninterested in acreage "on which a jack rabbit could hardly live."[97] Federal land disposal policy through the nineteenth and early twentieth centuries resulted in the existence of scattered and hard-to-manage plots; essential pieces, like watering holes, had been carved out for private control. Until recently few interests, much less the general public, knew or cared about the public range lands. (A 1970 congressional commission report estimated that the public lands accounted for just 3 percent of all the forage consumed by livestock in the United States).[98] Moreover, those interests which have cared about the Bureau's lands had a direct, economic stake in forestalling the creation of a strong federal range-managing agency. Philip Foss, in *Politics and Grass*, argued that Western ranchers wanted the Taylor Grazing Act administered so there would be both peace on the range and a halt to competing users of the range resource—in their interests, in other words. They would have foregone these benefits if it meant any drastic changes in grazing rights, closer regulation of use, or higher fees.[99]

The Bureau thus found itself in the unenviable position of being closely identified with a single interest; as such, it epitomized the "captured agency" phenomenon that public administration scholars long have studied and analyzed.[100] Bureau officials, even when they wanted to, found it difficult to build support for a broadly conceived range management program which might have partially neutralized the political power of the livestock industry. They received little support from non-Western congressmen, who exhibited sustained interest only in the budgetary aspects of the Bureau's program; they more or less ignored rangeland conservation and other issues of potential salience to them. Because of this situation, for most of its history the Bureau was not able to efficiently manage its large land holdings; rather, it negotiated. Few changes were put through over strong ranching opposition.[101] This continues to be the case in 1990's, as we discuss below.

The Bureau's "capture" by ranching interests can be more fully appreciated by comparing it to the Forest Service, an agency which most observers admit was more successful at neutralizing constituency pressures. A number of differences exist between these two land managers. First, the Bureau has been chronically underfunded when compared with the Forest Service. Culhane documented this, as did Dana and Fairfax in their 1980 book on forest and range policy, and as we do. The organizational result has been to make the Bureau more vulnerable to the demands of its local attentive public:

> BLM has never and will never control the land it administers the way the
> Forest Service does. ... BLM has roughly one-seventh the personnel, one-
> third the money, and four times the land of the Forest Service. ... Thus,
> BLM managers are on thin ground. They must, therefore, rely extensively
> on the cooperation of land-users to implement management programs.[102]

Whether budget and personnel resources are the cause or the effect of an organization's relative deprivation is difficult to determine; it is a "chicken and egg" question. But in either event the practical result for the BLM has been to place it in a catch-up position vis-à-vis the Forest Service, with the latter agency serving as a role model for the former. As Culhane noted, the early directors of the Grazing Service frequently were recruited from the ranks of the professional foresters of the Forest Service.[103] The current acting director of the BLM, Michael Dombeck, also is a forester who previously worked for the Forest Service.

A second factor making the BLM more susceptible to local grazing interests concerns management techniques. As Kaufman noted, in his classic study *The Forest Ranger*, the long-standing Forest Service policy of personnel rotation did much to guard against agency professionals "going native." Regular and routine rotation from one locale to another had the effect of reinforcing the national perspective, as opposed to local and regional perspectives, among Forest Service employees. The BLM, however, has not followed a strict rotation policy and so agency personnel have been subjected to more pronounced local pressures than have their cohorts in the Forest Service.

A third reason for the Bureau's dependence on its local constituency has to do with the professional orientation of the agency and with its personnel recruitment practices. Range management, which constitutes the agency's predominant profession, is offered in only a few colleges and universities in the country—primarily Western agricultural schools. In fact, appointment to its predecessor, the Grazing Service, was for a time officially biased toward the west. From 1936 to 1946, only bona-fide residents of Western states for at least one year were eligible for top management positions in the Service. At one point during the New Deal, Interior Secretary Harold Ickes became so exasperated with this situation that he vowed never again to appoint a "cow man" to head the agency.[104] The Taylor Grazing Act also recommended that the Civil Service Commission consider practical range experience

in hiring agency personnel. The result was that many Bureau employees were former ranchers, and many more were the sons of ranchers.
Bradley and Ingram noted in 1986 that "Even now, the line officers of
BLM are still predominantly Western natural resource professionals—
26 percent of the BLM's managers are Utah State University graduates;
55 percent are graduates from other Western universities."[105]

Finally, the social pressures on agency employees were, as Wesley
Calef suggested, in the direction of increasing Bureau dependence on
the livestock interests:

> Local BLM officials are quite probably strongly affected by adverse social
> pressures on themselves and their families. Most BLM offices are located
> in small western towns whose culture and livelihood are largely oriented
> to the range livestock industry. Public opinion is entirely that of the ranching
> interests. Consequently, a district manager who strongly antagonizes the
> local livestock interest will soon find himself and his family largely isolated
> from the social life of the community. Few managers or staff members
> experience this social disapproval, because they rarely antagonize the
> rancher community.[106]

In comparing the Bureau of Land Management with the more powerful
and independent Forest Service Calef, too, found that "the Bureau of
Land Management administration is much looser, more flexible and
more permissive."[107]

The ranchers' dominance over the BLM prevented the agency, for
most of its existence, from developing new activities and new constituencies. This resulted in what Dana and Fairfax refer to as "the
enduring obscurity of the Bureau of Land Management."[108] A good
example of this situation was the increasing political importance of
wilderness and recreation issues, which scholars claim bypassed the
agency in the 1960s:

> In spite of all the public outcry and congressional attention to parks and
> wilderness, the management of public domain lands continued to be
> underfunded and essentially unattended to. Although the BLM made
> some progress ... the best index of the stature of the BLM during this peri-
> od is probably to be found in the Wilderness Act. The act omitted public
> domain lands and did not mention the Bureau. This was not the result of

special pleadings or policy but simply an oversight. Four hundred and sixty-five million acres of public domain lands were simply forgotten.[109]

As of 1994, the Bureau still lagged behind all other federal land managers in the amount of acreage it administered as wilderness. It currently manages 1.6 million acres of congressionally designated wilderness. Official documents, however, point out that an additional 23 million acres are under study.[110] This compares with over 34 million wilderness acres managed by the Forest Service. As a 1994 Forest Service report noted, "This amounts to about 75 percent of the designated wilderness in the lower 48 states, and about 35 percent of all designated wilderness."[111]

Given this set of political and organizational conditions one may well have predicted a dreary future for the Bureau. In the 1970s, however, there were indications that the agency was breaking away from its impoverished and subservient position relative to range interests. In a 1979 article on the Bureau the authors noted that during the 1950s the agency started to become increasingly "professionalized": It began to move from being a dominant-use agency, as mandated by the 1934 Taylor Grazing Act, to incorporating a multiple-use philosophy like that of the Forest Service. They wrote:

> professional land management is dominated by a multiple-use philosophy. Thus, BLM officers desired a multiple-use mandate similar to that of the Forest Service. Such a mandate would have the same advantages for the Bureau as it had for the Forest Service, allowing the agency to moderate conflicting demands of single-use consumption-oriented clients.[112]

By the late 1970s, Culhane reported that the BLM professionals had become "indistinguishable" from their Forest Service counterparts in at least one crucial respect: that being their strong commitment to multiple-use management and progressive conservation values.[113]

The Bureau in fact got such a mandate from Congress in 1964 when it passed the Classification and Multiple Use Act. The act, however, was of a temporary nature and was due to expire in 1970. The reason for this was that Congress also passed legislation in 1964 creating the Public Land Law Review Commission, and it was the task of the commission "to conduct a review of existing public land laws and regulations and recommend revisions necessary therein."[114] A large part of the commission's task was to attempt to resolve what had been attempted several times in the past: To find a permanent political and organizational solution for the remaining public domain.

In 1970 the commission completed its study and issued its final report, *One Third of the Nation's Land*. Many of its recommendations concerned the plight of the Bureau of Land Management and its several hundred million acres. In particular, the report recommended against any large scale disposal of these lands and emphasized the necessity of an organic act—a firm, statutory base—for the Bureau. In 1976 Congress acted upon these and other recommendations by passing a fifty-page statute, the Federal Land Policy and Management Act (FLPMA), for the Bureau. A corrolary statute, the Public Rangeland Improvement Act (PRIA), was passed in 1978. Thus, after a long, insecure and conflict-ridden existence, the agency finally became legitimized.

The election of Jimmy Carter in 1976 was good news for the Bureau in terms of its efforts at diversifying. President Carter appointed Frank Gregg to head the BLM. Here was an individual from New England who boasted of having solid conservationist credentials. Unlike many of his predecessors, he was anything but a "typical cow man from the West." With Gregg as director, Cecil Andrus as interior secretary, and Jimmy Carter as president, the leadership was in place to bring the Bureau into line with the significant changes occurring in public attitudes toward the environment. Whereas in the past barren canyon country was criticized for having no economic value, by the mid-1970s it was being praised for its ruggedly scenic quality and its wilderness potential. Coal and oil deposits once thought unpractical to develop were identified as a key to solving the nation's energy crisis and its dependence on foreign oil. BLM lands also were discovered in the seventies not only by wilderness enthusiasts but by all-terrain-vehicle users and wild horse lovers. Thus, outdoor recreation began to emerge as an important component of the Bureau's new multiple-use mission, as mandated by FLPMA.

During the Carter administration, Bureau personnel moved to neutralize some of the ranchers' longstanding power over their agency by getting in on new presidential and congressional initiatives. These included: locating oil and gas deposits on the Outer Continental Shelf and on its own immense land holdings, participating in the "synfuels" program, and starting a wilderness inventory that was modeled after the Forest Service's RARE program. The agency planned to examine 175 million of its nearly 300 million acres for possible inclusion in the national wilderness system.

During this environmentally active period, the Bureau also was impacted by the passage of the Endangered Species Act, the clean air and water acts, and the eleventh-hour passage of ANILCA late in 1980. This act, which environmentalists consider a milestone in conservation history, finally resolved many of the local, state, and federal conflicts over land use that had raged for decades in America's last frontier. Under the act the BLM was given statutory authority to manage over 92 million acres of land in Alaska. These lands, which amount to one-third of its entire holdings, are, needless to say, ill-suited for ranching. ANILCA thus presented the BLM with another opportunity to escape capture by its cattle and sheep-raising clientele.

But what the Carter administration did to or for the BLM, the Reagan administration undid. Seeing that the BLM was vulnerable politically, the Sagebrush Rebels of the West immediately homed in on it and its new agenda. When the president appointed James Watt interior secretary, and the Colorado rancher, Robert Burford, to head the Bureau, the Western commodity interests got the appointments they wanted. They proceeded to lobby the administration for significant changes in the Bureau's priorities.

Although other resource managing agencies were affected by the Sagebrush Rebellion, it was clear that the BLM bore the brunt of the movement's disapproval with the policies of the 1970s. An exchange between Representative Sidney Yates and Secretary Watt during an appropriations hearing at the outset of the Reagan administration underscored the centrality of the BLM to the movement:

> *Mr. Yates:* Okay, tell us. What organized them [the Sagebrush Rebels]?
> *Secretary Watt:* The attitudes of the Bureau of Land Management.
> *Mr. Yates:* None of the other Bureaus?
> *Secretary Watt:* They are not on the cutting edge.
> *Mr. Yates:* Not the Forest Service?
> *Secretary Watt:* One of our objectives will be to make the Bureau of Land Management successful in building community relationships by adopting the management techniques they use in the Forest Service.[115]

Acting Director Edward Hastey also agreed that the Bureau of Land Management had become the lightning rod for the Sagebrush Rebellion: "It ended up centering pretty much on the BLM and the land we manage."[116] During the appropriations hearings, Watt offered a terse explanation as to why the Bureau was the primary target of the Sagebrush Rebels: "there has been an attitude of distance, arrogance, and disregard for local interests."[117] Of course, the local interests to which Secretary Watt was referring were the ranchers who dominated the Bureau's activities until the passage of FLPMA in 1976. The rebellion got most of its strength from grazing interests who objected to the Bureau's new policies concerning grazing fees, wildlife, native plants, and predator control. A 1981 article in *American Forests* accurately explained this viewpoint: "Ranchers become angry and are quick to blame the 'new' BLM, which suddenly, because of the recent 'organic act' [FLPMA] legislation has become an active management agency rather than a custodian."[118] The author of the article also quoted a prominent Utah rancher who complained bitterly about the Bureau's increasing professionalism: "The BLM hires young kids straight out of college who suddenly become experts and tell seasoned ranchers how to manage the rangeland ... . Federal employees sit around a big table and come up with a plan to manage the land you've grazed for a half-century or more."

The agency's problems with ranchers were exacerbated by a 1972 ruling in a case brought by the Natural Resources Defense Council charging the agency with inadequate preparation of its environmental impact statements. The court handed down a decision that ordered the Bureau to prepare 144 separate impact statements on grazing. Although the agency fought the decision, these court-mandated impact statements were cited by ranchers as a typical example of "useless paper work" produced by the Bureau of Land Management.[119] To some, it looked as though the Bureau was now getting trapped between the proverbial rock and a hard place, that is, between two extremist movements. The agency's political situation bore an uncanny resemblance to the land it managed.

Although the underlying thrust of the Sagebrush Rebellion was to force the transfer of federal lands to state or private ownership, Watt said that he opposed massive transfers of land unless the transfer met the criterion of being in the public interest. The following debate is drawn from an appropriations hearing, with Representative Yates again leading the attack:

> *Mr. Yates:* Does the Sagebrush Rebellion carry with it returning any of the federal lands to the states?
> *Secretary Watt:* Some of the proponents of the Sagebrush Rebellion advocate that. I do not.
> *Mr. Yates:* So to the extent that you have the power to do so you will not turn back any of the federal lands to the states except for the kinds of transfers of small holdings such as you described this morning?
> *Secretary Watt:* That is basically correct. We do not anticipate any massive land transfers. It will just be that which is done in the public and national interest.[120]

Watt did not further specify the criteria to be used in determining the public interest.

The priorities of the Reagan administration, which also were those of the Sagebrush Rebellion, were detailed in the agency's proposed FY 1982 budget to Congress. This was their first budget proposed for Congress' consideration. Under the "Management of Lands and Resources" item, the Reagan budget called for a $2 million increase (and 30 new positions) to accelerate oil and gas leasing on the Outer Continental Shelf (OCS), coupled with a $10 million reduction in OCS environmental studies. Thus, there would be more offshore leases granted but much less research done on the environmental impacts of those leases.[121]

Similar objectives were pursued with respect to onshore oil and gas leasing, with an increase of $1.5 million to cover the costs of intensified leasing and exploration efforts, and a concomitant reduction in the intensity of data collection related to resource considerations in the preparation of the environmental statement. This accelerated leasing activity represented a marked increase over the previous year when a moratorium was placed on oil and gas leasing because of alleged abuses in the program.[122] At that time the responsibility for managing the leasing program was shared by the Bureau of Land Management and the Geological Survey. According to the latter agency, the Bureau didn't maintain accurate records, resulting in lost revenue. BLM officials denied these charges.[123]

In Reagan's proposed FY 1982 budget the funding for the coal leasing program was reduced but the projected number of leases was expected to rise sharply.[124] The rangeland management program also was cut, although its workload was held constant. Part of this reduction was due to a $1.6 million decrease in funds for preparing the court-ordered environmental impact statements for the Bureau's grazing programs. This, of course, posed a difficult problem for the agency, since the court order contained a specific deadline for completion.[125] Monies for the agency's dam safety program were also cut, despite the fact that "serious problems are known to exist in several major structures."[126]

The planning program was reduced by nearly $1.5 million. According to the agency, planning was necessary in order to "insure that we don't have a serious impact on vegetation, soils, and cultural resources. We need to find out what is there so when we do cause an impact we know what we are impacting; or if we do find something we decide should not be impacted, at least we know what we are doing."[127] Such inventories were mandated by NEPA, The Endangered Species Act, and other statutes passed in the seventies. They were deeply disliked by political conservatives such as Ronald Reagan. Hence, it came as no surprise that the Reagan White House immediately cut expenditures for inventories in all resource programs. During appropriations hearings for FY 1982 Congressman Yates succinctly described the Reagan budget for resource planning:

> Under this proposal you are reducing the intensity of resource inventory into oil shale, you are reducing the level of inventories in grazing, you are reducing the level of intensity for inventory in natural cultural resources, you are reducing or actually you are deferring all inventories for recreation resources ... and you are also reducing the level of intensity for inventories under wildlife.[128]

The de-emphasis on planning, data collection, inventories, and EIS preparation was part of a push to reduce what Secretary Watt called "paralysis by analysis." Conversely, increases in funding for leasing programs were designed to accelerate those approvals with a minimum of interference from studies and regulations. He explained his philosophy to the Congress: "We have studied too many things too long. We need to make America move."[129] The catch-word used throughout the 1982 Reagan budget was "streamlining," which was the explanation for all such reductions. Some of these proposed deductions were large: The recreation and wilderness management program was cut by 29 percent, for example. This constituted a reduction of $7.12 million, of which $7.10 million was justified as "streamlining."[130]

The Bureau of Land Management's Wilderness Inventory was yet another target of the Reagan budget cutters in 1981 and 1982. They called not only for funding reductions but for a decrease of 400 permanent positions, almost all of which were related to the Bureau's recreation or wilderness programs.[131] This would result in a significant reduction in wilderness studies, reduced staffing on the Bureau's millions of acres used for outdoor recreational pursuits, and, in some cases, to the absence of law enforcement protection on these federal lands. An agency spokesman said bluntly: "As far as visitor protection is concerned, that is something that most visitors are going to have to take on at their own risk."[132] They simply didn't have the manpower to do more, which has been a chronic problem for the agency.

The 1982 budget was an important precedent, not only because it was Reagan's first budget, but because Congress acquiesced to most of the Presidents' proposals. The final 1982 budget for the BLM was about the same as the previous year's appropriation because the increases for resource extraction offset the reductions in environmental protection and related functions.

Reagan's budget proposals for FY 1983 and 1984 continued to stress the priorities set at the outset of his administration. Increases were requested from Congress for across-the-board resource development, but these initiatives became mired in a number of political, and very public, controversies. First, late in 1982 Secretary Watt made headlines with his plan to lease the entire Outer Continental Shelf for oil drilling. "In raw numbers alone, the plan staggered observers," one scholar wrote. "Between 1955 and 1982, about 3 percent of the *total* continental shelf surrounding the United States had been leased for oil exploration. In a single executive action, Watt opened almost the entire shelf."[133] Legislators from several states, including California, Florida, and the New England area, objected, however, and Congress voted to exempt those areas from BLM leasing.

A second area where the Reagan administration's leasing program met political resistance was in the coal leasing program. Secretary Watt planned to substantially increase coal leases, but the Congress placed a ban on them until after an *ad hoc* coal commission investigated the leases; a report by the General Accounting Office had concluded that the Watt leasing schedule had lost $100 million in revenues.[134]

A third area of controversy over BLM leasing involved the agency's Wilderness Study Areas (WSAs). The Bureau intended to study 24 million acres of land for possible inclusion in the National Wilderness Preservation System. Secretary Watt planned to open that land to mineral and oil development, but after a battle with Congress he announced a temporary ban on leasing in the potential wilderness areas.[135]

The accumulation of these and other controversies led James Watt to resign his position in 1983. He was succeeded in the secretary of the interior's office by less outspoken individuals whose agendas were virtually indistinguishable from his and the president's.

By the end of President Reagan's first term in office, the BLM was experiencing another fluctuation in its fortunes. Not only had it been the principal target of the Sagebrush Rebels, who were successful in stalling its diversification efforts, but a 1984 reorganization of the Interior Department took from the agency many of its offshore and onshore leasing functions. The reorganization created a new unit, called the Minerals Management Service (MMS), by combining some BLM programs with others from the U.S. Geological Survey. The reorganization was the result of considerable criticism, from both within government and outside of it, of the Bureau's minerals leasing program. As a consequence of the reorganization, the BLM's budget showed a significant decline by the end of Reagan's first four years in office. Manpower was also cut but not so drastically. Clearly it was not the story of a successful agency. In fact, one scholar described the impact of Reaganomics and departmental reorganization on the BLM as "devastating."[136]

But, as is the case with organizational shooting stars, the agency managed to rebound from its precarious position in 1984–85. Its total budget and workforce crept up through the late 1980s and early 1990s. In 1990 fire-fighting functions were consolidated within the Interior Department, and the BLM was given that responsibility. But the primary reason for the increases, we were told in interviews, was due to the fact that both the Reagan and Bush administrations pushed for increased resource exploitation on virtually all of the public lands, and the Bureau, with its huge land holdings, was central to that effort. Under Director Burford's hands-on leadership, BLM personnel generally accepted Reaganomics and proceeded to implement its pro-development agenda. No John Mummas or "AFSEEE" movements emerged within the BLM during the 1980s, as they did in the Forest Service, to challenge the development orientation.

For those who had expected to see the BLM transformed into a more influential, independent, and genuine multiple-use agency, the 1980s were disappointing. Those who were most disappointed with the BLM's performance naturally were environmentalists. So, by the end of a trying decade they turned their dismay into public criticism of the agency. The critique was familiar: That the BLM had fallen back into the role of a captured agency. The time had come again to reform it.

A 1991 report by the General Accounting Office captured much of the mounting criticism of the Bureau. Dubbed the "Hot Desert" report, the GAO criticized the Bureau's management of 20 million acres of desert land in the five states of Arizona, California, Nevada, New Mexico, and Utah. It concluded its analysis by stating that livestock grazing was singularly ill-suited for these desert lands, and then went so far as to suggest that Congress eliminate grazing on the *entire* 20 million acres in question.[137] Along with the Forest Service, the BLM also came in for its share of criticism in the Pacific Northwest, where it manages the "O & C lands" (Oregon and California public lands). Environmental organizations in that region charged the BLM with threatening critical wildlife habitat and other land uses by steeply increasing timber production. Court orders have halted, temporarily, timber harvests on BLM and Forest Service lands.

Despite the Bureau's clear commodity orientation during the Reagan-Bush presidencies, there was some evidence that multiple-use management was gaining a foothold, at least here and there, within the agency. Innovative thinking about how to manage 270 million acres of real estate was sprouting up from the grass roots; it was even getting the attention of Washington policymakers by the 1990s. For example, several of what Bureau officials presently call their "showcase projects" originated during the eighties or earlier. These include: The Anasazi Heritage Center in Dolores, Colorado; the San Pedro River Riparian Area in southeastern Arizona; the Hohokam Ruins Site near Phoenix;

and the Oregon Trails Interpretive Center in Baker City. Over the last ten years or so the agency attempted to take the lead, with some success, in the emerging area of concern known as riparian management.

With the changing of the guard in 1992 calls for reform on the range reached a minor crescendo in the United States. Consequently, expectations were high that President Clinton's secretary of the interior, Bruce Babbitt, the former governor of Arizona, would effect substantial changes in resource management generally and in particular within the BLM. Topping the new administration's list of priorities were reform of the 1872 Mining Law and the imposition of higher grazing fees. In other words, the Clinton administration confronted the most sacred of sacred cows in the West: The nineteenth-century law which allows prospectors, with their picks, shovels, and mule trains, to gain title for virtually nothing over large tracts of federal land, and the 1976 fee formula that charges ranchers a modest $1.86 per animal unit month (AUM) to graze their livestock on the public range. The market-driven fee, by contrast, at present varies from $6.00 to $12.00 per AUM. The government's proposal was merely to double the $1.86 fee.

The appointment of James Baca to head the BLM further heightened expectations that the agency was about to embark on another change cycle. Baca previously had been New Mexico's aggressive, reform-minded lands director, and in that position he imposed higher grazing fees on state lands. To environmentalists, Baca had both the professional credentials and the temperament to do what the Democratic administration claimed it wanted done: Push through substantial reform on the range.

Then came the "Baca debacle." Forced to resign in February of 1994, Jim Baca lasted only nine months in the director's office. He was, administration officials explained, too abrasive. He had a "different management style" from that of his immediate boss, Interior Secretary Babbitt. In attempting to implement reform he angered too many influential people including, quite naturally, ranchers and miners along with their political allies in governors' offices and in Congress.

But that was to have been expected. Baca himself had a different explanation for his firing: "It happened," he said, "because they [Secretary Babbitt and chief of staff Tom Collier] wouldn't stand up for their principles. I know how politics works. But I also know you have to stand up for your principles. And they wouldn't."[138] Upon leaving office, Baca predicted that the agency did not have a bright path ahead of it. "So they've kicked that poor agency in the teeth again. And things had been looking up," he mused.[139] To anyone knowing the history of the BLM, this was very familiar stuff.

The Baca debacle predictably had a negative effect on agency personnel. Although many within the Bureau continue to work on reinventing the agency—through such activities as holding a brainstorming session at Lake Tahoe in the spring of 1994 (the "Tahoe Summit," modeled after the Park Service's "Vail Agenda"), devising organization charts which employ horizontal imagery as opposed to ones depicting the traditional hierarchical power structure, and staffing the Washington office with more minorities and women with nontraditional credentials—the present administration's failure to get Congress to enact *any* range reform legislation does not bode well for the agency. The BLM continues to exhibit the characteristics of an organizational shooting star.

The obvious question that arises from a study of the recent history of the BLM is how long the American public, and its elected representatives, will stand for the agency's capture. Here is a federal entity whose employees are responsible for the proper management of 270 million acres of public land. That is a lot of land, amounting to a little over one acre for every American. And yet some 20,000 ranchers with grazing rights set public land priorities for the entire country. In other words, a fraction of one percent of the U.S. population still holds captive not only the Bureau of Land Management but also the varied economic, recreational, and aesthetic interests of the remaining 99 percent of the population. This remarkable situation appears to us to be a case of "gridlock *in extremis.*"

SUMMARY: MISSIONS ACCOMPLISHED AND INTERRUPTED

To a greater extent than the five other agencies discussed in this study, the Bureau of Reclamation and the Bureau of Land Management have had what might be termed a variegated history. That is, their development is characterized by more ups and downs than is typically the case. They neither display the steady, impressive growth that sets the Corps and the Forest Service apart, nor do they move along at the slower but steady pace of the other three agencies. Unpredictability and uncertainty are almost built in to the character of these organizations.

In the case of the Bureau of Reclamation, it got off to an impressive start but just a decade later it ran into financial difficulties. These problems were eventually ameliorated, and so the Bureau made a comeback during the FDR era; many of its most impressive accomplishments date from the 1930s and 1940s. But this zenith was again followed by a sustained period of organizational decline that began about 1950 and continued until 1981. The agency enjoyed considerable support from the Reagan administration—unlike the other agency discussed in this chapter—but that changed when Bill Clinton captured the White House in 1993. One also might have thought that the energy crisis of the 1970s would have breathed new life into the agency, but the data indicate that the Bureau did not appreciably benefit from this crisis; it remains an agency with a very uncertain future.

The conditions that appear to have most constrained the agency's growth are these: From the outset, the Bureau was geographically limited to working in only the seventeen westernmost states of the nation. In other words, it has been a decidedly regional agency. This constraint was exacerbated by the existence of another federal agency, the Corps, which was not so delimited. Thus the Corps could literally build support for its activities throughout the country; it could challenge, often successfully, the Bureau even on its own turf.

Furthermore, as a former interior secretary pointed out, the Bureau had to act under a set of legislative directives far more stringent than those under which the Corps operated. Monetary payments by beneficiaries of Bureau projects were unable to keep the agency solvent over the long term; and even after Congress liberalized the sources of money going into the reclamation fund, it never entirely let go of the idea that the Bureau should work with earmarked monies. In contrast, Corps projects were not so conceived until recently. As time went on, the competition between the two water developers became increasingly uneven: As the Corps's fortunes snowballed, the Bureau's diminished.

Unlike the Bureau of Reclamation, the Bureau of Land Management did not get off to a fast start. It came into existence through a 1946 Executive Order, but its creation was not quickly followed by Congressional action. Thus for some thirty years the agency was forced to act as a holding company until the federal government could decide what it wanted to do with the enormous public landholdings under the Bureau's jurisdiction.

Once Congress passed an organic act for the Bureau, however, it embarked on what appeared to be an impressive take-off stage of development; by 1977 the future looked bright indeed. Moreover, the agency fared very well under Carter. The president appointed an intelligent individual with a strong pro-conservation record to head the agency during these critical, agency-building years. Both the president and the Bureau's director, Frank Gregg, were committed to transforming the agency from being a single-use, rancher-dominated organization into a multiple-use, professionalized one. The bureaucratic model used to effect these changes was that of the U.S. Forest Service, and the Carter-Gregg alliance even bore some distant resemblance to the happy alliance between Theodore Roosevelt and Gifford Pinchot which gave the Forest Service its strong start some seventy years earlier. As the data presented in chapter 5 show, the Bureau's budget increased substantially between 1976 and 1980, an indication that the agency was on the move.

During the 1970s, the Bureau not only benefited from this presidential interest in its mission but from changing public values and concerns. As we discussed previously, what were once thought of as utterly useless, unproductive lands now promised to contain both material and spiritual wealth for a nation concerned about resource depletion. For example, one of the Carter administration's primary solutions to solving the energy crisis was in switching from expensive imported oil to abundant, domestically produced coal. Bureau lands were a virtual treasure trove for that particular resource. They contained not only valuable energy resources, however. The rugged, "god-forsaken" character of much of this land began to be valued for precisely those features that earlier were viewed as its drawbacks. The result was that the hundreds of millions of acres under Bureau management became the focal point of competition for use of them.

But the agency's take-off was barely launched when a new president, with a quite different ideology, entered the picture. Ronald Reagan, together with Secretary Watt, and a new Bureau director, Robert Burford, halted the agency's take-off in mid-air. These policy-makers were sympathetic to the so-called Sagebrush Rebellion and therefore considerably less interested than their predecessors were in creating a strong and autonomous Bureau of Land Management. In fact, they were interested in just the opposite.

Public expectations that the Bureau would develop into another Forest Service therefore have been disappointed by the changes in the political environment which began with Reagan and which continue through Clinton. The agency's future, as has been the case often in the past, is again up for grabs. We suspect that this situation has not escaped the attention of the Republican majority in the 104th Congress.

A Cross-Validation of Agency Power:

Budget, Personnel, and
Status Rankings

The extensive research on the histories of these seven resource agencies goes a long way toward accounting for the observable differences among federal bureaucracies in how each uses its power and influence in the political process. In this chapter we are interested in broadening the historical analysis of agency power by examining other indicators of organizational strength. We do so because the statistical and attitudinal data presented here are not only intrinsically interesting but also because these measures provide an important check on the interpretations drawn from the historical records of each agency. In this endeavor we follow the methodological advice of the authors of *Unobtrusive Measures*, who argue for cross-validation of this type:

> No research method is without bias. Interviews and questionnaires must be supplemented by methods testing the same social science variables but having *different* methodological weaknesses. ... [T]he issue is not choosing among individual methods. Rather, it is the necessity for a multiple operationism, a collection of methods combined to avoid sharing the same weaknesses.[1]

Two of the most frequently compared categories across organizations are budgets and personnel. From the relative size of an agency's budget and workforce, inferences can be drawn about that organization's power. The Corps and the Forest Service, for example, with their annual budgets in the $3–4 billion range, and workforces of 28,000 and 35,000, are far ahead of the five other agencies in this study. Moreover, budgets and personnel are not just indicators of strength but are themselves among the most valuable resources upon which an agency draws to further enhance its position. Thus over time they become both cause and effect of an agency's power in the executive establishment.

A third indicator has to do with an organization's reputation. In answer to the question, "How does one know who is powerful and who is not?," a simple way to find out is to ask people. This is what we have done. Agencies, like people, have reputations for power and influence. So in order to complement the historical research and the budget and personnel statistics, we personally interviewed policymaking staff in each of the seven agencies in our sample. They were asked to rank six agencies (excluding their own) according to four variables.[2] A second round of interviews, conducted mostly in 1994, used a less structured format to elicit the same data. These findings, as shown presently, strongly reinforce the conclusions obtained from the other data. These four essentially independent sources of information thus allow us to draw some rigorously tested generalizations concerning agency power differentials. Before reviewing those generalizations, however, the three variables of budgets, personnel, and perceptions will be briefly analyzed and discussed.

AGENCY BUDGETS

Budgets are an extremely useful source of information, as Wildavsky, Schick, and other scholars have shown. The data are regularly published and they provide a standard unit of comparison. But budget data have their limitations, so they should be used in conjunction with other methods of measurement and other kinds of information.

The principal limitation of budget data is that they do not, by themselves, explain anything. In other words, their interpretation depends on a familiarity with the political, social, and economic contexts in which budgets are made. For example, figure 5.1 displays the total annual budget appropriations of our seven agencies for the years 1950–80. One might make much of the fact that each agency's budget is absolutely larger in 1980 than it was in 1950. But this observation is less impressive when one considers the rate of inflation over this period.

Taking into account inflation means that agencies, like the rest of us, have to have more money just to stay even. A statement by an official of the Fish and Wildlife Service in 1972 illustrates the point:

> Using 1967 as a base, the fund level of available monies to the Bureau has actually decreased. You will also notice the committee has been most generous in the last several years in increasing the appropriations but with the degree of inflation. ... [3]

A related problem of working with budget data is the increasing complexity of the spending process. Wildavsky had a lot to say on this subject, for he spent nearly thirty years tracking the intricacies of government expenditures. From his original 1964 book, *The Politics of the Budgetary Process,* to the 1992 version, *The New Politics of the Budgetary Process,* he found a world of difference. He no longer was able to describe completely the process. "I would be surprised," he wrote in 1992, "if anyone claims to comprehend fully defense budgeting."[4]

Defense budgeting may be the extreme example, but greater complexity, to the point of obfuscation, appears to be the norm in other program areas as well. We discovered problems in collecting budget data for the years 1980–94 which weren't there previously. For example, the appendix to the annual budget doesn't always contain a "bottom line" for federal agencies and bureaus! In other words, the researcher can no longer go to the most readily available source on the federal budget and find the annual appropriation (budget authority) for a federal agency. The data in the budget appendix now must be supplemented and cross-checked by each agency's budget office and/or by appropriations hearings. This, we think, is inexcusable.

We also discovered in the budget appendix for FY 1982 a very useful "bottom line" for agency personnel, wherein each federal agency's permanent workforce (for 1980) was listed. Was this extremely useful data compilation continued in subsequent years? Don't ask.

In interpreting budgets one must also be sensitive to the impoundment issue. Our budget data are for annual budget authority (BA), which is what Congress authorizes the agency to spend in a given fiscal year. However, certain presidential administrations have had their own opinions about agency expenditures so the Office of Management and Budget sometimes restricted or impounded an agency's appropriation. This practice reached its extreme during the Nixon years, and in 1973 a statement by a Corps of Engineers official shows the potential for misinterpretation of raw budget figures.

> The total amount we are requesting for fiscal year 1974 for civil works is $1,479,000,000. This compares with an appropriation last year including supplementals of slightly over $1.85 million. However, linked with the budget request for new funds is a decision by the administration that $116 million of our fiscal year 1973 appropriation will be carried over unobligated for use in fiscal year 1974. The effect of this is to balance off the two fiscal years at close to the same level.[5]

With contextual considerations like these in mind, our budget data for the seven natural resource managing agencies yield interesting comparisons. Figures 5.1, 5.2, and 5.3 display funding levels for each agency over a forty-four-year time span. One obvious interpretation is that the Corps and the Forest Service lead the pack. The budgets of both of these agencies are significantly larger than those of the other five agencies included in this study. During the decade of the 1980s, however, the Corps' budget levelled off while the Forest Service's budget continued its upward trend. The Park Service also made impressive budgetary gains during the Reagan-Bush era, and that is shown in figure 5-3. It is less a "muddler through" than it was previously. The other four agencies still cluster at the bottom of the graph.

The Corps and the Forest Service best illustrate the budgetary characteristics of powerful agencies: From modest bases in 1950, these agencies have shown remarkable growth in the amount of money they have had to spend on programs and the workforce needed to implement those programs. On average, they have enjoyed absolute annual appropriations significantly larger than the other five agencies. Their budgetary growth, occurring during liberal and conservative political regimes, suggests the ability, previously discussed, to expand into new areas of activity without necessarily sacrificing traditional functions. Both agencies have been able to maintain congressional and/or executive approval for their programs.

We think that the Park Service could be approaching that category as well. It is possible that it may have experienced *its* take-off stage during the heyday of park barrel politics in the eighties. The agency's

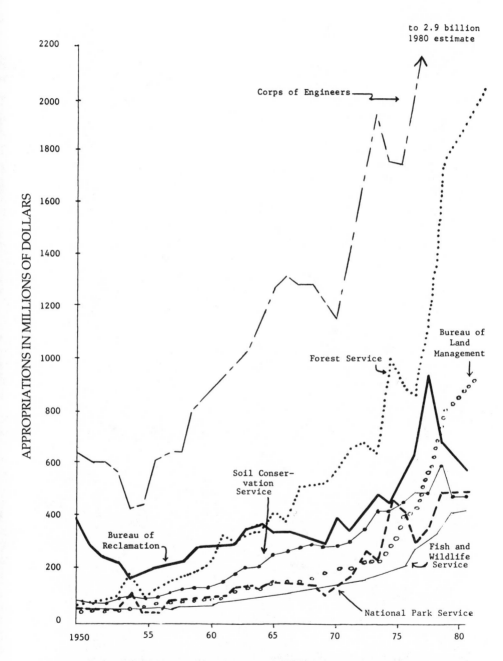

Figure 5.1 Total Annual Budget Appropriations of Seven Agencies for the Years 1950–1980. *Source:* Office of Management and Budget.

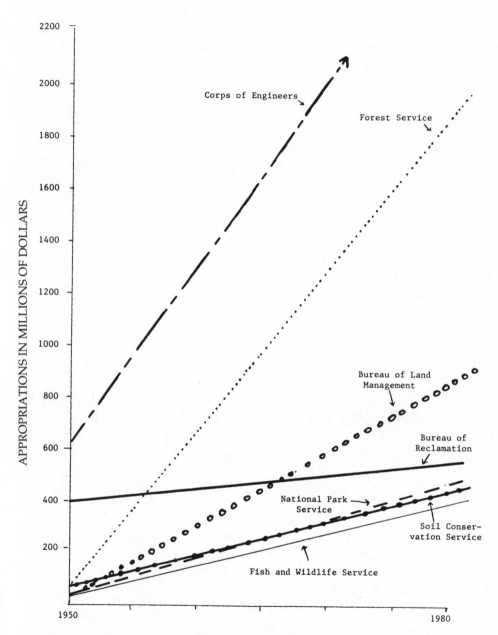

Figure 5.2 Total Annual Budget Appropriations of the Seven Agencies for 1950 and 1980. *Source:* Office of Management and Budget.

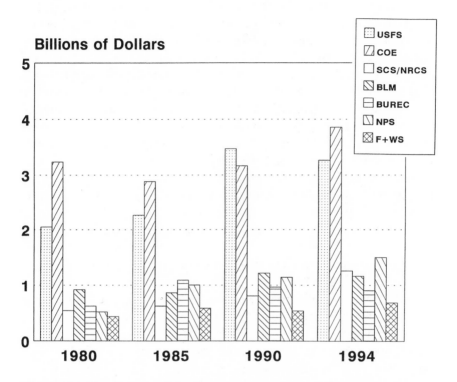

Figure 5.3 Total Annual Budget Appropriations of Seven Agencies
1980–94. *Sources:* Office of Management and Budget, Federal Agencies.

budget increase is still too recent, though, to predict with certainty
whether it is a short-lived gain, as has characterized the agency in the
past, or whether it represents a long-term trend. Early initiatives in the
104th Congress, however, point to the former interpretation.

Contrasting with the Forest Service and the Corps are the Bureau
of Reclamation, the Soil Conservation Service/Natural Resources and
Conservation Service, the Bureau of Land Management, the Fish and
Wildlife Service, and (until recently) the National Park Service. The
budgets for these agencies show a different pattern. Their budgets
increase incrementally. In the case of some of these agencies, their
budgets also have decreased rather dramatically. These five agencies
generally are subjected to greater fluctuations in their financial fortunes
than are the superstars.

There is thus displayed in figures 5.1 and 5.2 a gradual widening of the gap between the rich and not-so-rich agencies. Figure 5.2, showing only the years 1950 and 1980, illustrates this more forcefully than does figure 5-1. For example, the budgetary woes of the National Park Service during this period are amply documented.[6] Although national park visitation rose dramatically during the 1950s and 1960s, and while the number of national parks also was augmented, the Service failed to achieve a commensurate increase in funding for operations and park management.[7] This forced it into deficit spending in 1969.[8] The director of the agency went to the extreme of threatening Congress that he would close down the parks if it didn't respond more generously to the Service's impoverishment, which in 1970 Congress did.[9] But this generosity didn't last through the decade.

Also evident in these figures is the Bureau of Reclamation's decline from a position of relative strength. The Bureau's competition with the Corps, which is discussed in the histories of the two agencies, is seen in figures 5.1 and 5.2, where a "mere" 250 million dollars separate them in 1950, but where a whopping $2.3 billion in 1980 is testimony to the Corps' increasing monopoly on water resources development and related activities. The Bureau in this critical time period failed to broaden its activities while the Corps successfully assumed responsibility for an increasing diversity of operations.

To a somewhat lesser extent, the Park Service and the Fish and Wildlife Service have also suffered from competing with the formidable strength of the Forest Service in a number of overlapping program areas. The Bureau of Land Management was successful in recent years to the extent that it was able to imitate the Forest Service. But that behavior, as we show in chapter 4, had its costs as well. Fenno's research, as does ours, corroborates the finding that powerful agencies marshal their resources in a cumulative manner and often at the expense of their less powerful rivals.[10] Defining agency power as the ability to get Congress to appropriate what the agency requested, Fenno found the Forest Service to have strong committee support, while the Park Service, Fish and Wildlife Service, Bureau of Land Management, and the Bureau of Reclamation were characterized by weak committee support.[11] Fenno's study was for a time period of fifteen years—from 1947 to 1962. One can infer from the budget data displayed in figures 5.1 and 5.2 that this situation did not change during the 1970s.

Figures 5.1 and 5.2 thus provide an illustration of the total expenditures for the seven agencies and how they have increased or decreased over time. We can extend our understanding of these budgets by taking a closer look at how they change over time. A number of methods have been developed in the public policy literature which examine budgetary change in terms of percentage increase or decrease.[12] These measures are appropriate for examining the rate of change occurring in a particular agency's budget, but they are less useful for a comparative study, such as this one, because percentages do not take into account absolute differences. For example, both the Corps of Engineers and the Soil Conservation Service experienced a mean annual budget increase between 1950 and 1980 of about 7.5 percent. This is an interesting comparison, but it must be kept in mind that the Corps' budget is so much larger than the Soil Conservation Service's budget that a 7.5 percent rate of increase for one is not the same as a 7.5 percent increase for the other. Thus we argue that for comparative purposes changes in agency budgets are best explained in terms of absolute amounts, since these provide a clearer picture of what each agency has to work with.

Table 5.1 provides the mean annual change in appropriations for each of the seven agencies. The data are divided into three columns. The first column gives the mean annual increases only and indicates the number of years (out of a total of 33) that the agency experienced an increase in funding. The second column shows decreases, while the third column totals all thirty-three years to arrive at the mean annual change in appropriations from 1951 to 1983 (appropriations for 1983 are estimates).

A number of observations can be made regarding the data displayed in table 5.1. The Bureau of Reclamation sustained budget reductions in 15 of the 33 years. These reductions average about $60 million. The two agencies with the largest budgets, the Corps and the Forest Service, also have received substantial average cuts but they, unlike the Bureau of Reclamation, compensated for these reductions by substantial increases in other years. Still, the Bureau was not totally deprived of significant increases, for it ranks a distant third—behind

*Table 5.1 Mean Annual Change in Appropriations, 1951–1983
in THOUSANDS OF DOLLARS*

Agency	Increase	Decrease	Total
Corps of Engineers	159,603 (N=20)	64,573 (N=13)	71,291
Forest Service	102,260 (N=24)	68,957 (N=9)	55,564
Bureau of Land Management	42,532 (N=29)	21,106 (N=4)	34,818
Bureau of Reclamation	74,332 (N=18)	59,998 (N=15)	13,272
National Park Service	60,976 (N=21)	39,216 (N=12)	24,543
Soil Conservation Service	27,338 (N=25)	27,476 (N=8)	14,050
Fish & Wildlife Service	20,422 (N=25)	9,132 (N=8)	13,257

Source: U.S. Budget, 1952–84.

the Corps and Forest Service—in terms of dollar increases. The data indicate that the Bureau of Reclamation has experienced a rather capricious budgetary history that parallels its organizational history as discussed in chapter 4.

Some of the Bureau's funding fluctuations can be traced to the organizational difficulties which the Bureau of Reclamation has had to endure. However, since both the Bureau and the Corps of Engineers have been subjected to a larger number of decreases than the other agencies in this study, one may also conclude that water resources development as a program area has been the object of greater capriciousness on the part of the purse holders than is the case with other program areas. The Corps has survived these vagaries quite well, however, while the Bureau has not. As a result, the latter agency has experienced a very low mean annual budget growth. Only the budget of the Fish and Wildlife Service has averaged a lower annual growth.

The budget of the Bureau of Land Management also presents an interesting case. Prior to 1976, the year in which the Bureau's organic act was passed, the agency had a mean annual budget growth of only $15.4 million. But after Congress passed the Federal Land Policy and Management Act the Bureau's budget increased dramatically. Also, the agency managed to escape a large number of annual budget decreases, sustaining in fact only four negative growth years from 1951 through 1983.

In sum, a principal finding of table 5.1 is that the Corps of Engineers and the Forest Service have experienced high levels of budgetary growth *despite* significant losses during negative growth years. The overall growth of their budgetary bases is impressive. The Bureaus of Reclamation and Land Management present a different picture. These two agencies have experienced greater fluctuation and hence greater inconsistency in their fiscal development. It becomes difficult, therefore, to predict their future funding situations. Both agencies have experienced success but it has been generally short-lived. Finally, a third pattern emerges with the National Park Service, the Soil Conservation Service, and the Fish and Wildlife Service, three agencies which demonstrated relatively unremarkable annual budgetary growth. The budget for the Park Service shows a cyclical funding pattern, but overall it has grown at a rate which is only half that of its major competitor, the Forest Service. The Soil Conservation Service and the Fish and Wildlife Service, the tortoises of the pack, creep slowly but steadily along.

Next, we analyze the budgetary fortunes of these seven agencies during the decade of the 1970s and through the critical first two years of the Reagan administration. During the seventies, numerous issues came to the forefront of public attention which related directly to natural resources policy and which had an impact on these seven resource managers. First, the country witnessed the environmental crisis. Shortly thereafter—that is, about 1973 or 1974—the nation was confronted with the energy crisis, which continued through the Carter administration and which was a preoccupation of the president's. By 1980 these issues had culminated and coalesced into a generalized public concern over shortages of all kinds, with the 1980 presidential election largely being fought over who, Carter or Reagan, could better deliver on bringing economy and frugality to the nation's capital.

What impact did this substantial public concern over environmental crises and energy shortages, and the concomitant 1980 changing of the guard, have on the agencies? First of all, the data support the thesis that the rich get richer and, by comparison, the poor stay poor. One might have suspected that pro-development agencies such as the Corps and the Forest Service would have been materially hurt by the environmental quality issue, and conversely that those agencies with a clearer preservationist orientation, like the Park Service and the Fish and Wildlife Service, would have been rewarded. This seems not to be the case. Long-term trends in agency budgets predominated over what Anthony Downs has described as relatively short-term "issue-attention cycles."[13] To some extent, all seven resource agencies benefitted from increased public attention to these issues, but those benefitting the most turned out to be the two agencies in the best position to capitalize on both the environmental and energy crises. Those agencies, the Corps and the Forest Service, are the two organizations whose histories show a marked ability to incorporate new missions and new programs into their repertoire. The agencies faring less well were those that saw "nothing new" in the National Environmental Policy Act of 1969, or that resisted it, or that were in a precarious position to begin with. A point that we will return to in the conclusion of this study is the observation that the fortunes of agencies, as measured by the size of their budgets, has more to do with what Matthew Holden described as the organization's "disposition"[14] than it has to do with the nature of the agency's mission. Preservation-oriented agencies do not, in other words, automatically or necessarily benefit from an era of environmental awareness; this is especially true when it is immediately followed by an energy crisis that would logically have an opposite effect on the agencies.

The decade of environmentalism was followed by the era of "Reaganomics" and with it came unprecedented presidential attempts at budget-cutting. Budget data for his first term are presented in table 5.2. The table compares presidential requests and congressional appropriations for the fiscal years 1981 to 1984. It should be noted that the presidential requests for both 1981 and 1982 are the former Carter administration's figures; the 1983 and 1984 requests belong to the Reagan administration. It was not possible to derive a Reagan request for 1982 because, upon his election, the Carter requests went through a complicated series of revisions at the hands of the new administration. No exact figures were readily available. However, since the Congress largely accepted the Reagan administration's proposed changes in the

Carter budget requests during the transition year, it is the "congressional appropriation" for fiscal year 1982 which fairly accurately reflects Reaganomics during the transition year.

Table 5.2 Presidential Requests and Congressional Appropriations, 1981–1984 in THOUSANDS OF DOLLARS

Agency	1981 Req.	1981 App.	1982 Req.	1982 App.	1983 Req.	1983 App*	1984 Req.
Corps of Engineers	2,991,764	3,073,597	3,340,500	2,970,052	2,197,000	2,958,188	2,315,108
Forest Service	2,028,279	2,141,866	2,206,201	1,877,066	1,985,607	1,904,715	1,684,972
Bureau of Land Management	996,795	1,034,346	1,099,074	1,239,476	1,255,630	1,162,421	584,177
National Park Service	809,452	788,180	906,7123	773,205	936,520	810,922	974,910
Bureau of Reclamation	518,900	868,959	562,395	801,192	734,578	885,576	737,525
Soil Conservation Service	535,247	588,233	566,354	577,044	515,816	518,330	474,406
Fish & Wildlife Service	445,684	424,225	459,904	438,253	412,353	465,194	472,382

*Estimate

A comparison of the 1981 and 1982 appropriations shows that Reagan initially succeeded in reducing the budgets of the seven agencies by an average of 2.26 percent. This is not an impressive amount. But what must be kept in mind is that the administration's cuts were made more according to functional categories and less in terms of the agency *per se*. As we discussed in the previous three chapters, pro-development programs were increased and pro-environment activities were decreased in virtually all of the seven agencies. In other words, the Reagan strategy of changing the priorities of the executive branch was to get within the agency or bureau, and alter specific behaviors or activities at that level. His successors, Bush and Clinton, continued this approach, which is sometimes referred to as micro-management. Therefore, it now is imperative for scholars to do likewise in order to appreciate fully a presidential administration's impact on the bureaucracy.

The 1983 appropriation figures are only preliminary estimates, but they nevertheless reveal a significant change in support for the president from the previous year. In 1982 President Reagan's budget proposals were accepted over Carter's without major revision. In 1983, however, the president's honeymoon was over and so his influence over Congress had likewise eroded somewhat; as a result appropriations differ substantially in some cases from the presidential request. This is evident in the budget for the Corps of Engineers which Reagan proposed to cut by a phenomenal 26.8 percent. However, Congress refused to accept such a cut and increased the president's proposal by 36.2 percent, thereby allowing the Corps to maintain a "status quo" budget. It also becomes evident in the Park Service's budget which, beginning in the mid-eighties increased dramatically as a result of "park barrel politics" (See figure 3.1. in chapter 3). Working in the opposite direction, Congressional budget-makers decreased the president's proposal for the Bureau of Reclamation by 13.4 percent.

While nearly everyone now agrees that President Reagan was initially quite successful in meeting his objectives, it is important to assess what has been the long-range impact of the "Reagan Revolution" on resource management. Figure 5.3, Annual Budget Appropriations for Seven Agencies, 1980–1994, provides data to help make that assessment. What, in short, happened to the budgets of these seven resource managing agencies over those fourteen years—years that spanned three presidential administrations, one change in party control of the White House, and one change in party control of the Senate?

First, the overall picture in 1994 looks similar to that for 1980. The budgets of the two superstars, the Corps and the Forest Service, far exceed the budgets of the other five agencies. But whereas the Bureau of Land Management was the rising star in the earlier period, that designation now belongs to the National Park Service. The Park Service made the greatest gains of all of the seven agencies during the last fourteen years, nearly tripling its budget. The other four agencies, the Soil Conservation Service, now reorganized into the Natural Resources and Conservation Service, the Bureau of Land Management, the Bureau of Reclamation, and the U.S. Fish and Wildlife Service carry on with the smallest budgets. As in 1980, the Fish and Wildlife Service brings up the rear.

Second, if we look at the budgets of each of the agencies in more detail, the impact of Reaganomics is apparent in figure 5.3. The Reagan White House succeeded in holding the line on the Corps of Engineers' budget, thereby reversing what had been a period of phenomenal growth for the agency. It also achieved what previous administrations failed to do, and that was to impose stricter cost-sharing provisions on Corps projects. The Water Resources Development Act of 1986, pushed by an interesting coalition of fiscal conservatives and environmentalists (who thought they saw the demise of the Corps in the new law), was the major national water policy accomplishment of the decade. Thus by 1990 the Corps' budget was about the same as it was in 1980. As a result, a number of agency employees became alarmed over what they perceived as stagnation—but what we suggested was, in the conclusion to the first edition of this book, an "optimal size" for an organization.

But if the Corps' traditional opponents expected WRDA and Reaganomics to eviscerate the agency, they were wrong. Stories about the death of the agency proved to be greatly exaggerated. One reason had to do, oddly, with the supercollider project in Texas. Analysis of congressional appropriations hearings during the Bush administration shows that the president relinquished the high moral ground of the office to achieve parochial objectives. In insisting on appropriations for the supercollider, the White House was in no position to deny a myriad of demands from congresspersons for public works projects in *their* districts and states. The four years of the Bush presidency therefore resemble one gigantic logrolling session, with the Corps a major beneficiary of this political free-for-all. By 1994, its budget had shot up to $3.8 billion. However, by the 1990s it is important to note that Corps projects were "greener" than they had been previously. It wasn't quite back to the traditional pork barrel, although the process was the same.

The impact of Reaganomics on the Forest Service is also apparent. The agency's budget increased substantially from 1980 to 1990, largely as a result of the administration's insistence on a stepped-up timber production program. In passing the Timber Supply Relief Act in 1984, however, the Congress showed that it concurred with President Reagan's objectives. Thus the agency's budget went from a little over $2 billion in 1980 to $3.5 billion in 1990. "Most of that increase was tied to timber sales," we were told by a number of individuals. But a disastrous fire year also contributed to the agency's record budget year of 1990: Approximately $790 million of the $3.5 billion was expended on fire fighting activities.[15]

The agency's budget declined under Presidents Bush and Clinton principally because it was impossible to keep timber production at previous levels. As we discussed in chapter 2, Reaganomics placed great strains on the capabilities of the Forest Service to produce the volume of timber it was told to produce. Agency officials currently are dealing with the consequences of years of record harvests coming from the national forests. A major problem is how to compensate for the precipitous decline in annual timber receipts which, in the heyday of Reaganomics, were "in excess of $791 million."[16]

Bringing in money like that to the U.S. Treasury has been one of the agency's sources of power; now its officials are having to demonstrate once again their flexibility and ingenuity by looking for other revenue sources. With annual harvests currently in the 5 BBF range, as opposed to the 10 BBF of the 1980s, Forest Service policymakers are responding by increasing fee receipts from other uses of the national forests. In its FY 1995 budget, for example, the agency projects substantial increases in both grazing and recreational user fees: For grazing fees, the increase is from $9.2 million in 1993 to nearly $16 million for 1995; and in recreational use, from $49.2 million in 1993 to $61 million.[17] Even with increases such as these, however, it is unlikely that the agency will soon experience another period of growth such as it did in the 1980s. Trees take a long time to grow back. The 104th Congress, however, is "helping out" with its introduction of the controversial timber salvage bill in 1995.

Two of the three agencies that muddle through—the Soil Conservation Service and the Fish and Wildlife Service—did just that through difficult political times. The budget for the SCS increased incrementally from 1980 to 1990, despite serious discussions emanating from the Reagan and Bush administrations over abolishing the agency. But the lobby for the country's agricultural sector historically has been strong, and farmers had a special friend in Secretary John Block, who kept the SCS from OMB's cutting block. In addition, the nature of the mission of the SCS, to conserve and improve topsoil, although not widely appreciated by urban Americans, is in fact an essential one.

For these reasons, the SCS survived into the 1990s. An overdue reorganization of the entire department was a top priority of President

Clinton's agriculture secretary, Michael Espy, and in 1994 the SCS was reorganized, along with parts of the ASCS, into the Natural Resources and Conservation Service (NRCS). Its FY 1994 budget of about $1.2 billion indicates continued modest growth, since approximately $340 million of that appropriation went for activities connected with the disastrous Midwestern floods of 1993. All in all, budget analysis reveals that the NRCS is not doing badly.

However, the same cannot be said for the Fish and Wildlife Service. It continues to be plagued by the kinds of problems that it has had for virtually all of its existence. Its budget from 1980 to 1990 increased by only $100 million, largely due to the fact that the Reagan administration was utterly opposed to one of its principal functions, that of enforcing the Endangered Species Act. Then, one of the first actions taken by Clinton's interior secretary, Bruce Babbitt, was to create by secretarial order a National Biological Service (NBS). If this wasn't a vote of no confidence for the Fish and Wildlife Service, nothing was. Although a relative handful of employees of other Interior Department agencies were transferred to the NBS, most of its employees came from the USF&WS. Thus Reaganomics, followed by Clinton's reinventing government effort, hit the Service hard. We consider its 1994 budget of $681 million as one which stretches the capabilities of the agency to the breaking point. But that is nothing new.

The third agency characterized as a muddler through, the National Park Service, did more than that during the last fourteen years. Its budget increased from about $515 million in 1980 to $1.5 billion in 1994. That is impressive growth. It was due principally to the fact that Congress rediscovered the agency in the 1980s, when money for traditional pork barrel projects was shrinking, and when, after the collapse of the Soviet Union, even the defense budget started declining. The vast changes in the political landscape during this period forced congresspersons to look for popular but relatively inexpensive projects to bring home to their districts and states. The park barrel was born.

Although the Park Service enjoyed a rare period of substantial growth during the last ten years, few agency officials in 1994 *feel* rich. We discussed in chapter 3 the various reasons for this; it boils down to the perennial problem of the agency, which is that appropriations never have kept up with system expansion. During the last fourteen years many new park units were added to the system, and appropriations indeed tripled. But the Park Service is still underfunded in critical program areas like operations and maintenance. Agency officials, and their support groups, estimate that there is at least a $1 billion backlog for such activities as rehabilitating roads and trails, and in improving public buildings and employee housing. The agency thus requires appropriations in the $2.5 billion range in order to do everything it is supposed to do.

The Bureaus of Reclamation and Land Management, agencies characterized as shooting stars, continued in that pattern during the Reagan, Bush, and Clinton years. The budget of the Bureau of Reclamation initially increased during the first few years of Reaganomics, and then declined. The BLM's budget did the opposite; it took a nosedive in the mid-1980s and then began to increase under Bush and Clinton. The fluctuating fortunes of these two agencies are once again evident in the most recent budget data.

Huge reclamation projects, like the Central Arizona Project and the Central Utah Project, account for much of the Bureau of Reclamation's budget increases in the early eighties. By 1985 the agency's budget had climbed to nearly $1.1 billion, quite a jump from what Carter had held it to. With the changing of the guard in 1981 the Bureau was back in favor. Analysis of appropriations hearings in the 1980s reveals that both Western congresspersons and the president (a pro-development Westerner) saw eye to eye on the Bureau's budget. However, when the Clinton administration took office in 1993 and appointed a longstanding critic of the agency as Commissioner of Reclamation, its fortunes, predictably, changed. The Bureau's budget is again sloping downward.

The fortunes of the BLM were largely the reverse of Reclamation's. Leaders of the Sagebrush Rebellion succeeded in putting the agency back into what they perceived as its proper place. With the creation in the early eighties of the Minerals Management Service, the Bureau's budget plummeted as it lost programs to the new agency. Its appropriation for FY 1986 of $653 million marked the decade's trough. After 1986, however, the BLM's budget began climbing again, and in 1990 its budget was further augmented when all departmental firefighting functions were transferred to the Bureau.

As of 1994, therefore, the BLM's budget shows a modest increase from its 1980 level. But given the vast acreage it manages, and the new programs it is supposed to implement such as riparian area management, the Bureau continues to be underfunded. This is especially the case when it is compared with the Forest Service, and now even the National Park Service.

AGENCY WORK FORCES

Another useful measure of power is the agencies' workforces. Figures 5.4 and 5.5 show the total number of personnel for these seven agencies over a forty-four-year time span. Figure 5.4 compares the agencies between 1950 and 1980, while figure 5.5 covers the years from 1980 to 1994.

As was the case with their budgets, figure 5.4 demonstrates the substantial growth in the Corps' and the Forest Service's workforces during their take-off period. The Corps moved from second to first place by overtaking the Bureau of Reclamation, and the Forest Service moved from third to second place. The Park Service, the Bureau of Land Management, the Soil Conservation Service, and the Fish and Wildlife Service slowly increased their personnel base during this thirty-year period. Also very apparent is the Bureau of Reclamation's decline, which began around 1950 when the agency had the largest workforce of the seven agencies and was the largest agency within the Interior Department. The Bureau's powerful position as of 1950 was due largely to FDR's New Deal which, with help from the Bureau and other federal construction agencies, literally built the nation's infrastructure.

With the average salary for federal employees increasing about 118 percent between 1950 and 1976,[18] even a modest increase in workforce required a significant growth in an agency's budget. In view of this, the rapid growth of the Forest Service and the Corps is even more impressive than it appears in figure 5.4. It speaks of an unusual ability to acquire new positions necessary for expanding and diversifying agency operations even during a period when inflation and salary increases were neutralizing much of the organization's real, or noninflationary, growth.

Thus in terms of personnel, by 1980 the two superstars were two to three times larger than their cohorts. This strongly suggests that these agencies were far better off than the smaller agencies in terms of enjoying slack resources. With workforces of 25,000 to 30,000, organizational

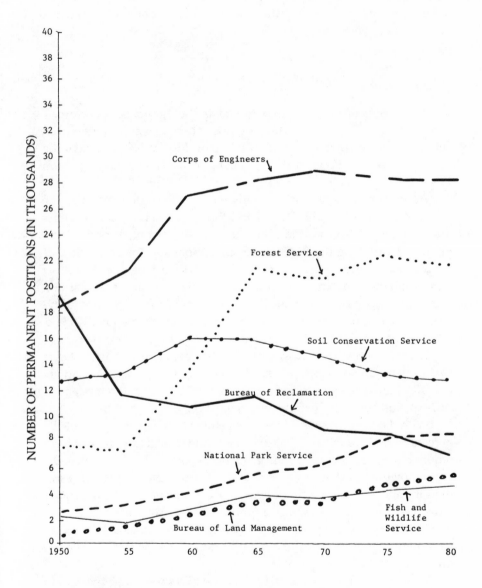

Figure 5.4 Total Number of Permanent Positions in Seven Agencies for the Years 1950–1980, in five-year intervals. *Source:* Office of Management and Budget.

flexibility clearly is more assured than when an agency's workforce is stretched to the limit. The plight of the Fish and Wildlife Service during the late 1960s and the 1970s is the best example of this condition. In a variation of the current unfunded mandates controversy, an activist Congress thrust numerous new responsibilities of coordination, enforcement, and research upon an agency unequipped to handle the great increase in workload. Consequently, its traditional programs suffered and the agency was criticized, as it had been in the past, for not doing its job. The Park Service and the BLM also were put in a similar budgetary and personnel bind during this period. Park Service employees complained that they had to be the lowest-paid workers in the entire federal government, while the BLM, with the "discovery" in the 1970s of its valuable energy resources, also was stretched very thin due to only modest increases in its budget and workforce.

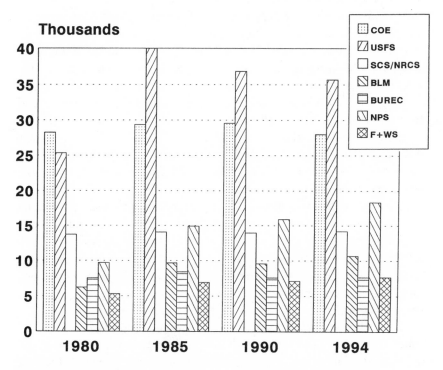

Figure 5.5 Total Number of Permanent Positions/FTEs in Seven Agencies 1980–1994. *Sources:* Federal Agencies, OPM, Budgets of U.S. Gov't.

Figure 5.5 displays agencies' work forces from 1980 to 1994. The picture looks remarkably similar to that showing the agencies' budgets for this period (figure 5.3). Of the seven agencies, the Corps and the Forest Service still have the largest number of employees. By 1985, however, the Forest Service surged ahead of the Corps and has remained out in front ever since. The National Park Service, for reasons previously discussed, made significant gains in personnel during this period. To a lesser extent, so did the BLM. The remaining three agencies, the NRCS, the Bureau of Reclamation, and the Fish and Wildlife Service, essentially held their own.

In comparing figures 5.4 and 5.5 one computational change must be noted. In FY 1982 the government converted its earlier method of calculating the federal work force, called manpower ceilings, to full-time equivalent positions (FTEs). The effect was to produce an increase in all of the seven agencies' workforces after 1982, but the increase was especially evident in the Forest Service, the Bureau of Land Management, and the National Park Service. What these three agencies have in common is a seasonal workforce to take care of the influx of summer vacationers heading for the great outdoors. We thus assume that the change to FTEs incorporated the seasonal workforce of federal agencies.

Over the last fifteen years or so two primary issues dominated debates and decisions about the federal work force. One was quantitative and the other was qualitative. Figure 5.5 shows evidence of the quantitative concern, which is but another term for Reaganomics and its successor, reinventing government. In short, elected officials demanded that the federal bureaucracy perform more efficiently—or, in the words of a park official, that it "do more with less." Beginning about 1981, tremendous pressures have been placed on federal agencies to reduce the size of their workforces. With two exceptions, the Park Service and the Forest Service, the success of downsizing is reflected in figure 5.5. Five agencies, including the powerful Corps of Engineers, are doing more work with either the same number of employees or fewer. However, they also are doing more contracting out.

The other workforce issue is qualitative. It concerns diversity. Policymakers in all of the seven agencies in this study have made efforts at diversifying their professional base in a number of different directions: Efforts have been made at hiring more women, at hiring more people of color, and at hiring more "greens", that is, individuals with environmental science degrees and/or backgrounds. We discovered considerable evidence that these natural resource agencies are responding to societal pressures to more accurately reflect the heterogeneous composition of American society.

Although the evidence primarily is anecdotal, it is compelling. The present director of the Fish and Wildlife Service is a female forester from New England who, we were told, is the first nonhunter to head the agency. An associate director of the Bureau of Land Management is a black woman from the East; as such she can be considered a nontraditional senior official of that Western-based agency on three counts. The associate chief of the Natural Resources and Conservation Service currently is an Afro-American with a strong environmental record, and the head of the NRCS is, one official said, "clearly the greenest chief the agency has ever had."

"It used to be that the Forest Service wouldn't waste a forester's position on a woman," a high-ranking official of the agency bluntly admitted. But that bias is disappearing at the same time as the agency increases diversity in its professional ranks. A 1994 listing of the Forest Service's professional workforce contains 32 separate occupations.[19] Foresters remain the most numerous, with 5,063 (or nearly 15 percent of the agency's total workforce), but the agency employs significant numbers of people with other degrees as well. For example, to cite a few, there presently are 301 archaeologists, 967 general biologists and ecologists, 341 fisheries biologists, 890 wildlife biologists, and 272 landscape architects working for the Forest Service.

The Corps of Engineers also has made efforts at diversification over the last fifteen years. Like the Forest Service it has hired more of what are referred to as "Ologists." The agency's headquarters also keeps track of the ethnic and gender composition of its workforce. A 1993 Affirmative Action Table, for example, shows that 31 percent of the agency's 38,925 employees were women; 11.3 percent were black; 2.9 percent were Hispanic; 3.6 percent were Asian American/Pacific Islander; and 1.2 percent were Native American. Although white males still run the agency—there are no women and no blacks in the Senior Executive Service and Grades 16–18 category—nevertheless women and minorities gradually are making their way up the career ladder in the Corps: They comprise 16 percent of those in grades 13–15.[20]

One of the most laudable features of the civil service in the United

States has been its commitment to equal opportunity. In doing the research for the second edition of this book, we have been impressed with the extent of the efforts made by officials in these seven agencies to achieve that goal. There is still room for improvement, of course, but we think that it is important, in this era of government-bashing, to recognize accomplishments when they have occurred. [21]

PERCEPTIONS ABOUT AGENCY POWER

Finally, how do bureaucrats view each other? Are the perceptions of agency personnel in these seven organizations consistent with the findings presented above? Despite, or perhaps because of, some intense interagency rivalry, do they see a hierarchical pattern of agency power?

The answers to the above questions are yes. In order to cross-check the historical research and the budgetary and personnel data, we interviewed agency personnel in each of the seven agencies. We did so in 1979–80 and again in 1992–94. The 1979 sample (N=20) consisted of mid- to upper-level officials working in the agencies' Washington offices, and whose positions were associated with policy analysis and/or environmental programs. Each respondent was asked, among other things, to rank six agencies (excluding his or her own) on four variables. The variables were: (1) the agency's relative power within the executive branch; (2) the agency's relationship with Congress; (3) the range of its interest group support; and (4) the quality of its response to the National Environmental Policy Act.

Table 5.3 gives the mean rankings for all seven agencies on the four variables. The means are also presented in graph form in figure 5.6. A score of one (1.0) represents the highest possible ranking; each successive score indicates a lower ranking. This scoring system allowed each respondent to choose only one agency for each position, thus emphasizing the more extreme scores: Only one agency could receive a score of one, and one had to be ranked sixth.

For variable one (relative power within the executive branch) a clear hierarchy emerges. With a mean score of 1.8, the Corps of Engineers is ranked well above the other agencies. The Forest Service is

Table 5.3 Mean Rankings

	Overall Mean	Variable 1 Relative Power within Executive Branch	Variable 2 Close Relation- ship with Congress	Variable 3 Interest Group Support	Variable 4 Quality of Response to NEPA
Bureau of Reclamation	4.1	4.2	3.4	4.2	4.5
Bureau of Land Management	4.5	4.4	4.4	4.5	4.7
Corps of Engineers	2.1	1.8	1.4	3.0	2.3
Fish & Wildlife Service	3.9	3.6	4.6	3.9	3.6
Forest Service	2.7	2.6	2.8	2.7	2.5
National Park Service	3.5	3.2	4.0	3.0	3.7
Soil Conservation Service	3.7	4.1	3.8	3.3	3.7

ranked second, while the other four agencies scored moderate to low rankings. For variable two (close relationship with Congress), the Corps of Engineers again scored well above all other agencies with a mean of 1.4. The Forest Service again ranked second.

The findings for variable three (interest group support) are less stark. Although the Corps of Engineers and the Forest Service still scored high, so did the Park Service. The results therefore are less definitive, with all of the scores clustering at the moderate and low ranks. What might account for this is that there may have been some confusion over our reference to "interest groups." Since much of the discussion in the interviews centered around natural resources policy and the environmental movement, respondents may have assumed that this variable was concerned only with *environmental* interest group support and not with pro-development lobbies. This is only one possible explanation for the results on this variable, however. It may be that the results accurately reflect the perceptions of the respondents, that is, that a consensus does not exist concerning which agencies have the strongest network of alliances.

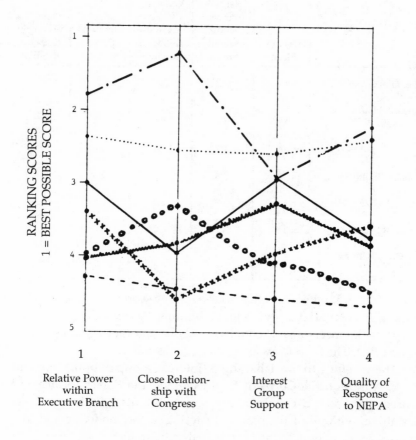

RANKING SCORES
1 = BEST POSSIBLE SCORE

| 1 | 2 | 3 | 4 |

Relative Power within Executive Branch

Close Relation-ship with Congress

Interest Group Support

Quality of Response to NEPA

VARIABLES

Key:

— · — Corps of Engineers
········· Forest Service
ʁ ʁ ʁ ʁ ʁ ʁ Fish & Wildlife Service
— — — Bureau of Land Management

——— Park Service
▬▬▬ Soil Conservation Service
o o o o Bureau of Reclamation

Figure 5.6 Mean Rankings (1 = best possible score)

On variable four (quality of response to NEPA) the Corps of Engineers and the Forest Service once again received the highest scores by a considerable margin. We were interested in the agencies' responses to NEPA because in the policy literature it frequently is used as a measure of an agency's ability to change and innovate. This in turn is related to agency survival.

To provide a general ranking for the four variables combined, we calculated an overall mean which includes all the scores across all four variables contained in table 5.3. These scores average the results from each of the four variables, and emphasize the first-place ranking of the

Table 5.4 First-Place Ranking for Each Agency on Each Variable

	Mean	Variable 1 Relative Power within Executive Branch	Variable 2 Close Relation- ship with Congress	Variable 3 Interest Group Support	Variable 4 Quality of Response to NEPA
Bureau of Reclamation	3 (1.7)	0	0	1 (6.7)	0
Bureau of Land Management	0	0	0	0	0
Corps of Engineers	10 (57.8)	10 (55.6)	15 (83.3)	4 (23.5)	11 (68.8)
Fish & Wildlife Service	1.8 (11.2)	0	2 (12.5)	4 (25.0)	1 (7.1)
Forest Service	4.4 (27.5)	6 (37.5)	3 (18.8)	4 (25.0)	4 (28.6)
National Park Service	1.3 (8.3)	3 (20.0)	0	2 (13.3)	0
Soil Conservation Service	1.3 (7.7)	0	2 (11.8)	3 (18.8)	0

Note: Total number is given first. Number in parentheses is adjusted percentage.

Corps of Engineers and the second-place ranking of the Forest Service. One of the advantages of using this type of ranked scoring system is the exclusivity of the highest rank. Since only one agency can be ranked first, the respondent must carefully select the one agency that would receive the highest rank. Table 5.4 gives the total number of respondents that ranked each agency first on each variable. The stark contrast between agencies is apparent. The Corps of Engineers dominated the highest ranking. For variables one, two, and four, the Corps received 55.6 percent, 83.3 percent, and 68.8 percent, respectively. The exception again is variable three (interest group support), where no agency received a clear lead. It should be noted, however, that the Corps and the Forest Service were the only agencies in the sample to score first-place rankings on all four variables. The other five agencies received no first-place ranking on at least one of the four variables.

The other extreme is the lowest ranking, number six. Again, the scoring system requires all respondents to rank one agency last on each variable. Table 5.5 gives the total number of respondents that ranked each agency last on each variable. Again the Corps of Engineers and the Forest Service scored impressively with the lowest number of last place rankings. At the other extreme, the Bureau of Land Management received, by a substantial margin, the greatest number of last place scores.

These findings lend support to the initial hypothesis concerning power differentials among federal agencies. Among natural resources agencies, the Corps of Engineers and the Forest Service by 1980 had clearly established reputations as powerful, innovative agencies. Furthermore, support for this perception was not limited to one or two rival agencies but, rather, was broad-based. At least one respondent from every agency in our sample ranked the Corps first on variables one, two and four. There was also across-the-board support for ranking the Forest Service either first or second on all variables. For variable four (quality of response to NEPA), at least one respondent from each agency in the sample ranked the Forest Service either first or second.

For the other agencies, however, there was little consistency or agreement among respondents. For example, scores for the Soil Conservation Service and for the Fish and Wildlife Service varied dramatically, often covering the entire range of possible rankings. This

Table 5.5 Last-Place Ranking for Each Agency on Each Variable

	Mean	Variable 1 Relative Power within Executive Branch	Variable 2 Close Relation-ship with Congress	Variable 3 Interest Group Support	Variable 4 Quality of Response to NEPA
Bureau of Reclamation	2.5 (16.6)	3 (18.8)	1 (06.3)	3 (20.0)	3 (21.4)
Bureau of Land Management	5.8 (37.1)	6 (37.5)	4 (25.0)	8 (50.0)	5 (35.7)
Corps of Engineers	.75 (04.7)	0	0	0	3 (18.8)
Fish & Wildlife Service	1.6 (11.2)	2 (12.5)	2 (12.5)	2 (12.5)	1 (07.1)
Forest Service	.5 (03.4)	0	0	1 (06.3)	1 (07.1)
National Park Service	2.5 (16.7)	3 (20.0)	5 (33.3)	2 (13.3)	0
Soil Conservation Service	2.6 (16.7)	3 (16.6)	5 (29.4)	1 (06.3)	2 (13.3)

may indicate that these agencies have yet to establish a clear reputation as either strong or weak agencies within the executive establishment.

In contrast to the scores described above, the Bureau of Reclamation and the Bureau of Land Management consistently scored well below the other five agencies. There was widespread agreement among agency personnel in the sample to rank these two agencies at the lowest rankings.

These data also showed evidence of competitive attitudes between agencies, resulting in a form of mutual, if grudging, respect. This was most obvious between the Forest Service and the National Park Service, where respondents from each agency consistently ranked the other higher than average. All of the Park Service respondents ranked the Forest Service first on variable one (relative power within the executive branch). Conversely, all of the Forest Service respondents ranked the Park Service either first or second on the same variable. The competition over management practices and policy which gave rise to the creation of these two agencies in the early part of the century has continued through much of the twentieth century.

A second round of interviewing was conducted between 1992 and 1994. We interviewed a total of 36 individuals: 21 were high-level officials working in the agencies' Washington headquarters; 10 were district or regional officials; and 5 were natural resources scholars not employed by the agencies. Most of the interviews were conducted in person; they lasted usually an hour or more. Although we chose not to use the structured questionnaire that we employed previously, we asked the same questions of all of the respondents. A number of these questions were designed to measure perceptions of agency power.

From these interviews we discovered that perceptions have changed rather significantly over the past fifteen years. Nearly everyone said that the distinctions that were very clear among the seven agencies ten or fifteen years ago are no longer so clear. The two leaders a decade ago, the Corps and the Forest Service, have become slightly dimmer superstars. Many respondents, including personnel within the agency, noted that the Corps' budgetary and personnel growth levelled off in the 1980s. At the same time a strong competitor emerged, the Environmental Protection Agency, to challenge the Corps' preeminence in the water resources field. The Bureau of Reclamation, all agreed, is a distant third in the competition for control of the water arena. In fact Clinton's first commissioner made every effort to further downsize the agency. The Fish and Wildlife Service and the Natural Resources and Conservation Service continue to play their traditional auxiliary roles in water management. However, the 1994 reorganization of the SCS into the NRCS is, we think, a positive sign for that agency.

In the case of the Forest Service, its budgetary and personnel gains over the past fifteen years are impressive. But in the midst of this growth, Smokey the Bear received a black eye; as we previously discussed, the agency took a severe public relations beating over the timber harvesting issue. Even officials within the Forest Service acknowledge that they have much work to do to change public attitudes and win back the trust of environmentalists.

At the same time, the Forest Service's principal competitor, the National Park Service, is closing ranks. Of the seven agencies covered in this study, arguably it has made the greatest gains in power over the past fifteen years. In interviews we noted a modest increase in the confidence level of agency officials; but, because of its continuing problems, officials in the Park Service continue to be cautious about the future. They may be doing better, but, to paraphrase Aaron Wildavsky, they are not feeling very much better. In fact, the same uncertainties that beset Americans generally also gnaw at agency personnel in all of these organizations. No one feels very rich or powerful any longer.

Still, the Forest Service and the Corps continue to be well-funded and well-staffed agencies within the executive establishment. As such they remain powerful organizations. An additional reason that this is the case, besides the ones already discussed, has to do with the leadership variable (see table 1.1 in chapter 1). In doing the most recent interviews for this study we uncovered an "unobtrusive measure" of effective leadership. Although we made every effort to accommodate the busy schedules of the heads of these seven agencies—we made two separate trips to Washington in 1994 to conduct these interviews—we were granted appointments with only three of the seven heads: with the commissioner of reclamation, the chief of Engineers, and the chief of the Forest Service. Only two of the three had prepared for the interview by reading some or all of our book: the chief of Engineers and the chief of the Forest Service. The point of course is *not* that we consider (necessarily) our book as the *sine qua non* of scholarship, but that the two chiefs of the superstars were both accessible to "the public" and informed about their concerns. That is an example of astute leadership.

CONCLUSION

The combination of archival research, budget and personnel statistics, and data from the interviews concerning agency power reinforce one another. Without belaboring the point, two federal agencies have pulled out from the pack of seven to distinguish themselves within the executive establishment. A third agency, the Park Service, may be in a take-off stage. The other four bureaus either move along at a slower pace or experience alternating periods of growth and decline. We consider this finding to be highly interesting and empirically verified. In the final chapter we will speculate on the likely future of these federal agencies, and of natural resources policy generally, as we approach the twenty-first century. Especially given the revolutions that have taken place, or are taking place, in transportation, communications, and national politics, we offer some suggestions about the necessity for further reform and reorganization of natural resource management.

6

From Staking Out the Terrain
to Searching for Common Ground

The ten years that have elapsed since the publication of the first edition of this book have wrought significant and measurable changes within the federal bureaucracy. What President Ronald Reagan began in 1981, Washington politicians are continuing in 1995. This attempt at reinventing government promises to have profound effects on the seven natural resource agencies analyzed in this book. Already, however, our research shows that these organizations are significantly altered from what they were a decade or so ago. Not only have their political environments changed, but internally generated pressures for reform also have had their effects. A decade hence it is possible that these agencies will be barely recognizable—mere shadows of their former selves, if they survive at all.

Despite some fundamental changes in natural resources policy over the past decade, this research also found elements of continuity. Understandably so: Even convulsive historical eras like the 1930s and the 1980s must connect with the past. Politicians rarely have the luxury of writing on a *tabula rasa,* and when one is dealing with organizations designed for permanence, like the bureaucracy, it is no surprise that change is evolutionary rather than revolutionary. Thus we found that the relative strengths and weaknesses of the seven agencies are still evident. We also found that the original model of agency power, and the typology developed from it, continue to have validity. The nature of the agencies' missions, their sources of expertise, and their constituency support may have changed appreciably over the last ten years but the overall significance of these elements remains. All things being equal, the bureau that is seen to contribute to the nation's economic vitality, that has a respected scientific base, that is run by professionals, and that is supported by a network of organized interests still has the edge over those that do not.

The concluding chapter assesses the crosscutting political forces of continuity and change in natural resources policy in this manner. Moving from the particular to the general, we first discuss trends in (1) public lands management, and (2) water resources policy. Then we examine more general political and administrative changes that probably will have a long-term impact on the entire natural resources policy arena. A final section addresses the prospects for the most fundamental of changes, that of the replacement of one intellectual paradigm with another. Although it is impossible to predict whether such a change in world view will occur as the twentieth century gives way to the twenty-first, there surely are signs that humans are reexamining their relationship with nature, and that they are using new tools to do so.

In the spirit of millennial change, then, we conclude by offering a reorganization proposal that is both politically achievable and intellectually compelling. It is designed to push our resource managers in the direction of further institutionalizing the emerging paradigm, that of ecosystems management, which we and others see as the wave of the future.

TRENDS IN LAND MANAGEMENT

The most significant recent development in managing the nation's public lands is the introduction of the concept of ecosystems management (EM). It has been defined as "a management philosophy which focuses on desired conditions rather than system outputs, and which recognizes the need to protect or restore critical ecological components, functions, and structures in order to sustain resources in perpetuity." It encompasses five subprinciples: (1) socially defined goals and management objectives; (2) integrated, holistic science; (3) broad spatial and temporal scales; (4) collaborative decision building; (5) adaptable institutions.[1]

Although EM still is in a definitional stage, the idea is accumulating adherents and gaining public attention. Developing out of such statutes as NEPA and the Endangered Species Act, and incorporating the new information-gathering technologies, ecosystems management is a serious attempt at putting back together the pieces of resource management. So far, federal and state land managers have addressed the jurisdictional problems which EM highlights primarily through increased interagency coordination and cooperation. Personnel within the BLM, the Forest Service, the Park Service, and the Fish and Wildlife Service—and their state counterparts—will find themselves coordinating even more as an EM regime emerges. Interagency cooperation, in the form of memoranda of understanding (MOUs) and memoranda of agreement (MOAs), will proliferate in the foreseeable future.

Eventually, the new paradigm will force major institutional reorganizations. As we learn more about ecosystems, and map them (the Forest Service already has begun this critical task, along with a few other agencies), traditional boundaries will not make much sense. New organizations will be fashioned from existing ones. Needless to say, there will be a high degree of conflict engendered within the political system as this occurs. Containing the conflict within reasonable bounds will be a major task of policymakers in the twenty-first century.

A second trend in land management is an overtly political one. As has been true for other policy arenas, there has occurred over the past ten to fifteen years a proliferation in the number of interest groups clamoring to be heard. Land managers not only are at their wits' end in trying to placate all of them, but they are nearly unanimous in observing that the iron triangle construct, which dominated the scholarly literature for years, is outdated.[2] Today's land managers are part of not one, but several, triangles of interests. Perhaps a new term for this changed situation would be tangles of interests. Each knot in the tangle would represent what is now called (ironically, we find, given this book's title) a "stakeholder." Whatever the terminology, the reality is that land managers find their actions more circumscribed than ever before. It is a political environment in which it is hard to accomplish even the simplest objective.

Frankly, it is difficult to discern an immediate solution to this form of political gridlock. Possibly, as resource managers accumulate more and better data from the new technologies they have at their disposal, they then will be in a better position to defend their actions as being in the public interest. Perhaps their actions *will be* more in the public interest. Perhaps, too, the current demands for decentralizing decision-making will produce less conflict. Certainly that is one of the objectives of those who espouse the new federalism.

Maybe bypassing the federal government altogether is another solution to gridlock. Organizations such as the Nature Conservancy and the Trust for Public Lands have protected millions of acres of land simply by purchasing and then managing them. This strategy appears to have been a popular one with the public. Finally, agencies may have to rely more and more on so-called experts in conflict resolution—for example, social psychologists, sociologists, and political scientists—to forge consensus among stakeholders. Some scholars report that mediation has resolved several conflict-ridden environmental disputes in recent years.[3]

While all of these approaches show promise, in the short run it appears that federal land managers will have to continue to muddle through. The political arena will remain fragmented and fractious for some time, until a new equilibrium is reached. In this respect, the end of twentieth century is not unlike the end of the last century, when progressive conservation found its unifying voice only in 1901, with Theodore Roosevelt's fortuitous accession to the presidency. There is nothing like intelligent and inspired leadership to break through political stalemate.

Another change is in the staffing of the land managing agencies. During the 1980s and 1990s efforts were made to politicize positions at the top and to diversify the workforce throughout the organization. We observe that the considerable effort made by the Reagan administration to gain control of these agencies was successful. The SCS joined the NPS, the BLM, and the Fish and Wildlife Service in having a political appointee, rather than a careerist, head the agency. The only holdout has been the Forest Service, but even that traditionally powerful agency has been under great pressure to capitulate. Its current chief, for instance, is seen to be too closely connected with the Clinton administration for his—and the agency's—own good.

Although there are obvious compelling reasons for the politicization of the bureaucracy, overall we cannot consider it a positive trend. It is demoralizing for agency employees. It weakens the image of the agency in the minds of the public. It does not provide the kind of politically disinterested leadership that is essential in running a professional organization. One of the problems, for example, with the Environmental Protection Agency throughout its twenty-five year existence has been a vacuum of knowledgeable leadership at the very top. Through both Democratic and Republican administrations, the agency generally has been headed by political cronies. Thus, we would rather see a trend in the opposite direction; that is, toward making the heads of these resource agencies careerists who are promoted for excellence, and "from the ground up." Gifford Pinchot's model of the ideal bureaucracy continues to be, in our view, the best one around.

Diversification of agency workforces is a more positive development. It is occurring in two ways. First, there have been serious efforts at recruiting minorities and women to professional positions within the agencies. With increasing frequency, we found that these traditionally disadvantaged groups are represented at the uppermost levels. Overall, the land managing agencies are doing a good job at hiring and promoting professionals who are other than white males. They should, we think, continue this effort.

Second, professionally based diversification is occurring in the agencies. More of what are referred to as "ologists"—biologists, entomologists, geologists, and so on—are being hired. So are greater numbers of social scientists, especially economists and accountants. This aspect of diversification is, of course, related to the move toward ecosystems management, and in the long run it is a positive trend.

In the short run, however, it poses problems for those agencies, such as the Forest Service, which have had a long history of enjoying an undisputed "dominant profession." Forestry has been the cement that has held the Forest Service together, and the transition from traditional forestry to a more inclusive science of forest management is causing organizational problems for the agency. As the current chief said, what the agency needs is "a new dominant profession." It is, he believed, in the process of being created, in academe and in the agency itself, but it is far from being realized.

All of the land-managing agencies have a stake in both creating a new ecosystems management discipline and in extending professionalism and expertise throughout their agencies. In this regard, the decision made by the Office of Personnel Management several years ago to *not* require a college degree for a ranger's position within the National Park Service was a step backwards. Resource management in the twenty-first century will require more, not less, expertise.

Finally, there is a clear trend in land management towards internationalization. Like national economies, the lands and resources of the world's countries are becoming intertwined. There already exist numerous relationships between land management in the United States and events and conditions throughout the world. The ones perhaps getting the most media attention are physical in nature: global warming, ozone depletion, acid rain deposition, and global deforestation. Other connections are economic: the controversial timber exports to Japan and recent trade agreements such as NAFTA and GATT.

In response, land management agencies are developing international perspectives. The Forest Service has an international forestry program, the Fish and Wildlife Service maintains a separate list of foreign endangered species, and the Park Service has established professional relationships with park managers in other countries. These are positive initiatives, and in the future we expect to see both greater emphasis on global resource management and on regional resource management. There will be a concomitant de-emphasis on the national level, as resource managers develop the capability to "think globally, act locally."

NEW DIRECTIONS IN WATER RESOURCES POLICY

Water policy will continue to be in a state of flux for some time to come, as new issues arise and as traditional ones persist. We see at least five emerging issues that likely will shape future water policy.

First, both the Corps of Engineers and the Bureau of Reclamation —and to a lesser extent the Natural Resources and Conservation Service—have an enormous mission in environmental restoration and mitigation. Much of this work is the result of their own projects, but there exists a host of clean-up problems caused by other public activities as well. For example, the Corps and the Bureau have done work on behalf of EPA and its water quality mission; the Corps has also assisted in the clean-up of military installations around the country. This effort is likely to continue as part of the Defense Department's base closure program. Also, if the 104th Congress succeeds in abolishing the

Department of Energy, it is very likely that some of its clean-up and restoration programs will be transferred to the Corps and the Bureau.

On the farthest edge of this emerging environmental mission is dam decommissioning. Presently there is serious consideration to remove the Elwha and Glines Canyon Dams on Washington's Olympic Peninsula; according to a GAO study the hydropower produced by them is worth less than the Salmon runs that have been damaged or destroyed.[4] In Oregon local governments also are debating the removal of two dams.[5] The widespread debate throughout the Pacific Northwest over salmon restoration, siltation behind dams, impaired water quality, and the virtues of white water rafting may result in even more proposals to remove dams, or at least to significantly modify them. This clearly is work for the agencies' engineers.

There are impediments, however, to an enhanced environmental mission for the traditional water resources agencies. One is the Environmental Protection Agency. The EPA, the "new kid on the block," may usurp much of this work as its own. President Clinton's proposed budget for FY 1995, for instance, increased funding for EPA by 9 percent but cut the Corps' budget by 20 percent. Even more disturbing was a recent draft of the Clean Water reauthorization act that would transfer water planning to the EPA. One Corps official whom we interviewed called the EPA "the decade's darling," and expressed a concern shared by many that the traditional water planning experts in the federal government were losing ground to the newer agency.

Another roadblock to an expanding environmental mission for the Corps and the Bureau is the present Congress. Early indications are that the Republican majority is going to effect major changes in the federal government's entire environmental agenda. These legislative changes would, of course, significantly affect the Corps, the Bureau, the EPA, and other water-managing agencies. Virtually everything of an environmental nature is on the table in the 104th Congress.

A second mission trend involves increasing the efficiency of existing projects, of enhancing water conservation, and of moving toward water marketing. Much of the new management strategy of the Corps and Bureau will focus on managing demand rather than increasing supply. New "sources" of water are likely to be unconventional. For example, the Bureau could keep itself busy well into the next century by lining its porous canals and ditches. The water saved could then be marketed—at a nonsubsidized price—to growing communities. Such a program could garner the support of environmentalists, urban dwellers, the construction industry, and many farmers. However, there is always resistance to such fundamental change, and several Western states would have to revise their water laws before a free market in conserved water became a reality.[6]

A third area of growing interest is in providing water for Native Americans. In the last fifteen years more than a dozen tribes have signed water settlements, many of which require some form of water development.[7] The Bureau, long criticized for its inattention to American Indians, has finally recognized them as part of its new constituency. Commissioner Beard's "Blueprint for Reform," for example, identified the water needs of Native Americans as "an important new program area for Reclamation."[8] For its part, the Corps currently is engaged in a Native American outreach effort; it also might find itself occupied with the large task of mitigating the impacts that its Upper Missouri River dams have had on Indian reservations.[9]

Then, there is infrastructure development and rehabilitation. This could prove to be the largest, and most politically popular, area of activity for federal engineering agencies. In recent years there have been dire predictions about infrastructure collapse, with equally dire predictions about how much money it will take to repair it. Cost estimates from a few representative studies are listed below:

- The National Infrastructure Advisory Committee, established by Congress, estimated in 1984 that "water [development] needs are projected to be nearly $100 billion through the year 2000."[10]
- The Association of General Contractors published a study in 1982 that concluded the nation should spend these amounts on water infrastructure: urban water needs, $140 billion; drainage, flood control, $170 billion; locks, $15 billion; ports, $4 billion; waterways, $33 billion; and dams and reservoirs, $84 billion.[11]
- The Corps of Engineers and the Bureau of Reclamation completed in-house studies of America's water infrastructure needs. Their recommended spending totals were on the same order as the study by the Association of General Contractors.[12]
- The National Council on Public Works Improvement recom-

mended in 1988 that $90 billion needs to be spent annually on infrastructure, much of it on water resources.[13]

If the nation decides to embark on a massive new public works program, it could well keep the Corps, the Bureau, and other agencies busy for decades. The problem, of course, is money. As everyone knows, until the uncontrollables in the federal budget are put under control, there can be no new major federal initiatives.

Finally, the most pervasive new trend is towards a general goal of service. Like the economy in general, water agencies are moving from basic production and construction to the provision of services. For example, one of the fastest growing activities for these agencies is tourism and outdoor recreation. In the 1988 appropriations hearings the assistant secretary of the army for civil works explained that Corps projects account for 500 million visitor-use days per year: "That places us second as the most-visited agency, behind only the National Forest Service, and ahead of the National Park Service."[14] The expanding service mission also will include more passive roles, such as serving as mediators, facilitators, information specialists, and planners.

In summary, there are new opportunities to do much-needed work for the Corps and the Bureau of Reclamation. But it is a fickle political climate, and old habits die hard. It would be naive, for instance, to assume that the days of the pork barrel are over. The Clinton administration already learned this; in 1994 members of the House Appropriations Committee added $62 million to fund their favorite projects, including nineteen new starts that were not in the president's recommended budget. These attempts to increase spending were among the last acts of many Democrats in Congress.

Notwithstanding their efforts to severely cut federal spending, the new Republican majority in the 104th Congress may only add to the tendency, since a number of the strongest proponents of water development spending are Republicans. For example, the 1994 Republican victory could help fund the stalled Animas–La Plata Project. A recent *Los Angeles Times* headline read: "Animas–La Plata Dam will cost $687 million. Critics cry pork, but Republican backers are newly empowered."[15]

Continuing in this vein, The *CQ Weekly Report* described Senator Mark Hatfield, the new chair of the Appropriations Committee, as a "skillful hand at pork barreling. ... [L]ikely to use the position to help get funding for harbors, hydroelectric plants and federal lands in his home state."[16] The House's Appropriations Subcommittee for Energy and Water Development now is chaired by John Myers of Indiana, who has "battled against cuts to the energy and water appropriations bill."[17] Thus the Republicans' control of Congress could revive funding for traditional water projects while cutting back on new environmental initiatives. As in natural resources policy generally, the old politics and the new coexist.

The network of interest groups that help to shape national water policy also has changed a great deal in recent years. In a word or two, the water lobby has been decentralized, fragmented, and overrun with special interests. Traditionally, a few big associations, such as the National Rivers and Harbors Congress and the National Irrigation Association, played a dominant role in water politics. Today nearly everyone has a hired gun. For example, the list of new national lobby registrations for just one month in 1991 contained the following: The small town of Globe, Arizona, hired a Phoenix firm to negotiate Native American water claims; the Colorado-Ute Electric Association Inc. hired a D.C. firm to protect its water rights; Empire District Electric of Missouri hired a firm with a D.C. office to further its interests in flood control; the Sabine River Authority of Texas hired a D.C. firm to monitor congressional appropriations for water projects; the San Juan Water Commission of New Mexico hired a Denver firm for the Animas–La Plata Project; Tex-La of Texas, hired a D.C. firm for its interest in the Denison Dam; Wasatch County, Utah, hired a Salt Lake City firm to lobby for the CUP completion bill; and the American Water Works Association hired a D.C. firm to protect municipal water interests.

The same thing has occurred on the other end of the political spectrum. New grassroots environmental groups, the Western Urban Water Coalition, and fiscally conservative groups such as the National Taxpayers' Association and Citizens for Responsible Government all are lobbying for fundamental reform in water policy. Altogether, the interest group portrait of American politics looks like democracy running amok.

In view of these sea-changes within Congress and within their traditional interest group networks, the Corps and the Bureau find themselves in a precarious political situation. They have to present themselves as both agents of change and supporters of tradition. The

Corps, we found, is especially adroit at presenting this somewhat paradoxical picture. "In these times of change," a Corps spokesman recently told Congress, "the Army takes pride in the Corps of Engineers' long history of service to the Nation in water resources development and looks forward toward the challenges that will accompany the President's program of investing in the future of the Nation."[18]

Toward that end, one of the Corps' most recent initiatives is a thorough examination of *all* of its missions and programs to determine what should remain and what should go. The Bureau of Reclamation has been doing much the same thing under its present leadership. Thus we can expect these two agencies to be significantly transformed as they embark on their third and second centuries of service, respectively.

THE NEW POLITICS OF RESOURCE MANAGEMENT

Although each of the seven agencies examined in this book has responded to the changed political environment in its own historically determined way, we nevertheless found some general trends in natural resources management that apply to all of them. These broader changes promise to have a long-term impact on the entire natural resources arena.

First, we discovered an increased emphasis on policy and program analysis among resource managers. Contemporary forms of policy analysis reach far beyond the limited, "number-crunching," analyses of the past. Today federal agencies use much more sophisticated approaches that encompass a wide range of variables, factors, and inputs. From computer modelling of critical habitats to the setting up of formal advisory boards and commissions, agency personnel presently are engaged in significant analytical exercises.

Such analyses help agencies to justify their budgets in an era of scarcity, and they also help protect them from parochial interests that want to control agency policy. In other words, policy analysis can be a form of anti-capture insurance. They also can serve to elevate the stature of the agency with the public and with key policymakers. Recent examples of complex scientific analyses include the Bureau of Reclamation's environmental impact statement for Glen Canyon Dam, the substantial efforts by biologists and other experts to justify claims of endangered habitat, such as the Thomas report on the spotted owl, the Galloway report on flood policy, and the extensive studies performed by the Garrison Diversion Unit Commission for a Bureau of Reclamation project in North Dakota.

The present Social Darwinian political climate is such that all federal agencies must be able to justify what they do. Those agencies that do not have competent analytical units clearly are disadvantaged over those that do. We thus see strenuous efforts being made within these agencies to strengthen their analytical capabilities. Recent legislation proposed by the Republican majority in Congress would push this effort even further: If agencies are required to do benefit-cost analyses on all of their major activities, they obviously will need the experts to do those economic and social impact analyses. (Although this particular legislation was designed to cut down the size of the federal bureaucracy, it may, perversely, have just the opposite effect.)

In a broad sense, we are seeing a return to the old politics/administration dichotomy. At a time when federal agencies have been overrun by special interests, and by pressures to politicize them, they are fighting back with the weapon of scientific expertise. When we recently asked a forest supervisor, for example, how he coped with the present litigious environment in which nearly every action was challenged, he replied, "We prepare and justify our decisions as thoroughly as possible. We defend ourselves with facts."

A second trend is administrative decentralization, which we already have discussed. Suffice it to say that the present political regime is barreling down in this direction, and encountering relatively little opposition. Both liberals and conservatives agree that government in general and the federal bureaucracy in particular need to be reinvented. They are divided, of course, on the specifics. But there is no question that all of the resource managing agencies covered in this study are engaged in efforts to reduce central control and thus place greater power in the hands of those "closer to the ground." The matrix-type organizational model that we have seen for some time in business is now coming to the public sector.

The move toward decentralization was given impetus by the passage of recent legislation. Statutes such as NEPA, ESA, and other environmental laws require extensive public participation, scoping processes, comment periods, and so on. These of course have the effect of increasing input into administrative decision-making from scattered and diverse sources. The recent resurgence in grass-roots politics clearly is connected with these laws, as is the increase in legal challenges to administrative action. The net result is that resource decisions in the future are bound to be more locally and regionally based.

Yet another trend, hardly confined to the natural resources arena, is policymaking via budgeting. This practice began in earnest during the Reagan years and probably will become even more pronounced in the future. It is connected to deficit spending and the astronomical growth of the national debt in the eighties. As Aaron Wildavsky wrote in 1992, "Budgeting has become the major issue of American political life because it brings to a head questions about what kind of government we will have and, therefore, what kind of people we will be."[19] He also discovered that, along with the budgetary process taking center stage in national politics, there has occurred a breakdown in political consensus. "Budget control [in the form of traditional norms] gives way to a free for all."[20]

Policymaking via budgeting means that agencies' budgets are increasingly scrutinized by OMB, the GAO, the CBO, congressional appropriations committees, and legions of others outside of the formal institutions of government. The smallest details can give rise to the most heated, and sometimes meaningless, debates. Virtually every aspect of an agency's budget becomes a vehicle for policymaking. If a balanced budget amendment and the line-item veto become law, there will be an even greater tendency to make basic policy decisions through the budgetary process. Wildavsky called this budgetary overload, and it shows no signs of abating.

The politics of budget-cutting in the 104th Congress already is having an impact on natural resources policy. The new Republican leadership immediately targeted several environmental programs for budget cuts, including the Endangered Species Act, some national parks appropriations, nuclear waste cleanup, and soil erosion programs.[21] For their part, Democrats led by Congressman George Miller introduced the "Public Resources Deficit Reduction Act of 1995," which would "establish fair market pricing" for all timber, minerals, and forage produced on federal lands, and for all hydropower produced at federal facilities.[22] Thus agencies must be more prepared than ever to defend every line-item in their budgets.

Last, there is a trend among natural resources agencies away from the iron triangle. That is, there is occurring a shift from providing goods and services to select private interests and towards providing more general services to "the public." Access is being democratized— although we wouldn't want to take this generalization too far. The poor, for example, continue to have very limited access to resource management decisions. And small, well-organized interests with a vested economic stake in policy still have a greater potential for influencing legislation than do broad, diverse, and loosely organized groups.

A test to see whether "policy democratization" has occurred is to ask the question: Who can be a beneficiary? In the past, benefits often were targeted: Federal grazing policy was designed and implemented for cattle and sheep ranchers in the west, national forest policy benefited first and foremost timber companies, and the nation's mineral wealth was there for mining companies. Now, however, the uses to which our common pool resources are put have been expanded. Many more people are choosing to participate, whether it is to increase their outdoor recreation opportunities, to save endangered species, or to ensure cleaner air, land, and water in their communities.

Another way of stating this is by noting that natural resources management, like the American economy in general, is moving from basic production to the provision of services. In the former system, beneficiaries were concentrated, whereas in the latter they are dispersed. Policymaking arrangements are becoming not only democratized but balkanized. That is the downside to increased participation and to a service orientation.

We think that the real challenge today is how natural resources managers can bring coherence, continuity and common sense to a fragmented policy arena where the clamor arising from non-negotiable group demands can be deafening. In the words of a BLM official, "We need to move towards the radical middle." But he admitted that such a move would be hard, given that the groups on the political extremes are not interested in resolution. "That would put them out of business," he bluntly noted.

Thus, federal managers are faced with a contradiction that will take considerable time to resolve: Resource policy is most effective when it is based on natural ecological units and a long-term perspective, as opposed to constructed political and jurisdictional boundaries aggravated by demands for immediate gratification. But the present political climate is characterized by just that. The existence of strong centrifugal forces has served to increase conflict and division and has resulted in gridlock. Finding the political middle ground is what resource management in the twenty-first century will be about.

NEW PARADIGMS AND OLD POLITICAL REALITIES: A PROPOSAL FOR IMPLEMENTING ECOSYSTEMS MANAGEMENT

In the most general sense, the political stalemate which characterizes contemporary natural resources management is the result of competing paradigms, the old and the new.[23] The old paradigm is based on the highly successful, utilitarian public philosophy that was formulated about one hundred years ago. It was premised on the interrelated precepts that the *federal* government was a necessary, countervailing power to society's vested economic interests, that *federal* agencies were the repositories of expertise and information, that a network of competing interest groups, with government as the final arbiter, would serve the public interest, and that specialization and differentiation were an integral part of the proper functioning of government. As one of its founders, Gifford Pinchot, put it, conservation meant: "The greatest good for the greatest number in the long run."

In its most positive aspect, utilitarianism created systems of national forests, national parks, and national wildlife refuges. It built the nation's infrastructure largely during the New Deal era, it spread the benefits of affordable electricity to the rural sector, it built an inland waterways transportation network, it watered the West, it created a wilderness system, and much else. But in its most negative aspect, and over time, it legitimized the carving up of natural resources management into tight little iron triangles. It led to agency capture, excessive fragmentation of decision-making, and a lot of unnecessary regulation and subsidies.

As the great scholar of bureaucracy, Max Weber, foresaw, the period from the 1880s to about 1980 was an era of organizational differentiation. Bureaucracies permeated European and American society. Scientific inquiry became increasingly specialized, as did economic and political endeavor. By the 1970s, however, the scientific and technological revolutions of the twentieth century were bearing fruit. Industrial society was being transformed into postindustrial society. In the natural resources field a new paradigm, ecosystems management, began to take form. Currently its adherents are challenging many of the fundamental propositions of the older, utilitarian paradigm.

Substantively, the ecosystems paradigm is founded on the wealth of new information that is being generated by the latest developments in communication, transportation, and data collection and analysis. For example, we now have the capability to see not only our immediate surroundings but whole continents and even the entire planet via satellites. It is commonplace to travel half-way around the world in less than a day. One can communicate virtually instantaneously with someone six thousand miles away. How could this information explosion *not* have a profound effect on how we manage our natural resources? There can be little doubt that society is undergoing a great transformation; we are moving from an era of differentiation to an era of integration.

We discovered that officials in all of the seven agencies included in this study were searching for ways to incorporate the new ecosystems paradigm into their organizations. This new management philosophy is still in its formative stage, so consequently there is a great deal of experimentation, wheel-spinning, and soul-searching currently going on. Few people know precisely what ecosystems management is, but they do know that it is different from the traditional way of managing resources.

Officials in the Bureau of Land Management, for example, are drawing up new organization charts that employ horizontal imagery as opposed to the traditional hierarchical model. The commissioner of reclamation is turning his agency away from a construction orientation to a service orientation. The Army Corps of Engineers has drawn up plans for a comprehensive reorganization (which has yet to be approved by Congress). The chief of the Forest Service is returning that agency to its original multiple-use philosophy after several decades of being captured by interest group demands for high timber yields. And the Soil Conservation Service, as part of a departmentwide reorganization, is now the Natural Resources and Conservation Service. Its new mission emphasizes agricultural production carried out in an ecologically sound manner, with greater attention paid to wetlands, more interest in organic farming, and so on.

But at the same time as agency officials struggle with an abundance of new scientific information, new methods of communication, changing workforces, and a new paradigm, they must also work within the traditional political system. It is a system that is slow to change. Those groups and institutions that have benefited the most from what Theodore Lowi characterized as "interest group liberalism" continue to be powerful forces in the political process. Pork and park barrels frequently win out over the bigger picture. New initiatives are easily sidetracked. The 104th Congress, elected in 1994, promises to be different, and to break the gridlock in Washington. That is an estimable goal. However, some of its suggestions for reform, such as turning the federal lands over to the states in which they lay, would set back natural resources management in the United States by one hundred years. It was not a good idea in 1929, it wasn't a good idea in 1981, and it is an even worse idea in 1995, since we are just now developing the capability to manage entire watersheds and ecosystems. Watersheds and ecosystems generally don't conform to state boundaries.

Other proposals have more merit. The efforts at downsizing the Washington offices of these agencies, reducing the layers of bureaucracy, and giving more decision-making responsibility to the local level, are clearly in tune with what citizens want: more control over their immediate environments. Devolution and decentralization, moreover, fit well with the politics of ecology, which is to "think globally, act locally." The capacity to think globally is becoming possible; the power to act locally should follow. Rethinking the entitlement programs, which consume so much of the federal budget, also is an idea whose time has come. In the natural resources field, this would entail cutting back on the entitlements that go to agribusiness, and the cattle, mining and timber industries. Market-based pricing for commercial uses of the public lands and waters is a long-overdue reform. Increased fees for recreational use, including wilderness uses, also should be seriously considered.

Among the seven agencies whose histories are traced in this study, four are working well. It goes without saying that there is much room for improvement within these four agencies, but the point to emphasize is that they have developed into coherent and cohesive organizations with clearly defined missions and with promising futures. They are: The National Park Service in the Interior Department, the Natural Resources and Conservation Service and the U.S. Forest Service in Agriculture, and the Army Corps of Engineers. They include two that muddle through and two superstars.

The other three agencies, the U.S. Fish and Wildlife Service, the Bureau of Land Management, and the Bureau of Reclamation, continue to have serious problems. We documented these political and organizational difficulties in this book, some of which go back nearly a century. Since all three of the bureaus are housed in the same department, we suggest that it is time to reorganize the Interior Department along the lines of the Agriculture Department's recent reorganization. Interior Secretary Babbitt made a start at this in 1993 when he created the National Biological Service; but that administrative unit was hastily conceived and not sufficiently comprehensive. A more fundamental reform, which would be in keeping with the new paradigm, is to merge these three agencies into a single agency and perhaps call it the Western Ecosystems Management Agency (WEMA).

All three agencies manage resources in the western United States, including Alaska. That is an important element they have in common. Another is that they are experiencing enormous difficulties in reinventing themselves to meet the needs of the twenty-first century. The Bureau of Reclamation is trying to transform itself into a water management, service-oriented organization. The Bureau of Land Management, due to significant political opposition, struggles with becoming a genuine multiple-use agency; and the Fish and Wildlife Service is given neither the personnel nor the resources to both manage its large system of fish hatcheries and wildlife refuges *and* to implement controversial statutes such as the Endangered Species Act.

Moreover, it is often the case that the lands administered by these agencies are adjacent to, or in close proximity with, the lands and structures of the other two agencies. In southeastern Arizona, for example, the BLM manages the San Pedro Riparian Area, while the U.S. Fish and Wildlife Service manages the Buenos Aires National Wildlife Refuge. The Bureau of Reclamation manages a nearby water delivery system, the Central Arizona Project (CAP). Tucson residents do not want CAP water, so perhaps there are better uses, related to wetlands and wildlife, for the Colorado River water.

For several reasons, then, we think it makes much sense to merge these three agencies of the Interior Department. The reorganization would be a move in the direction of streamlining government, it would further the goal of ecosystems management by combining water, land, and critical habitat missions, and it could give the new agency, WEMA, the resources essential to practice regional resource management.

A final point is that even with this reorganization there would still exist a number of different agencies operating in the natural resources arena. In the first edition of this book, we argued the virtues of having diversity and competition within the executive branch. We still do. With the Corps, the Forest Service, the National Park Service, the Natural Resources and Conservation Service, the Environmental Protection Agency, a new Western Ecosystems Management Agency, and others, as major players, there clearly remains sufficient organizational diversity to ensure that competition and cooperation will remain aspects of the federal bureaucracy.

THE LAST WORD

Over one hundred years of federal involvement in natural resources management is described and analyzed in this book. Although there has been much to criticize about the behavior and decisions of these seven agencies over those one hundred years, there is also much to commend. Overall, many generations of Americans have been well served by their federal resource managers. They continue to be. Consider this: The annual budgets for the Corps, the Forest Service, the National Park Service, the Natural Resources and Conservation Service, the Bureau of Reclamation, the Bureau of Land Management, and the U.S. Fish and Wildlife Service combined add up to less than $16 billion, or less than 1 percent of the current $1.6 trillion federal budget. Americans thus enjoy a nation-wide system of parks and forests, an abundance of reasonably priced food, little scarcity of drinkable water, the opportunity to see bald eagles, wolves, and grizzlies in the wild, and much else, all for relatively little money. We think that is quite a bargain.

Appendix

Could you please rank 6 of the 7 agencies listed below according to the criteria at the top of each column of blanks. Omit your own agency from consideration. Place a number one beside the agency that you think best meets the criteria. Number the rest of the agencies in consecutive fashion.

Relative Power within Executive Branch	Close Relationship with Congress	Interest Group Support	Quality of Response to NEPA	
_____	_____	_____	_____	Bureau of Reclamation
_____	_____	_____	_____	Bureau of Land Management
_____	_____	_____	_____	Corps of Engineers
_____	_____	_____	_____	Fish & Wildlife Service
_____	_____	_____	_____	Forest Service
_____	_____	_____	_____	National Park Service
_____	_____	_____	_____	Soil Conservation Service

Notes

CHAPTER 1. DIFFERENTIALS IN AGENCY POWER

1. Anthony Downs, "Up and Down with Ecology: The 'Issue-Attention Cycle'" *The Public Interest* 28 (Summer 1972): 38–50.

2. For example, under President Jimmy Carter the Department of Energy came into being; there were intensified efforts to decontrol natural gas prices; and laws to conserve fuels, such as the 55-mile-per-hour speed limit, were enacted.

3. For an excellent discussion of the nature of modern legislation and the policy process, see Theodore Lowi, *The End of Liberalism*, 2nd ed. (New York: W. W. Norton and Co., 1979), esp. ch. 5.

4. Francis Rourke, "Grappling with the Bureaucracy," in Arnold J. Meltsner, ed., *Politics and the Oval Office* (San Francisco: Institute for Contemporary Studies, 1981), p. 130.

5. Grant McConnell, *The Modern Presidency*, 2nd ed. (New York: St. Martin's Press, 1976), p. 65.

6. Francis Rourke, *Bureaucracy, Politics, and Public Policy*, 2nd ed. (Boston: Little, Brown and Co., 1976), p. 81.

7. Allan F. Wichelman, "Administrative Agency Implementation of the National Environmental Policy Act of 1969: A Conceptual Framework for Explaining Differential Responses," *Natural Resources Journal* 16 (April 1976): 263–300.

8. Richard N. L. Andrews, *Environmental Policy and Administrative Change* (Lexington, Mass.: D. C. Heath and Co., 1976).

9. Richard A. Liroff, *NEPA and Its Aftermath: The Formation of a National Policy for the Environment* (Bloomington: Indiana University Press, 1976).

10. See Herbert Kaufman, *Are Government Organizations Immortal?* (Washington, D.C.: The Brookings Institution, 1976).

11. Rourke, *Bureaucracy*, pp. 81–106.

12. Max Weber, "Politics as a Vocation," in H. H. Gerth and C. W. Mills, eds., *From Max Weber: Essays in Sociology* (New York: Oxford University Press, 1958), pp. 232-33.

13. Rourke, *Bureaucracy*, p. 83.

14. Richard Ellis and Aaron Wildavsky, "'Greatness' Revisited: Evaluating the Performance of Early American Presidents in Terms of Cultural Dilemmas," *Presidential Studies Quarterly* 21 (Winter 1991): 15–34.

15. Lowi, *End of Liberalism*, p. 120.

16. Kaufman, *Are Government Organizations Immortal?*, p. 4.

17. Rourke, *Bureaucracy*, p. 89.

18. Ibid., p. 90.

19. Arthur Maass, *Muddy Waters: The Army Engineers and the Nation's Rivers* (Cambridge, Mass. Harvard University Press, 1951).

20. We are using the concept of type or category here in the sense that Weber used "ideal type"—that is, as a heuristic device not intended to do damage to the idiosyncratic features of each organization. Likewise, no value judgments are necessarily implied by our categories.

21. Charles E. Lindblom, "The Science of 'Muddling Through'," *Public Administration Review* 19 (Spring 1959): 79–88.

CHAPTER 2. BUREAUCRATIC SUPERSTARS

1. Frank E. Smith, *The Politics of Conservation* (New York: Harper Colophon Books, 1966), p. 3.

2. 7th Congress, 1st sess., chap. 9, sec. 26, Mar. 16, 1802. "An act fixing the military peace establishment of the United States."

3. 18th Congress, 1st sess., chap. 139, sec. 2, May 24, 1824. "An act to improve the navigation of the Ohio and Mississippi Rivers."

4. Smith, *Politics of Conservation*, p. 12.

5. U.S. Congress, House, Committee on Appropriations, Hearings before the Subcommittee on Public Works, Apps. for FY 1975, Part I, 93rd Cong., 2d. sess., p. 229.

6. Andrews, *Environmental Policy and Administrative Change*, pp. 57, 141–3.

7. Smith, *Politics of Conservation*, p. 271.

8. Maass, *Muddy Waters*.

9. Smith, *Politics of Conservation*, p. 290.

10. U.S. Congress, House, Committee on Rivers and Harbors, "Pollution of Navigable Waters," Testimony of Thomas Robins, Deputy Chief of the Corps of Engineers, 79th Cong., 1st sess., 1945, p. 94.

11. Smith, *Politics of Conservation*, pp. 267–271.

12. See for example: Daniel Mazmanian and Jeanne Nienaber, *Can Organizations Change? Environmental Protection, Citizen Participation and the Corps of Engineers* (Washington D.C.: Brookings Institution, 1979); Richard Andrews, *Environmental Policy*; Richard Liroff, *A National Policy for the Environment: NEPA and its Aftermath* (Bloomington: Indiana University Press, 1976).

13. Mazmanian and Nienaber, *Can Organizations Change?*, p. 194.

14. *Appendix to the Budget for Fiscal Year 1981*, pp. 337–50, and *U.S. Budget 1981*, pp. 426–28, 1022.

15. *The New York Times*, 21 February 1977, p. 1; 22 February 1977, p. 13; 7 March 1977, p. 1.

16. Quoted in Phillip L. Fradkin, *A River No More* (New York: Knopf, 1981), p. 5.

17. Ibid., p. 9.

18. The letter was ambiguous on this point but could certainly be interpreted to apply to ongoing projects. The letter urges Mr. Carter to "halt the construction of unnecessary and environmentally destructive dams." Quoted in *The New York Times*, 13 March 1977, p. 24.

19. These were the Dickey-Lincoln in Maine, Paintsville Lake in Kentucky, and the Freeport project in Illinois. In *The New York Times*, 24 March 1977, p. 1.

20. Two projects—the Auburn-Folsom South in California, and the Narrows Unit in Colorado—were left unfunded pending further safety studies. In *The New York Times*, 16 April 1977, p 1.

21. *The New York Times*, 3 May 1977, p. 34.

22. Ibid., 17 April 1977, p. 1; and the *Congressional Quarterly Weekly Report*, 4 March 1978, p. 568.

23. Ibid. Congresswoman Boggs made an appropriate comment during congressional hearings: "When some of the few projects that were asked to be deleted are within your own state, and within your own district, of course you have an entirely different set of criteria to use." Senator Johnston made a similar comment. "Do I have a parochial interest in [the Atchafalaya project]? You bet I do." See: U.S. Congress, House Committee on Appropriations, Hearings before the Subcommittee on Public Works, 95th Cong., 1st sess., 1977, part 9, p. 52; *Congressional Quarterly Weekly Report*, 2 July 1977, p. 1338.

24. *Presidential Documents: Jimmy Carter, 1977*, vol. 13, no. 17, 18 April 1977, p. 557.

25. U.S. Congress, House, Committee on Appropriations, Hearings before the Subcommittee on Public Works on 1978 app. bill, 95th Cong., 1st sess., part 9, pp. 3–42.

26. Ibid, p. 4; and *National Journal*, 9 April 1977, p. 547.

27. *Presidential Documents: Jimmy Carter, 1977*, vol. 13, no. 17, 18April 1977, p. 558.

28. *The Washington Post*, 19 December 1977, p. 1.

29. U.S. Congress, House, Committee on Appropriations, Hearings before the Subcommittee on Public Works on 1978 app. bill, 95th Cong., 1st sess., part 9, pp. 4–5.

30. Ibid., p. 4.

31. Ibid.

32. Ibid., p. 45.

33. Quoted in *The New York Times*, 17 May 1979, p. 16.

34. *The Washington Post*, 19 December 1977, pp. 1, 4.

35. Ibid., 5 August 1977, p. 5; *The New York Times*, 9 August 1977, p. 17.

36. *The Los Angeles Times*, 10 June 1978, p. 1.

37. Ibid., 16 June 1978, p. 11.

38. Ibid., 12 October 1978, p. 7.

39. *Hoover Commission Report on Organization of the Executive Branch of Government* (New York: McGraw-Hill, 1949), p. 263.

40. U.S. Congress, House, Committee on Government Operations, Hearings on H.R. 6959, "Reorganization of Executive Departments," 91st Cong., 1st sess., 2 June 1971, part 1, p. 8.

41. *The New York Times*, 12 February 1979, p. 18.

42. Ibid., 19 July 1979, p. D-18.

43. U.S. Congress, House, Committee on Appropriations, Hearings, "The Federal Budget for 1979," 95th Cong., 2d sess., p. 109.

44. *The New York Times*, 19 July 1979, p. D-18; and U.S. Congress, House, Committee on Appropriations, Hearings, "The Federal Budget for 1979," 95th Cong., 2d sess., pp. 11, 21.

45. *The New York Times*, 24 January 1980, p. D-22.

46. U.S. Congress, House, Committee on Appropriations, Hearings, "Supplemental Appropriations and Rescission Bill, 1981." 97th Cong., 1st sess., part 1, p. 633.

47. U.S. Congress, Committee on Appropriations, Hearings before the Subcommittee on Energy and Water Development, Appropriations for 1982, 97th Cong., 1st sess., part 1, p. 9.

48. U.S. Congress, House, Committee on Appropriations, Hearings before the Subcommittee on Public Works, Appropriation Bill for 1978, 95th Cong., 1st sess., 1977, part 9, p. 2.

49. *The Chicago Tribune,* 29 December 1977, sec. 3, p. 2.

50. *The New York Times,* 13 December 1977, p. 16.

51. Ibid., 12 February 1979, p. 1.

52. U.S. Congress, Committee on Appropriations, Hearings before the Subcommittee on Energy and Water Development, Appropriations for 1982, 97th Cong., 1st sess., part 1, pp. 5–7.

53. Ibid., pp. 7–9.

54. Of the $230 million reduction proposed by Reagan, $167 million was in the construction program, and $117 million of that was due to reductions in these three projects. U.S. Congress, House, Committee on Appropriations, Hearings before the Subcommittee on Energy and Water Development. "Supplemental Appropriation and Rescission Bill for 1981," 97th Cong., 1st sess., part 1, pp. 560–62.

55. Ibid., p. 624.

56. Ibid., p. 578.

57. Ibid., pp. 581, 629.

58. Ibid., pp. 565, 610, 611, 639, 656.

59. Ibid., pp. 624–25.

60. Ibid., p. 611.

61. Ibid., pp. 562, 581, 626–27, 637.

62. *Congressional Quarterly Weekly Report,* 28 November 1981, p. 2352.

63. Executive Order 12322, 17 September 1981.

64. *National Journal,* 23 July 1983, p. 1559.

65. *The New York Times,* 12 February 1979, p. 18.

66. Ibid., 6 February 1980, p. 17.

67. U.S. Congress, Committee on Appropriations, Hearings before the Subcommittee on Energy and Water Development, "Appropriations for 1982," 97th Cong., 1st sess., part 1, pp. 143–149.

68. *The New York Times.,* 16 June 1981, p. B-12.

69. See Robert Reinhold's article in *The New York Times,* 9 August 1981, p. 1.

70. U.S. Congress, Committee on Appropriations, Hearings before the Subcommittee on Energy and Water Development, "Appropriations for 1982," 97th Cong., 1st sess., part 1, p. 327.

71. *Wall Street Journal,* 14 November 1985, p. 58.

72. For an excellent history of the bill see: Martin Reuss, "Reshaping National Water Politics: The Emergence of the Water Resources Development Act of 1986." Office of History, Headquarters, U. S. Army Corps of Engineers, IWR Policy Study 91-PS-1 (October 1991).

73. U. S. Congress, House Hearings before the Subcommittee on Energy and Natural Resources, Committee on Appropriations, 99th Cong., 2nd sess. 1986. "Energy and Water Development Appropriations for 1987," pp. 31–34.

74. *Congressional Record* 132 (17 October 1986): 16991. Remarks by Senator Abdnor.

75. *Congressional Record* 132 (17 October 1986): 16982.

76. U. S. Congress, House Hearings before the Subcommittee on Energy and Natural Resources. Comittee on Appropriations, 100th Cong., 1st sess. 1987. "Energy and Water Development Appropriations for 1988," p. 86.

77. Federal Water Pollution Control Act of 1972, Sec. 404 (b)(1). 40 CFR Part 230.

78. *Natural Resources Defense Council v. Calloway* (1975).

79. GAO Report (April 1993), "Wetlands Protection." GAO/RCED-93-26.

80. U. S. Congress, House, Hearings before the Subcommittee on Energy and Natural Resources, Committee on Appropriations, 102nd Cong., 1st sess. 1991. "Energy and Water Development Appropriations for 1992," p. 76.

81. *Congressional Record* (17 October 1991): E3129.

82. The "Wetlands Mitigation Banking Demonstration Study" was authorized by the Water Resources Development Act of 1990. The Corps has issued a series of reports titled "National Wetland Mitigation Banking Study": IWR Report 92-WMB-1 (July 1992); IWR Report 94-WMB-3 (January 1994); IWR Report 94-WMB-4 (February 1994); IWR Report 94-WMB-5 (March 1994).

83. For a summary of these see: *The National Journal* (2 April 1988), pp. 868–72.

84. U.S. Congress, House, Hearings before the Subcommittee on Energy and Natural Resources, Committee on Appropriations, 101st Cong., 2nd sess. 1990. "Energy and Water Development Appropriations for 1991," p. 5.

85. "Hard Choices: A Report on the Increasing Gap between America's Infrastructure Needs and Our Ability to Pay for Them." Summary Report prepared by the National Infrastructure Advisory Committee for the Joint Economic Committee of the U. S. Congress (February 1984), p. 7.

86. "Living Under Constraints: An Emerging Vision for High Performance Public Works." Concluding Report: Federal Infrastructure Strategy Program." U. S. Army Corps of Engineers, Water Resources Support Center, Institute for Water Resourses. IWR Report 94-FIS-20 (October 1994).

87. U.S. Congress, House, Hearings before the Subcommittee on Energy and Natural Resources, Committee on Appropriations, 103rd Cong., 1st sess. 1993. "Energy and Water Development Appropriations for 1994," p. 15.

88. U.S. Army Corps of Engineers, Water Resources Support Center, Institute for Water Resources, "Environmental Activities in Corps of Engineers

Water Resources Programs: Charting a New Direction." Prepared by Leonard Shabman (November 1993). IWR Report 93-PS-1.

89. U.S. Congress, House, Hearings before the Subcommittee on Energy and Natural Resources, Committee on Appropriations, 101st Cong., 2nd sess. 1990. "Energy and Water Development Appropriations for 1991," p. 311.

90. U.S. Congress, House, Hearings before the Subcommittee on Energy and Natural Resources, Committee on Appropriations, 102nd Cong., 1st sess. 1991. "Energy and Water Development Appropriations for 1992," p. 26.

91. "Sharing the Challenge: Floodplain Management into the 21st Century." Report prepared by the Interagency Floodplain Management Review Committee to the Administration Floodplain Management Task Force. Washington, D.C. (June 1994), p. 66.

92. "National Study of Water Management During Drought," Report to the U. S. Congress (Draft). IWR Report 94-NDS-12 (June 1994), p. vi.

93. "Vision 21: A Strategic Assessment of the Nation's Water Resources Needs," Directorate of Civil Works, Headquarters, U. S. Army Corps of Engineers (Draft). March 1990. See especially pp. 43–46.

94. *CQ Weekly Report*, 9 January 1988, p. 61; 8 July 1989, p. 1687; 23 June 1990, p. 1949; December 1991 (Special Issue), p. 68; 26 September 1992, p. 2934; 11 December 1993 (Special Issue); 65; 28 May 1994, p. 1379.

95. Smith, *Politics of Conservation*, p. 91.

96. Ibid., pp. 89–91.

97. Ibid., p. 97.

98. Gifford Pinchot, *Breaking New Ground* (New York: Harcourt and Brace, 1947), p. 27.

99. Ibid., p. 85.

100. Act of 3 March 1891, 51st Cong., 2d sess., Ch. 561. "An act to repeal timber-culture laws, and for other purposes."

101. Pinchot, *Breaking New Ground*, pp. 107–8.

102. Ibid., p. 140.

103. Samuel Trask Dana and Sally K. Fairfax, *Forest and Range Policy* (New York: McGraw-Hill, 1980), p. 96.

104. Pinchot, *Breaking New Ground*, pp. 506–7.

105. Dana and Fairfax, *Forest and Range Policy*, p. 121.

106. U.S. Congress, House, Committee on Appropriations, Hearings before the Subcommittee on Agriculture, 86th Cong., 2d sess., 1960, p. 18.

107. William L. O'Neill, *The Progressive Years: America Comes of Age* (New York: Dodd, Mead, and Co., 1975), p. 30.

108. Pinchot, *Breaking New Ground*, p. 140.

109. *U.S. Budget for FY 1981: Special Analysis,* p. 374.

110. U.S. Congress, House, Committee on Appropriations, Hearings before the Subcommittee on Agriculture, "Agriculture Department App. Bill for 1931," 71st Cong., 2d sess., 1930, p. 1.

111. U.S. Congress, House, Committee on Appropriations, Hearings before the Subcommittee on Agriculture, "Agriculture Department App. Bill for 1939," 75th Cong., 3d sess., p. 21.

112. Paul J. Culhane and H. Paul Friesema, "Land Use Planning for the Public Lands," *Natural Resource Journal* 19 (January 1979): pp. 43–74.

113. U.S. Congress, House, Committee on Appropriations, Hearings before the Subcommittee on the Department of the Interior and Related Agencies, App. for 1971, 91st Cong., 2d sess., p. 3.

114. U. S. Department of Agriculture, Forest Service, "RARE II: Final Environmental Statement, Roadless Area Review and Evaluation" (January 1979), p. 4.

115. Ibid.

116. The Forest and Rangeland Renewable Resources Planning Act, 16 U.S.C. 1601 (1974), and the National Forest Management Act, 16 U.S.C. 1600 (1976).

117. Culhane and Friesema, "Land Use Planning for the Public Lands," pp. 52–63.

118. For an excellent analysis of the problems and advantages associated with comprehensive planning in the Forest Service, see: Christopher Leman, "Resource Assessment and Program Development: An Evaluation of Forest Service Experience Under the Resources Planning Act, with Lessons for Other Natural Resource Agencies," mimeograph, 123.

119. Christopher Leman, "Political Dilemmas in Evaluating and Budgeting Soil Conservation Programs: The RCA Process," in Harold G. Halcrow, Earl O. Heady, and Melvin L. Cotner, eds. *Soil Conservation Policies, Institutions, and Incentives* (Ankeny, Iowa: Soil Conservation Society of America, 1982), p. 57.

120. U.S. Congress, House, Committee on Appropriations, Hearings before the Subcommittee on the Dept. of Interior and Related Agencies, App. for 1982, 97th Cong., 1st sess., part 10, p. 337.

121. Ibid., p. 314.

122. Appendices for the Budget of the United States Government, FY 1986, FY 1990, FY 1993. Executive Office of the President, Office of Management and Budget. Budgets for the U. S. Forest Service.

123. U.S. Congress, House, Committee on Appropriations, Hearings before the Subcommittee on Interior and Related Agencies, Apps. for 1982, 97th Congress, 1st sess., part 10, p. 455. Remarks by Chief Forester Max Peterson.

124. Charles O. Porter, "May Justice Come to Overcut National Forests," *The New York Times,* 10 April 1993, p. 10.

125. John Crowell, Memo to Chief Max Peterson, 7 January 1985, p. 1.

126. Ibid., p. 3.

127. Timothy Egan, "Forest Service Abusing Role, Dissidents Say," *The New York Times,* March 4, 1990, pp. A1, A26.

128. Personal Interview with John Mumma, 21 July 1993, Missoula, Montana. Also in "Testimony of John Mumma," presented to the Committee on Post Office and Civil Service, Civil Service Subcommittee, U.S. House of Representatives, 23 September 1991. Mimeograph.

129. Ibid.

130. Kenneth Gold, "A Comparative Analysis of Successful Organizations," U. S. Office of Personnel Management, July 1, 1981. Mimeograph. 33 pp.

131. Paul J. Culhane, *Public Lands Politics: Interest Group Influence on the Forest Service and the Bureau of Land Management* (Baltimore: Johns Hopkins University Press, 1981), p. 68.

132. Ibid.

133. Written communication from the Personnel Officer, Flathead National Forest, to Jeanne Clarke, 10 August 1992.

134. Table, National Park Service, Office of the Chief Personnel Officer, Washington, D.C., 6 June 1994.

CHAPTER 3. AGENCIES THAT MUDDLE THROUGH

1. Roderick Nash, *Wilderness and the American Mind* (New Haven: Yale University Press, 1967).

2. Act of 1 March 1872, 42d Cong., sess. II, ch. 24, pp. 32–33.

3. U. S. Department of the Interior, "Background Material On the National Park Service," Document 527–76, November 1976, p. 1.

4. William C. Everhart, *The National Park Service* (New York: Praeger, 1972).

5. Act of 25 August 1916 (39 Stat. 535; 16 USC 1).

6. Department of the Interior, "Background Material," p. 2.

7. Donald Swain, *Wilderness Defender* (Chicago: University of Chicago Press, 1970), p. 2.

8. Pinchot, *Breaking New Ground* pp. 26–27.

9. Everhart, *National Park Service,* p. 95.

10. Jeanne Nienaber Clarke, *Roosevelt's Warrior: Harold L. Ickes and The New Deal* (Baltimore: Johns Hopkins University Press, 1996.)

11. Swain, *Wilderness Defender*, p. 319.

12. F. Fraser Darling and Noel D. Eichhorn, *Man and Nature In the National Parks* (Washington D.C.: Conservation Foundation, 1967), p. 32.

13. Howard Bloomfield, "Quandary In the Campgrounds," *American Forests* 75 (July 1969): 6.

14. Culhane, *Public Lands Politics*, p. 52 .

15. Darling and Eichhorn, *Man and Nature*, p. 77.

16. Memorandum from Secretary of the Interior Stewart L. Udall, 10 July 1964. In "Administrative Policies for the Historical Areas of the National Park Service" (Washington: GPO, 1968), p. 73.

17. U.S. Department of the Interior, National Park Service, "Management Policies," 1975, introduction.

18. Darling and Eichhorn, *Man and Nature*, p. 36.

19. U.S. Department of the Interior, National Park Service, *Park Road Standards*, mimeograph, 1968.

20. *U.S. Budget*, "Detailed Budget Estimate," 1956, 1966, 1967, 1968.

21. National Park Service, *Management Policies*, p. V-1.

22. Ibid., pp. I-1, I-9, IV-1.

23. *U.S. Budget*, "Detailed Budget Estimate," 1964, 1968.

24. "The Degradation of Our National Parks," 24th Report by the House Committee on Government Operations, 30 June 1976, 94th Cong., 2nd sess.

25. Joseph Novogrod, Gladys O. Dimock, and Marshall E. Dimock, *Casebook in Public Administration* (New York: Holt, Rinehart and Winston, 1969), p. 96.

26. George B. Hartzog, "Management Considerations for Optimum Development and Protection of National Park Resources," in *Second World Conference on National Parks* (Lausanne, Switzerland: International Union for Conservation of Nature and Natural Resources), 1974, p. 158.

27. Bloomfield, "Quandary in the Campground," pp. 38–40.

28. William R. Lowry, "Land of the Fee: Entrance Fees and the National Park Service," *Political Research Quarterly* 46 (1993): 823, 832.

29. Stewart M. Brandborg, "The Wilderness Law and the National Park System in the U.S.," in J.G. Nelson, ed., *Canadian Parks in Perspective* (Quebec, Canada: Harvest House, 1970),p. 272.

30. Jeanne Nienaber and Aaron Wildavsky, *The Budgeting and Evaluation of Federal Recreation Programs; or, Money Doesn't Grow on Trees* (New York: Basic Books, 1973), p. 38.

31. Much of the information concerning problems with the reservation system was compiled from interviews with Park Service officials in the Washington headquarters. Also see U.S. Congress, Senate, Committee on Interior and Insular Affairs, "Proposed Reservation System In Selected National Parks," Hearings before the Subcommittee on Parks and Recreation, 93d Cong., 1st sess., 23 February 1973.

32. U.S. Congress, Senate, Committee on Interior and Insular Affairs, "Oversight-Park Reservation System," 93d Cong., 2d sess., 21 August and 19 Sept. 1974, pp. 2–4, 11, 16.

33. "Park Resource Survey, 1975," *National Parks and Conservation Magazine* (February 1976), pp. 11–16; and (March 1976), 9–14.

34. Nienaber and Wildavsky, *Budgeting and Evaluation*, p. 19.

35. James B. Craig, "Plusses and Minuses in the National Parks," *American Forests*, June 1976, p. 4.

36. "The Crisis in National Park Personnel," *National Parks and Conservation Association Magazine*, April 1975, p. 20.

37. "Budget Plans Starve the National Park Service," *National Parks and Conservation Association Magazine*, June 1975, p. 19.

38. U.S. Congress, House, Committee on Government Operations, "Degradation of the National Parks," 94 Cong., 1st, 2d sess., 4 December 1975, 30 January 1976, 7 April 1976, p. 74.

39. "Closing the Door on the National Parks," *National Parks and Conservation Association Magazine*, January, 1975, p. 23.

40. "Senate-House Views Expressed on National Parks," *National Wildlife Federation Newsletter* 24 (8 August 1976): p. 290.

41. In 1975, the Service operated 302 park areas. By the following year that number had dropped to 286. See *Appendix to the Budget Fiscal Year 1976*, p. 546, and fiscal year 1977, p. 456.

42. Brandborg, "Wilderness Law," p. 271.

43. Theodore Swem, "Planning of National Parks," p. 253.

44. Nienaber and Wildavsky, *Budgeting and Evaluation*, p. 42.

45. Charles Fraser, "Park Agencies for the Future," *Parks and Recreation*, August 1973, p. 38.

46. U.S. Department of Agriculture, Forest Service, "RARE II: Final Environmental Statement, Roadless Area Review and Evaluation," January 1979, p. 5.

47. Everhart, *National Park Service*, p. 182.

48. This survey questionnaire was administered by Daniel McCool to a sample of National Park Service employees at the Albright Training Center at Grand Canyon, Arizona.

49. Newton B. Drury, "Former Directors Speak Out," *American Forests,* June 1976, p. 30.

50. Craig, "Plusses and Minuses," p. 14.

51. The *Wall Street Journal,* 11 November 1983, p. 1.

52. *Appendix to the Budget for Fiscal Year 1984,* p. I-M28.

53. Richard Ganzel and Dorothy Olkowski, "The Politics of Coalition-Building: The Inholders Reach Out." Paper presented at the Western Social Science Association Meeting, Albuquerque, N.M., April 1983. Also see *Newsweek,* 25 July 1983, pp. 22–31.

54. *Appendix to the Budget for Fiscal Year 1983,* p. I-M38, and 1984, p. I-M33.

55. U.S. Congress, House Committee on Appropriations, Hearings before the Subcommittee on the Department of Interior and Related Agencies, 97th Cong., 1st sess., Appropriations for 1982, part 12, p. 694.

56. "State of the Parks 1980," report prepared by the Office of Science and Technology for the National Park Service, Department of the Interior (May 1980).

57. General Accounting Office, "Facilities in Many National Parks and Forests Do Not Meet Health and Safety Standards," CED-80-115, 10 October 1980.

58. U.S. Congress, House, Committee on Appropriations, Hearings before the Subcommittee on the Department of Interior and Related Agencies, 97th Cong., 1st. sess., Appropriations for 1982, part 12, p. 768.

59. Ibid., p. 686.

60. Ibid., p. 687.

61. U.S. Congress, House Committee on Appropriations, Hearings before the Subcommittee on the Department of Interior and Related Agencies, 97th Cong., 1st sess., Revised Justifications for Fiscal Year 1982, part 8, pp. 147–157.

62. U.S. Congress, House, Committee on Appropriations, Hearings before the Subcommittee on the Department of Interior and Related Agencies, 97th Cong., 1st sess., Appropriations for 1982, part 1, p. 698.

63. Ibid., pp. 708, 715.

64. Ibid., p. 710. Also see pp. 712, 717.

65. Ibid., p. 716–17.

66. Jack Ellis, *Presidential Lightning Rods* (Lawrence: University Press of Kansas, 1994), Ch. 3.

67. Aaron Wildavsky, *The New Politics of the Budgetary Process,* 2nd ed. (New York: HarperCollins, 1992), p. 405.

68. Smith, *Politics of Conservation,* p. 248.

69. Ibid., p. 247.

70. U.S. Congress, House Committee on Appropriations, Agriculture Department Apps. for 1936, 74th Cong., 1st sess., p. 63.

71. U.S. Congress, House Committee on Appropriations, Hearings before the Subcommittee on Agriculture, 88th Cong., 2d sess., 1964, p. 1015. Also see Smith, *Politics of Conservation*, p. 249.

72. Soil Conservation Act of 1935 (49 Stat. 163).

73. U.S. Congress, House, Committee on Appropriations, Hearings before the Subcommittee on Agriculture, Apps. for 1964, 88th Cong., 2d sess., p. 1015.

74. U.S. Congress, House Committee on Appropriations, Agriculture Department Apps. for 1936, 74th Cong., 1st sess., p. 63.

75. U.S. Congress, House Committee on Appropriations, Hearings before the Subcommittee on Agriculture, Apps. for 1938, 75th Cong., 1st sess., p. 1039.

76. U.S. Congress, House Committee on Appropriations, Hearings before the Subcommittee on Agriculture, Apps. for 1947, 79th Cong., 2d sess., p. 1001.

77. U. S. Congress, House Committe on Apps., Hearing before the Subcommittee on Agriculture, App. bill for 1937, 74th Cong., 2nd sess., p. 21.

78. Wayne D. Rasmussen, "History of Soil Conservation, Institutions, and Incentives," in Harold G. Halcrow et al., eds., *Soil Conservation Policies, Institutions, and Incentives* (Ankeny, Iowa: Soil Conservation Society of America, 1982), p. 8.

79. Ibid., p. 16.

80. Robert J. Morgan, *Governing Soil Conservation* (Baltimore: Johns Hopkins University Press, 1962), p. 169.

81. 49 Stat. 163, 1935.

82. Rasmussen, "History of Soil Conservation, Institutions and Incentives," p. 12.

83. Morgan, *Governing Soil Conservation*, p. 103.

84. U.S. Congress, House, Committee on Appropriations, Hearings before the Subcommittee on Agriculture, Apps. for 1944, 78th Cong., 1st sess., p. 954.

85. U.S. Congress, House, Committee on Appropriations, Hearings before the Subcommittee on Agriculture, Apps. for 1951, 81st Cong., 2d sess., p. 151.

86. U.S. Congress, House Committee on Appropriations, Hearings before the Subcommittee on Agriculture, Apps. for 1955, 83rd Cong., 2nd sess., part 3, p. 1361.

87. Rasmussen, "History of Soil Conservation, Institutions, and Incentives," p. 11.

88. Ibid., p. 12.

89. See Executive Orders 9060 (23 February 1942) and 9577 (29 June 1945).

90. U.S. Congress, House, Committee on Appropriations, Hearings before

the Subcommittee on Agriculture, Apps. for 1956, 84th Cong., 1st sess., part 2, pp. 834–35.

91. U.S. Congress, House, Committee on Appropriations, Hearings before the Subcommittee on Agriculture, Apprs. for 1964, 88th Cong., 2d sess., part 2, p. 1018.

92. U.S. Congress, House, Committee on Appropriations, Hearings before the Subcommittee on Agriculture, Apps. for 1977, 94th Cong., 2d sess., part 4, p. 238.

93. U.S. Congress, House, Committee on Appropriations, Hearings before the Subcommittee on Agriculture, Apps. for 1960, 86th Cong., 2d sess., part 2, p. 1062.

94. U.S. Congress, House Committee on Appropriations, Hearings before the Subcommittee on Agriculture, Apps. for 1977, 94th Cong., 2d sess., part 4, p. 279.

95. U.S. Congress, House Committee on Appropriations, Hearings before the Subcommittee on Agriculture, Apps. for 1965, 88th Cong., 2d sess., part 2, p. 504.

96. U.S. Congress, House, Committee on Appropriations, Hearings before the Subcommittee on Agriculture, Apps. for 1975, 93d Cong., 2d sess., part 2, p. 338.

97. Christopher Leman, "Political Dilemmas in Evaluating and Budgeting Soil Conservation Programs: The RCA Process," in Harold G. Halcrow et al., eds., *Soil Conservation Policies, Institutions, and Incentives*, p. 52.

98. Public Law 83-566, 16 USC. 1001–1008.

99. U.S. Congress, House Committee on Government Operations, Hearings before the Subcommittee on Conservation and Natural Presources, "Stream Channelization," 92d Cong., 1st sess., May 1971, p. 10.

100. Richard N. L. Andrews, *Environmental Policy and Administrative Change*, p. 96.

101. Ibid., p. 99.

102. Helen M. Ingram, "The Politics of Information: Constraints on New Sources," in John C. Pierce and Harvey R. Doerksen, eds., *Water Politics and Public Involvement* (Ann Arbor: Ann Arbor Science Publishers, 1976), p. 71.

103. Andrews, *Environmental Policy*, pp. 99, 119.

104. U.S. Congress, House Committee on Appropriations, Hearings before the Subcommittee on Agriculture, Apps. for 1975, 93d Cong., 2d sess., part 2, p. 393.

105. Leman, "Political Dilemmas in Evaluating and Budgeting Soil Conservation Programs," p. 84.

106. Douglas Helms, "New Authorities and New Roles: SCS and the 1985

Farm Bill," in *Readings in the History of the Soil Conservation Service* (Washington, D.C.: U.S. Department of Agriculture, Soil Conservation Service, Historical Notes number 1, September 1992), p. 160.

107. United States Department of Agriculture, Soil Conservation Service, Budget Table for FY 1935–1994, 2/24/94.

108. U.S. Congress, House Committee on Appropriations, Subcommittee on Agriculture, Rural Development and Related Agencies, Apps. for 1982, 97th Cong., 1st sess., part 5, p. 658.

109. "Number of farms in U.S. falls to lowest since 1850," *The Arizona Daily Star,* 10 November 1994, p. 3.

110. 41st Congress, sess. III, "Joint Resolution for the Protection and Preservation of the Food Fishes of the Coast of the United States," 9 February 1871.

111. Richard A. Cooley, *Politics and Conservation: The Decline and Fall of the Alaska Salmon* (New York: Harper & Row, 1963), p. 73.

112. Ibid.

113. Ibid., p. 78.

114. Ibid., pp. 124–25.

115. Ibid., p. xiv.

116. "An Act to enlarge the powers of the Department of Agriculture, prohibit the transporation by interstate commerce of game killed in violation of local laws, and for other purposes." 56th Congress, sess. I, ch. 553, 1900, pp. 187–88.

117. 73rd U.S. Congress, sess. II, Ch. 71, 16 March 1934, p. 451.

118. Public Land Law Review Commission, *One Third of the Nation's Lands* (Washington, D.C.: GPO, 1970), p. 21.

119. U.S. Congress, P.L. 1024, 8, August 1963, 70 Stat., p. 1120.

120. U.S. Congress, House Committee on Merchant Marine and Fisheries, Reorganization Hearings, 84th Cong., 2d sess., 1957, p. 148.

121. For a discussion of this point see Herbert Kaufman, *The Forest Ranger: A Study in Administrative Behavior* (Baltimore: Johns Hopkins University Press, 1960).

122. U.S. Congress, House Committee on Appropriations, Hearings before the Subcommittee on the Department of the Interior and Related Agencies, Apps. for 1973, 92d Cong., 2d sess., part 2, p. 825.

123. U.S. Congress, House Committee on Appropriations, Hearings before the Subcommittee on the Interior Department and Related Agencies, Apps. for 1972, 92d Cong., 1st sess., part 2, p. 220.

124. U. S. Congress, House Committee on Appropriations, Hearings before the Subcommittee on the Department of Interior and Related Agencies, Apps for 1973, 92nd Cong., 2nd sess., part 2, p. 837.

125. Appendix to the Budget for Fiscal Year 1981, pp. 569–575.

126. U.S. Congress, House Committee on Appropriations, Hearings before the Subcommittee on Energy and Water Development, Appropriations for FY 1982, 97th Cong., 1st sess., part 3, pp. 7–9.

127. Ibid., part 10, pp. 16, 44.

128. Ibid., pp. 41–42, 109.

129. Ibid., pp. 40–41.

130. U.S. Congress, House Committee on Appropriations, Subcommittee on the Department of the Interior and Related Agencies, "Department of the Interior and Related Agencies Appropriations for 1993," 102nd Cong., 2nd sess. part 12, p. 552.

131. The Endangered Species Act of 1973. 16 U.S.C., Sec. 1531-1544.

132. Benjamin Simon, Craig Leff, and Harvey Doerksen, "Allocating Scare Resources for Endangered Species Recovery," *Journal of Policy Analysis and Management,* 14 (Summer 1995): 415-32. Also see: Tom Abate, "A Threatened Statute," *The Environmental Forum* 9 (March/April 1992): 16.

133. "Federal and State Endangered Species Expenditures," Fiscal Year 1991. Unpublished report compiled by U.S. Fish and Wildlife Service, July 1992. See table 2 of report.

134. "Endangered and Threatened Species Recovery Program," Report to Congress. U.S. Department of the Interior, U.S. Fish and Wildlife Service, December 1992.

135. U.S. Congress, House Hearings before the Subcommittee on Energy and Natural Resources, Committee on Appropriations. 103rd Cong., 1st. sess., 1993, part 1. "Energy and Water Development Appropriations for 1994," p. 209.

136. U.S. Congress, House. Committee on Appropriations, Subcommittee on the Department of the Interior and Related Agencies. 101st Congress, 2nd sess. "Department of the Interior and Related Agencies Appropriations for 1991," part 10, p. 27.

137. The Endangered Species Act of 1973. 16 U.S.C., Sec. 1533 (a) and (b). In 1979 Congress amended the act by creating an Endangered Species Interagency Committee that reviews listing and critical habitat decisions in light of their economic impact. This committee is authorized to overturn a decision if it concludes the economic impact is too great. Also see: *TVA v. Hill* 437 U.S. 153 (1978).

138. These data were provided by the National Biological Survey's Fort Collins Research Center to the authors.

139. General Accounting Office, "Endangered Species: Factors Associated with Delayed Listing Decisions." GAO/RCED 93-152 (August 1993).

140. U.S. Congress, House. Committee on Appropriations, Subcommittee on the Department of the Interior and Related Agencies. 102nd Congress, 1st sess. "Department of the Interior and Related Agencies Appropriations for 1992," part 9, p. 640.

141. Ibid, p. 676.

142. U.S. Congress, House. Committee on Appropriations, Subcommittee on the Department of Interior and Related Agencies. 102nd Congress, 2nd sess. "Department of Interior and Related Agencies Appropriations for 1993," part 12, p. 593.

143. *Solutions* (September 1994). U. S. Department of the Interior Newsletter.

144. Cited in U. S. Congress, House. Committee on Appropriations, Subcommittee on the Department of the Interior and Related Agencies. 102nd Congress, 1st sess. "Department of the Interior and Related Agencies Appropriations for 1992," part 9, p. 676.

145. Ibid.

146. Lettie McSpadden Wenner, "The Courts in Environmental Politics: The Case of the Spotted Owl," in Zachary Smith, ed., *Environmental Politics and Policy in the West* (Dubuque, Iowa: Kendall-Hunt, 1993); pp.45–62; also Steven Lewis Yaffe, *The Wisdom of the Spotted Owl* (Washington, D.C.: Island Press, 1994).

147. Laura Kirwan and Daniel McCool, "Environmentalists, Tribes, and Negotiated Water Settlements." Paper prepared for delivery at the annual meeting of the American Political Science Association, August 31-September 3, 1995. Chicago, Il.

148. U.S. Congress, House, Hearings before the Subcommittee on Energy and Natural Resources, Committee on Appropriations, 103rd Cong., 1st sess., 1993, part 1, "Energy and Water Development Appropriations for 1994," p. 213.

149. K. William Easter and Melvin L. Cotner, "Evaluation of Current Soil Conservation Strategies," in Harold G. Halcrow et al., eds., *Soil Conservation Policies, Institutions, and Incentives* (Ankeny, Iowa: Soil Conservation Society of America, 1982), p. 286.

CHAPTER 4. ORGANIZATIONAL SHOOTING STARS

1. Bernard DeVoto, *The Year of Decision: 1846* (Boston: Houghton Mifflin Co., 1942), p. viii.

2. George Sibley, "The Desert Empire," *Harper's*, October 1977, p. 53.

3. Smith, *Politics of Conservation*, p. 50.

4. Sibley, "Desert Empire," p. 54.

5. Reclamation Act of 1902 (43 USC 391), p. 388.

6. U.S. Congress, House, Committee on Appropriations, Hearings before the Subcommittee on Public Works, Apps. for 1971, 91st Cong., 2d. sess., part 3, pp. 28–46.

7. Reclamation Act of 1902 (43 USC 391), p. 389.

8. U.S. Congress, House, Committee on Appropriations, Hearings before the Subcommittee on the Interior Dept., Apps. for 1923, 67th Cong. 2d. sess., p. 619.

9. Sibley, "Desert Empire," p. 56.

10. U.S. Congress, House, Committee on Appropriations, Hearings before the Subcommittee on the Interior Dept., Apps. for 1940, 76th Cong., 1st. sess., p. 250.

11. Owen Stratton and Phillip Sirotkin, *The Echo Park Controversy* (University, Ala.: University of Alabama Press, 1959), p. 10.

12. Arthur Maass, *The Kings River Project: Case Studies in Public Administration and Policy Formation* (University, Ala.: University of Alabama Press, 1950).

13. U.S. Congress, House, Committee on Appropriations, Hearings before the Subcommittee on the Interior Dept., Apps. for 1946, 79th Cong., 1st sess., p. 1377.

14. Elmo Richardson, *Dams, Parks and Politics* (Lexington, Ky.: University Press of Kentucky, 1973), p. 48.

15. U.S. Congress, House, Committee on Appropriations, Hearings before the Subcommittee on the Interior Dept., Apps. for 1966, 89th Cong., 1st sess., part 1, p. 13.

16. U.S. Congress, House, "Appropriations Bill for FY 1975," Committee on Appropriations, Subcommittee on the Department of Interior and Related Agencies, 93rd Cong., 1st sess., part 2, p. 154.

17. Richard L. Berkman and W. Kip Viscusi, *Damning the West* (New York: Grossman Publishers, 1973).

18. U.S. Congress, House, "Appropriation Bill for FY 1978," Committee on Appropriations, Subcommittee on Public Works, 95th Cong., 1st sess., part 3, p. 225.

19. Ibid., p. 220.

20. *The New York Times*, 12 March 1977, p. 11.

21. Ibid., 7 March 1977, p. 20.

22. *Congressional Quarterly Weekly Report*, 2 July 1977, p. 1338.

23. Ibid., 30 July 1977, p. 1585.

24. Ibid., 2 July 1977, p. 1338.

25. *Los Angeles Times,* 10 June 1978, p. 1.

26. U.S. Congress, House, "Appropriations Bill for 1979," Committee on Appropriations, Subcommittee on Public Works, 95th Cong., 2d. sess., part 3, pp. 2–3.

27. 438 U.S. 645 (1978).

28. Ibid., pp. 665–667.

29. Executive Order 12113, 4 January 1979.

30. *The New York Times,* 12 February 1979, p. 5. Also see: U.S. Congress, House, "Appropriations Bill for 1980," Committee on Appropriations, Subcommittee on Energy and Water Development, 96th Cong., 1st sess., part 1, p. 46.

31. Department of the Interior News Release, 6 November 1979.

32. Ibid.

33. U.S. Budget for Fiscal Years 1979, 1982.

34. U.S. Congress, House, "Appropriations Bill for 1980," Committee for Appropriations, Subcommittee on Energy and Water Development, 96th Cong., 1st sess., part 1, pp. 193–95.

35. Speech before the American Water Resources Association by R. Keith Higginson, Denver, Col., 6 November 1979.

36. *Arizona Daily Star,* 15 November 1981, p. 1.

37. *The New York Times,* 18 September 1981, p. 15.

38. Christopher Leman, "Political Dilemmas in Evaluating and Budgeting Soil Conservation Policies: The RCA Process," in Harold G. Halcrow et al., eds., *Soil Conservation Policies, Institutions and Incentives,* p. 54.

39. U.S. Congress, House, "Appropriations for 1982," Committee on Appropriations, Subcommittee on Energy and Water Development, 97th Cong., 1st sess., part 3, p. 27.

40. Ibid., pp. 11–12.

41. Ibid., p. 26.

42. Ibid., pp. 26–27.

43. *Congressional Quarterly Weekly Report,* 19 June 1982, p. 1461.

44. General Accounting Office, "Federal Charges For Irrigation Projects Reviewed Do Not Cover Costs," PAD-81-07, March 3, 1981.

45. U.S. Congress, House, Committee on Appropriations, Hearings Before the Subcommittee on Energy and Water Development, Appropriations for FY 1984, 98th Cong., 1st sess., part 3, p. 71.

46. General Accounting Office, Report, "Impact Uncertain From Reorganization of the Water and Power Service," CED-81-80, 29 April 1981.

47. *Congressional Quarterly Weekly Report*, 8 May 1982, p. 1072.

48. Ibid., 23 June 1990, p. 1949. The headline reads: "Super Collider Paves the Way for Members' Pork Projects." Also see *CQ Special Issue*, 7 December 1991, 68.

49. The Central Arizona Irrigation and Drainage District filed bankruptcy in 1994; it owes $91 million to CAP. Seven months earlier the New Magma Irrigation and Drainage District filed. See: *Arroyo* (Fall-Winter 1993): 2–3; *Arizona Water Resource* 3 (June/July 1994): 4.

50. See the special issue on the CUP in *High Country News*, 15 July 1991.

51. Tom Melling, "The CUP Holds the Solution: Utah's Hybrid Alternative to Water Markets." *Journal of Energy, Natural Resources, and Environmental Law* 13 (1993): 159–207; Daniel McCool, "The Central Utah Project Completion Act," in *The Waters of Zion*, ed. by Daniel L. McCool (Salt Lake City: University of Utah Press, 1995).

52. *Four Corners Coalition v. Underwood* (1992). U.S. District Court of Colorado, Docket #92-2-2106.

53. *BNA Environmental Law Update*, 21 December 1992.

54. U.S. Department of the Interior, Office of Inspector General. Audit Report. "Development Status of the Dolores and the Animas–La Plata Projects, Bureau of Reclamation." Report no. 94-I-884 (July 1994).

55. U.S. Congress, House, Hearings before the Subcommittee on Energy and Natural Resources, Committee on Appropriations, 103rd Cong., 1st. sess., 1993, part 1, "Energy and Water Development Appropriations for 1994," p. 220.

56. Robert V. Bartlett, "Adapt or Get Out: The Garrison Diversion Project and Controversy," *Environmental Review* 12 (Fall 1988): 57–74.

57. David Lewis Feldman. *Water Resources Management* (Baltimore: Johns Hopkins University Press, 1991), p. 86.

58. Daniel McCool, *Command of the Waters* (Berkeley: University of California Press, 1987; reissued in 1994 in paperback by the University of Arizona Press), chapter 7.

59. Richard Wahl, *Markets for Federal Water* (Washington, D.C.: Resources for the Future, 1989), p. 38.

60. Irrigators do not have to pay interest on the money they borrow to finance the Bureau's water development; thus it constitutes a subsidy. However, when the Bureau calculates the costs of projects it does not include this subsidy, which in some cases costs more than the project itself. Currently, the total annual interest subsidy exceeds the total construction budget of the agency.

61. U. S. Congress, House, Hearings before the Subcommittee on Energy and Natural Resources, Committee on Appropriations, 100th Cong., 2nd sess., 1988, "Energy and Water Appropriations for 1989," p. 64.

62. U.S. Senate, Hearings before the Subcommittee on Water and Power, Committee on Energy and Natural Resources, "Miscellaneous Water Resources Measures," 9 June 1988, p. 2.

63. *Congressional Record* (13 June 1990): H3565. Remarks of Congresswoman Schneider.

64. "Irrigation and Crop Subsidy Programs," Bureau of Reclamation, U.S. Department of the Interior, Office of the Inspector General, Report no. 90-106 (September 1990).

65. GAO Report, "Reclamation Law: Changes Needed Before Water Service Contracts Are Renewed." GAO/RCED-91-175 (August, 1991), p. 17.

66. U. S. General Accounting Office, "Views on Proposed Reclamation Reform Legislation." Testimony of James Duffus III before the Subcommittee on Water and Power, Committee on Energy and Natural Resources, U. S. Senate, GAO/RCED-91-90 (12 September 1991), p. 3. Also see: "Water Subsidies: Basic Changes Needed to Avoid Abuse of the 960-acre Limit." General Accounting Office, GAO/RCED-90-6 (12 October 1989); and "Water Subsidies: The Westhaven Trust Reinforces the Need to Change Reclamation Law," General Accounting Office, GAO-RCED-90-198 (5 June 1990).

67. "Reclamation Law: Changes Needed before Water Service Contracts are Renewed," U.S. General Accounting Office, GAO/RCED-91-175 (August 1991); Wahl, *Markets for Federal Water*, pp. 197–219.

68. U.S. Congress, House, Hearings before the Subcommittee on Energy and Natural Resources, Committee on Appropriations, 100th Cong., 2nd sess., 1988, "Energy and Water Development Appropriations for 1989," p. 14.

69. This act was incorporated into the Reclamation and Projects Authorization and Adjustment Act of 1992, discussed in the text below.

70. *Colorado River Studies Office Newsletter* 8 (Fall 1994).

71. Interview with regional public affairs officer, Upper Colorado River Region. 25 November 1994.

72. Before the CVP was built, the Sacramento River salmon run was in excess of 84,000 fish; in 1991 biologists counted only 191 salmon returning to spawn. It now may be too late to save the run. See: *CQ Weekly Report*, 7 March 1992: p. 527.

73. *U.S. Water News*, November 1994, p. 1. The headline reads: "'New' Bureau of Reclamation Enters Era of Environmental Cleanup."

74. U.S. Congress, House, Hearings before the Subcommittee on Energy and Natural Resources, Committee on Appropriations. 100th Cong., 1st. sess., 1987, part 3, "Energy and Water Development Appropriations for 1988," p. 32.

75. *CQ Weekly Report*, 10 October 1992, p. 3150.

76. P.L. 102-575, "The Reclamation Projects Authorization and Adjustment Act," signed 30 October 1992.

77. *CQ Weekly Report*, 5 October 1992, p. 2626.

78. U.S. Congress, House, Hearings before the Subcommittee on Energy and Natural Resources, Committee on Appropriations, 100th Cong., 2nd sess., 1988,"Energy and Water Development Appropriations for 1989," p. 12.

79. U.S. Congress, House, Hearings before the Subcommittee on Energy and Water Development, Committee on Appropriations, 101st Cong., 1st sess., 1989,"Energy and Water Development Appropriations for 1990," p. 638.

80. U.S. Bureau of Reclamation, "Strategic Plan: A Long-Term Framework for Water Resources Management, Development, and Protection," June 1992.

81. This reorganization is far more comprehensive than past reorganizations. For example, the following is a statement from the newsletter of the Upper Colorado River Region office: "In the past 12 months, across this region, we have faced RIF's, two rounds of buy outs and early retirements, the complete reorganization of the Regional Office, the shift to Area Offices from Projects Offices, and the change of status in the Cortez, Durango, and El Paso Offices." *The Spillway*, December 1994, p. 1.

82. Daniel P. Beard, commissioner of Reclamation. "Blueprint for Reform: The Commissioner's Plan for Reinventing Reclamation," November 1993. Commissioner Beard used the reorganization to eliminate 1,300 positions in the agency. See: *The Spillway*, the Newsletter of the Upper Colorado River Region, January 1995, p. 1. In June, 1995, commissioner Beard announced his resignation.

83. Ibid.

84. Wesley Calef, *Private Grazing and Public Lands* (Chicago: University of Chicago Press, 1960), p. 250.

85. Roy M. Robbins, *Our Landed Heritage: The Public Domain, 1776–1936* (Lincoln, Neb.: University of Nebraska Press, 1962), p. 257.

86. Samuel P. Hays, *Conservation and the Gospel of Efficiency* (Cambridge, Mass.: Harvard University Press, 1959), pp. 49–50.

87. Ibid., pp. 63–65.

88. Robbins, *Landed Heritage*, p. 411.

89. Ibid., pp. 413–15.

90. Quoted Ibid., p. 416.

91. Ibid., p. 417.

92. Ibid., p. 418.

93. Ibid., p. 421.

94. Paul J. Culhane, *Public Lands Politics: Interest Group Influence on the Forest Service and the Bureau of Land Management*, p. 83.

95. Robbins, *Landed Heritage*, p. 423.

96. Culhane, *Public Lands Politics*, p. 88.

97. Robbins, *Landed Heritage*, p. 413.

98. Public Land Law Review Commission, *One Third of the Nation's Lands*, p. 105.

99. Philip Foss, *Politics and Grass* (Seattle: University of Washington Press, 1960), p. 202.

100. Paul J. Culhane and H. Paul Friesema, "Land Use Planning for the Public Lands," *Natural Resources Journal* 19 (January 1979): pp. 43–74.

101. Calef, *Private Grazing*, p. 261.

102. Dana and Fairfax, *Forest and Range Policy*, p. 342.

103. Culhane, *Public Lands Politics*, 86–88.

104. In Clarke, *Roosevelt's Warrior*, chap. 15.

105. Cited in Dorotha M. Bradley and Helen M. Ingram, "Science vs. the Grassroots: Representation in the Bureau of Land Management," *Natural Resources Journal* 26 (Summer 1986): 502–3.

106. Calef, *Private Grazing*, p. 262.

107. Ibid., p. 265.

108. Dana and Fairfax, *Forest and Range Policy*, p. 229.

109. Ibid.

110. Bureau of Land Management, U.S. Department of the Interior, "The President's Proposed FY 1995 Budget Request for the BLM" (Washington, D.C.: n.d.), p. 2.

111. William E. Shands, et. al., "U.S. Forest Service: Meeting Society's Changing Needs. Factbook" (Washington, D.C.: U.S. Forest Service, U.S. Department of Agriculture, June 1994), p. 6.

112. Culhane and Friesema, "Land Use Planning," p. 45.

113. Culhane, *Public Lands Politics*, p. 105.

114. Public Land Law Review Commission, *One Third of the Nation's Lands*, p. ix.

115. U.S. Congress, House, Committee on Appropriations, the Department of the Interior and Related Agencies, Appropriations for 1982, 97th Cong., 1st sess., part 5, p. 190.

116. Ibid., Part 9, p. 441.

117. Ibid., Part 5, p. 175.

118. Jim Zumbo, "Rebellion Rationale," *American Forests* 87, 3 (March 1981): 25.

119. *Natural Resources Defense Council v. Morton*, 458 F. 2d 827 (D.C. Cir., 1972).

120. U.S. Congress, House, Committee on Appropriations, *Hearings before the Subcommittee on the Department of the Interior and Related Agencies, Appropriations for 1982*, 97th Cong., 1st. sess., part 9, p. 175.

121. Ibid., part 8, pp. 2, 13.

122. Ibid., pp. 8–11.

123. Ibid., part 9, pp. 293–296.

124. Ibid., pp. 402–4, and part 8, pp. 4–5.

125. Ibid., pp. 22–23, and *NRDC v. Morton* 458 F. 2d. 827 (D.C. Cir., 1972).

126. Ibid., *Appropriations for 1982*, part 9, p. 399.

127. Ibid.

128. Ibid.

129. Ibid., part 3, p. 10.

130. Ibid., part 8, p. 38.

131. Ibid., part 9, pp. 355–56.

132. Ibid., pp. 358–59.

133. C. Brant Short, *Ronald Reagan and the Public Lands* (College Station: Texas A & M University Press, 1989), pp. 63-4.

134. General Accounting Office, Report, "Analysis of the Powder River Basin Federal Coal Lease Sale: Economic Valuation Improvements and Legislative Changes Needed," RCED-83-119, 11 May 1983.

135. *Congressional Quarterly Weekly Report*, 25 June 1983, p. 1306.

136. Robert F. Durant, *The Administrative Presidency Revisited: Public Lands, the BLM, and the Reagan Revolution* (Albany: SUNY Press, 1992), p. 59.

137. Steve Johnson, "Scorched Earth—Eating the Southwest Desert," *Inner Voice* (July/August 1993): 5.

138. Tony Davis, "BLM chief Jim Baca leaves amidst cheers and boos," *High Country News*, 21 February 1994, p. 3.

139. Ed Marston, "Jim Baca says the Department of Interior is in deep trouble," ibid.

CHAPTER 5. A CROSS-VALIDATION OF AGENCY POWER

1. Eugene J. Webb, Donald T. Campbell, Richard D. Schwartz, and Lee Sechrest, *Unobtrusive Measures: Nonreactive Research in the Social Sciences* (Chicago: Rand McNally, 1966), pp. 1–2.

2. See appendix for the questionnaire schedule.

3. U.S. Congress, House Committee on Appropriations, Hearings before the Subcommittee on the Department of the Interior and Related Agencies, Apps. for 1973, 92d Cong., 2d sess., part 2, p. 837.

4. Aaron Wildavsky, *The New Politics of the Budgetary Process*, 2nd ed (New York: Harper Collins, 1992), p. xxiii.

5. U.S. Congress, House Committee on Appropriations, Hearings before the Subcommittee on Public Works, Apps. for 1974, 93rd Cong., 1st sess., part 1, p. 26.

6. See, for example, Jeanne Nienaber and Aaron Wildavsky, *The Budgeting and Evaluation of Federal Recreation Programs.*

7. In 1950 there were 28 national parks and an annual visitation of 33 million. In 1976 there were 38 national parks and an annual visitation of 240 million, plus the additional responsibility for executing the Bicentennial Program. Source: U.S. Annual Budgets 1950–1976.

8. A deficit was mentioned again in 1971. U.S. Congress, House Committee on Appropriations, Hearings before the Subcommittee on the Department of the Interior and Related Agencies, Apps. for 1972, 91st Cong., 2nd sess., part 3, p. 455.

9. Nienaber and Wildavsky, *Budgeting and Evaluation of Federal Recreation Programs*, pp. 107–8.

10. For a concise statement of this proposition, see Matthew Holden, Jr., "'Imperialism' in Bureaucracy," *The American Political Science Review* 60 (December 1966): 943–51.

11. Richard Fenno, *The Power of the Purse* (Boston: Little, Brown, 1966), p. 412. His study did not include the Corps of Engineers.

12. Fenno, *Power of the Purse*; Ira Sharkansky, "Agency Requests, Gubernatorial Support, and Budget Success in State Legislatures," *American Political Science Review* 62 (December 1968): 1223–35; Otto Davis, M.A.H. Dempster, and Aaron Wildavsky, "On the Process of Budgeting II: An Empirical Study of Congressional Appropriations," in R.F. Byrne, A. Charles, W. W. Cooper, O. A. Davis, and Dorothy Gifford, eds., *Studies in Budgeting*, (New York: Elsevier, 1971); Harvey Tucker, "Budgeting Strategy: Cross-Sectional Versus Longitudinal Models," *Public Administration Review* 41 (November/December 1981): 644–49.

13. Downs, "Up and Down with Ecology."

14. Holden, "'Imperialism' In Bureaucracy," pp. 943–51.

15. Office of the Chief, Program Development and Budget, U.S. Forest Service, Washington, D.C., 30 September 1994, facsimile transmission.

16. *Appendix to the Budget for FY 1990* (Washington, D.C.: GPO, 1989), p. I-E101.

17. *Appendix to the Budget for FY 1995*, pp. 225–26.

18. Bureau of Labor Statistics, *Current Wage Developments* (Washington D.C.: U.S. Department of Labor, March 1975), table 1, p. 47.

19. "Annual Service-Wide Skills," Office of the Chief, Program Development and Budget, U.S. Forest Service, facsimile transmission, 30 September 1994.

20. "Breakdown by Affirmative Action Category as of 9/30/95," HQ USACE, Washington, D.C., 5 pp. Note that total workforce figure includes civil *and* military components of the Corps.

21. For a full treatment of this subject, see Charles T. Goodsell, *The Case for Bureaucracy: A Public Administration Polemic*, 3rd ed (Chatham, NJ.: Chatham House, 1994).

CHAPTER 6. SEARCHING FOR COMMON GROUND

1. Hanna J. Cortner, et. al. "Institutional Barriers and Incentives for Ecosystems Management, a Problem Analysis," Water Resources Research Center, College of Agriculture, University of Arizona, Issue Paper 16 (December 1994), p. 8.

2. See: Hugh Heclo, "Issue Networks and the Executive Establishment," in Anthony King, ed., *The New American Political System* (Washington, D.C.: American Enterprise Institute, 1978), 95–105; Daniel McCool, "Subgovernments as Determinants of Political Viability," *Political Science Quarterly* 105 (Summer 1990): 269–93.

3. See: Lawrence Bacow and Michael Wheeler, *Environmental Dispute Resolution*, (New York: Plenum Press, 1984); Douglas Amy, *The Politics of Environmental Mediation*, (New York: Columbia University Press, 1987); John Gamman, *Overcoming Obstacles in Environmental Policymaking*, (Albany: State University of New York Press, 1994).

4. General Accounting Office, "Hydroelectric Dams: Interior Favors Removing Elwha Dams, but Who Should Pay is Undecided." GAO/RCED-92-168 (June 1992).

5. *U. S. Water News*, December 1994, p. 3.

6. See: Marc Reisner and Sarah Bates. *Overtapped Oasis* (Washington, D.C.: Island Press, 1990), pp. 78–110.

7. See: Daniel McCool, "Intergovernmental Conflict and Indian Water Rights: An Assessment of Negotiated Settlements," *Publius* 23 (Winter 1993), 85–101; Daniel McCool, "Indian Water Settlements: The Prerequisites of Successful Negotiation," *Policy Studies Journal* 21, 2 (1993), 227–42.

8. Daniel P. Beard, commissioner of reclamation. "Blueprint for Reform: The Commissioner's Plan for Reinventing Reclamation," November 1993, p. 3.

9. See: Michael Lawson, *Dammed Indians* (Norman: University of Oklahoma Press, 1982).

10. "Hard Choices: A Report on the Increasing Gap between America's Infrastructure Needs and Our Ability to Pay for Them." Summary Report prepared by the National Infrastructure Advisory Committee for the Joint Economic Committee of the U.S. Congress, February 1984, p. 7.

11. "America's Infrastructure: A Plan to Rebuild." Prepared by the Association of General Contractors of America, May 1983, p. 5.

12. Ibid, p. 8.

13. *National Journal,* 12 March 1988, p. 685; *National Journal,* 2 April 1988, pp. 868–72.

14. U. S. Congress, House, Hearings before the Subcommittee on Energy and Water Development, Committee on Appropriations. 100th Cong., 2nd. sess., 1988, "Energy and Water Development Appropriations for 1989," pp. 32–33.

15. *Los Angeles Times,* 27 December 27, 1994, p. A5.

16. *CQ Weekly Report,* 12 November 1994, p. 3275.

17. *CQ Weekly Report,* 10 December 1994, p. 3507.

18. U.S. Congress, House, Hearings before the Subcommittee on Energy and Natural Resources, Committee on Appropriations, 103rd Cong., 1st. sess., 1993, part 1, "Energy and Water Development Appropriations for 1994," p. 9. Statement by Dr. Edward Dickey, Acting Assistant Secretary of the Army.

19. Aaron Wildavsky, *The New Politics of the Budgetary Process,* p. 415.

20. Ibid., p. 421.

21. *CQ Weekly Report,* 4 February 1995, pp. 349–54.

22. H.R. 721, "Public Resources Deficit Reduction Act of 1995," 104th Congress, 1st sess. 27 January 1995.

23. See Thomas S. Kuhn, *The Structure of Scientific Revolutions* (Chicago: The University of Chicago Press, 1962); also Hanna J. Cortner and Margaret A. Moote, "Trends and Issues in Land and Water Resources Management: Setting the Agenda for Change," *Environmental Management* 18, 2: 167–73.

Bibliography

BOOKS

Alexander, Charles C. *Holding the Line: The Eisenhower Era, 1952-1961*. Bloomington: Indiana University Press, 1975.

Allen, Frederick Lewis. *The Lords of Creation*. Chicago: Quadrangle Books, 1966.

Amy, Douglas. *The Politics of Environmental Mediation*. New York: Columbia University Press, 1987.

Andrews, Richard N. L. *Environmental Policy and Administrative Change*. Lexington: D. C. Heath and Co., 1976.

Bacow, Lawrence and Michael Wheeler. *Environmental Dispute Resolution*. New York: Plenum Press, 1984.

Berkman, Richard L. and W. Kip Viscusi. *Damning the West*. New York: Grossman Publishers, 1973.

Calef, Wesley. *Private Grazing and Public Lands*. Chicago: University of Chicago Press, 1960.

Clarke, Jeanne Nienaber. *Roosevelt's Warrior: Harold L. Ickes and The New Deal*. Baltimore: Johns Hopkins University Press, 1996.

Cooley, Richard A. *Politics and Conservation: The Decline and Fall of the Alaskan Salmon*. New York: Harper & Row, 1963.

Culhane, Paul J. *Public Lands Politics: Interest Group Influence on the Forest Service and the Bureau of Land Management*. Baltimore: Johns Hopkins University Press, 1981.

Dana, Samuel T., and Sally K. Fairfax. *Forest and Range Policy*. New York: McGraw-Hill, 1980.

Darling, F. Fraser and Noel D. Eichhorn. *Man and Nature in the National Parks*. Washington, D.C.: The Conservation Foundation, 1967.

Devoto, Bernard. *The Year of Decision: 1846*. Boston: Houghton Mifflin, 1942.

Durant, Robert F. *The Administrative Presidency Revisited: Public Lands, the BLM, and the Reagan Revolution*. Albany: SUNY Press, 1992.

Ellis, Jack. *Presidential Lightning Rods*. Lawrence: University Press of Kansas, 1994.

Everhart, William C. *The National Park Service*. New York: Praeger, 1972.

Feldman, David Lewis. *Water Resources Management*. Baltimore: Johns Hopkins University Press, 1991.

Fenno, Richard. *The Power of the Purse*. Boston: Little, Brown, 1966.

Foss, Phillip. *Politics and Grass*. Seattle: University of Washington Press, 1960.

Fradkin, Phillip L. *A River No More*. New York: Alfred A. Knopf, 1981.

Galbraith, John Kenneth. *The New Industrial State*. New York: Signet Books, 1967.

Gamman, John. *Overcoming Obstacles in Environmental Policymaking*. Albany: SUNY Press, 1994.

Gerth, H. H., and C. Wright Mills, eds. *From Max Weber: Essays in Sociology*. New York: Oxford University Press, 1958.

Goodsell, Charles T. *The Case for Bureaucracy: A Public Administration Polemic*. 3rd ed. Chatham, N.J.: Chatham House, 1994.

Halcrow, Harold G., Earl Heady and Melvin Cotner, eds. *Soil Conservation Policies, Institutions, and Incentives*. Ankeny, Iowa: Soil Conservation Society of America, 1982.

Hays, Samuel P. *Conservation and the Gospel of Efficiency*. Cambridge, Mass.: Harvard University Press, 1959.

Heclo, Hugh. *A Government of Strangers: Executive Politics in Washington*. Washington, D.C.: Brookings Institution, 1977.

Hofstadter, Richard. *Social Darwinism in American Thought*. Boston: Beacon Press, 1955.

Hoover Commission. *Report on Organization of the Executive Branch of Government*. New York: McGraw-Hill, 1949.

Ingram, Helen and Steven Rathgeb Smith, eds. *Public Policy for Democracy*. Washington, D.C.: Brookings Institution, 1993.

Kaufman, Herbert. *The Forest Ranger: A Study in Administrative Behavior*. Baltimore: Johns Hopkins University Press, 1960.

_____. *Are Government Organizations Immortal?* Washington D.C.: Brookings Institution, 1976.

Kuhn, Thomas S. *The Structure of Scientific Revolutions*. Chicago: University of Chicago Press, 1962.

Lawson, Michael. *Dammed Indians*. Norman: University of Oklahoma Press, 1982.

Liroff, Richard. *A National Policy for the Environment: NEPA and Its Aftermath*. Bloomington: Indiana University Press, 1976.

Lowi, Theodore. *The End of Liberalism*. 2nd ed. New York: W. W. Norton, 1979.

Lowry, William R. *A Capacity for Wonder*. Washington, D.C.: Brookings Institution, 1993.

Maass, Arthur. *The Kings River Project: Case Studies in Public Administration and Policy Formulation*. University, Ala.: University of Alabama Press, 1950.

_____. *Muddy Waters*. Cambridge Mass.: Harvard University Press, 1951.

Mazmanian, Daniel and Jeanne Nienaber. *Can Organizations Change? Environmental Protection, Citizen Participation and the Corps of Engineers*. Washington D.C.: Brookings Institution, 1979.

McCool, Daniel. *Command of the Waters*. Berkeley: University of California Press, 1987; paperback ed., Tucson: University of Arizona Press, 1994.

McConnell, Grant. *The Modern Presidency*. 2d ed., New York: St. Martin's Press, 1976.

Morgan, Robert J. *Governing Soil Conservation*. Baltimore: Johns Hopkins University Press, 1962.

Nash, Roderick. *Wilderness and the American Mind*. New Haven: Yale University Press, 1967.

Nienaber, Jeanne and Aaron Wildavsky. *The Budgeting and Evaluation of Federal Recreation Programs: Or, Money Doesn't Grow on Trees*. New York: Basic Books, 1973.

Novogrod, Joseph, Gladys O. Dimock, and Marshall E. Dimock. *Casebook in Public Administration*. New York: Holt, Rinehart and Winston, 1969.

O'Neill, William. *The Progressive Years: America Comes of Age*. New York: Dodd, Mead and Co., 1975.

Pinchot, Gifford. *Breaking New Ground*. New York: Harcourt and Brace, 1947.

Reisner, Marc and Sarah Bates. *Overtapped Oasis*. Washington, D. C.: Island Press, 1990.

Richardson, Elmo. *Dams, Parks and Politics*. Lexington: University of Kentucky Press, 1973.

Robbins, Roy M. *Our Landed Heritage: The Public Domain, 1776–1936*. Lincoln, Neb.: University of Nebraska Press, 1962.

Rourke, Francis. *Bureaucracy, Politics, and Public Policy*. Boston: Little, Brown, and Co., 1976.

Short, C. Brant. *Ronald Reagan and the Public Lands*. College Station: Texas A & M University Press, 1989.

Smith, Frank E. *The Politics of Conservation*. New York: Harper Colophon Books, 1966.

Stratton, Owen, and Phillip Sirotkin. *The Echo Park Controversy*. University, Ala.: University of Alabama Press, 1959.

Swain, Donald. *Wilderness Defender*. Chicago: University of Chicago Press, 1970.

Von Bertalanffy, Ludwig. *General Systems Theory*. New York: George Braziller, 1968.

Wahl, Richard. *Markets for Federal Water*. Washington, D.C.: Resources For the Future, 1989.

Webb, Eugene J., Donald Campbell, Richard Schwartz, and Lee Sechrest. *Unobtrusive Measures: Nonreactive Research in the Social Sciences*. Chicago: Rand McNally, 1966.

Wildavsky, Aaron. *The New Politics of the Budgetary Process*, 2nd ed. New York: HarperCollins, 1992.

Yaffe, Steven Lewis. *The Wisdom of the Spotted Owl*. Washington, D.C.: Island Press, 1994.

ARTICLES AND BOOK CHAPTERS

Abate, Tom. "A Threatened Statute." *The Environmental Forum* 9 (March/April 1992): 16.

"America's Infrastructure: A Plan to Rebuild." Prepared by the Association of General Contractors of America, May, 1983.

Bartlett, Robert V. "Adapt or Get Out: The Garrison Diversion Project and Controversy." *Environmental Review* 12 (Fall 1988): 57–74.

Bloomfield, Howard. "Quandary In the Campgrounds." *American Forests* 75 (July 1969): 6.

Bradley, Dorotha M. and Helen M. Ingram. "Science vs. the Grassroots: Representation in the Bureau of Land Management." *Natural Resources Journal* 26 (Summer 1986): 493-518.

Brandborg, Stewart. "The Wilderness Law and the National Park System in the U.S." In *Canadian Parks in Perspective*, ed. by J.G. Nelson. Quebec, Canada: Harvest House, 1970. pp. 270-291.

Brown, David S. "Reforming the Bureaucracy: Some Suggestions for the New President." In *Bureaucratic Power in National Politics*, ed. Francis E. Rourke. Boston: Little, Brown, and Co., 1978. pp. 377–389.

Clarke, Jeanne Nienaber. "Grizzlies and Tourists." *Society*, March/April 1990: 23-32.

Cortner, Hanna J., Margaret A. Shannon, Mary G. Wallace, Sabrina Burke, and Margaret A. Moote. "Institutional Barriers and Incentives for Ecosystems Management: A Problem Analysis." General Technical Report PNW – GTR 354. Portland Ore: USDA, Forest Service, Pacific Northwest Research Station (forthcoming 1995).

Cortner, Hanna J. and Margaret A. Moote. "Trends and Issues in Land and Water Resources Management: Setting the Agenda for Change,"*Environmental Management* 18, no. 2: 167–73.

Craig, James B. "Plusses and Minuses in the National Parks,." *American Forests* (June 1976): 4.

Culhane, Paul J. and H. Paul Friesema, "Land Use Planning for the Public Lands." *Natural Resources Journal* 19 (January 1979): 43–74.

Davis, Otto, M. A. H. Dempster, and Aaron Wildavsky. "On The Process of Budgeting II: An Empirical Study of Congressional Appropriations." In *Studies in Budgeting*, Ed. R. F. Byrne et al. New York: American Elsevier Publishing Co., 1971.

Davis, Tony. "BLM chief Jim Baca Leaves amidst Cheers and Boos." *High Country News*, 21 February 1994, 3.

Downs, Anthony. "Up and Down with Ecology: The 'Issue-Attention Cycle'." *The Public Interest* 28 (Summer 1972): 38–50.

Drury, Newton B. "Former Directors Speak Out." *American Forests* 82 (June, 1976): 30.

Egan, Timothy, "Forest Service Abusing Role, Dissidents Say." *The New York Times*, 4 March 1990, A1, A26.

Ellis, Richard and Aaron Wildavsky, "'Greatness Revisited': Evaluating the Performance of Early American Presidents in Terms of Cultural Dilemmas." *Presidential Studies Quarterly* 21, no. 1 (Winter 1991): 15–34.

Easter, K. William and Melvin L. Cotner. "Evaluation of Current Soil Conservation Strategies." In *Soil Conservation Policies, Institutions, and Incentives.*, ed. Harold G. Halcrow, et al. Ankeny, Iowa: Soil Conservation Society of America, 1982.

Francis, John. "The West and the Prospects for Rebellion: An Analysis of State Legislative Responses to the Public Lands Question." In *Resource Conflicts in the West.* ed. Richard Ganzel. Reno, Nev: Nevada Public Affairs Institute, 1983.

Fraser, Charles. "Park Agencies for the Future." *Parks and Recreation* 8 (August 1973): 21-23, 35-38.

Heclo, Hugh. "Issue Networks and the Executive Establishment." In *The New American Political System*, ed. Anthony King. Washington, D.C.: American Enterprise Institute, 1978: 95–105.

Holden, Matthew, Jr. "Imperialism in Bureaucracy." *The American Political Science Review* 60 (December 1966): 943-951.

Ingram, Helen. "The Politics of Information: Constraints on New Sources." In *Water Politics and Public Involvement*, John C. Pierce and Harvey R. Doerksen. ed. Ann Arbor, Mich.: Ann Arbor Science Publishers, 1976.

Johnson, Steve. "Scorched Earth—Eating the Southwest Desert." *Inner Voice* 5, No. 4 (July/August 1993): 5.

Landau, Martin. "Redundancy, Rationality, and the Problem of Duplication and Overlap." In *Bureaucratic Power in National Politics*, ed. Francis Rourke. Boston: Little, Brown, and Co., 1978.

Leman, Christopher. "Political Dilemmas in Evaluating and Budgeting Soil Conservation Programs: The RCA Process." In *Soil Conservation Policies, Institutions, and Incentives*, ed. Harold G. Halcrow, Earl O. Heady, and Melvin L. Cotner. Ankeny, Iowa: Soil Conservation Society of America, 1982.

Lindblom, Charles E. "The Science of 'Muddling Through'." *Public Administration Review* 19 (Spring 1959): 79-88.

Lowry, William R. "Land of the Fee: Entrance Fees and the National Park Service." *Political Research Quarterly* 46 (1993): 823–32.

Marston, Ed. "Jim Baca Says the Department of the Interior is in Deep Trouble." *High Country News*, 21 February 1994, 3.

McCool, Daniel. "Subgovernments as Determinants of Political Viability." *Political Science Quarterly.* 105 (Summer 1990): 269–93.

_____. "Intergovernmental Conflict and Indian Water Rights: An Assessment of Negotiated Settlements." *Publius* 23 (Winter 1993): 85–101.

_____."Indian Water Settlements: The Prerequisites of Successful Negotiation." *Policy Studies Journal* 21, no. 2 (1993): 227–42.

_____. "The Central Utah Project Completion Act,." In *The Waters of Zion*, ed. D. McCool. Salt Lake City: University of Utah Press, 1995.

Melling, Tom. "The CUP Holds the Solution: Utah's Hybrid Alternative to Water Markets." *Journal of Energy, Natural Resources, and Environmental Law* 13 (1993): 159–207.

Porter, Charles O. "May Justice Come to Overcut National Forests." *The New York Times*, 10 April 1993, 10.

Rasmussen, Wayne D. "History of Soil Conservation, Institutions, and Incentives." In *Soil Conservation Policies, Institutions, and Incentives*, ed. Harold G. Halcrow et al. Ankeny, Iowa: Soil Conservation Society of America, 1982.

Rourke, Francis. "Grappling with the Bureaucracy." In *Politics and the Oval Office*, ed. Arnold J. Meltsner. San Francisco: Institute for Contemporary Studies, 1981.

Sharkansky, Ira. "Agency Requests, Gubernatorial Support, and Budget Success in State Legislatures." *American Political Science Review* 62 (December 1968), pp. 1223-35.

Sibley, George. "The Desert Empire." *Harpers*, 1977, 49-68.

Simon, Benjamin, Craig Leff, and Harvey Doerksen. "Allocating Scarce Resources for Endangered Species Recovery." *Journal of Policy Analysis and Management*, 14 (Summer 1995) pp. 415–32.

Swem, Theodore. "Planning of National Parks." In *Canadian Parks in Perspective*. Ed. J. G. Nelson. Quebec, Canada: Harvest House, 1970, 253–269.

Tucker, Harvey. "Budgeting Strategy: Cross-Sectional versus Longitudinal Models." *Public Administration Review* 41 (November/December 1981): 644–49.

Weber, Max. "Politics as a Vocation." In *From Max Weber: Essays in Sociology*, ed. H. H. Gerth and C. W. Mills. New York: Oxford University Press, 1958, 232–33.

Wenner, Lettie McSpadden. "The Courts in Environmental Politics: The Case of the Spotted Owl." In *Environmental Politics and Policy in the West*, ed. Zachary Smith. Dubuque: Kendall-Hunt, 1993, 45–62.

Wichelman, Allan F. "Administrative Agency Implementation of the National Environmental Policy Act of 1969: A Conceptual Framework for Explaining Differential Responses." *Natural Resources Journal* 16, no. 2 (April 1976): 263–300.

Zumbo, Jim. "Rebellion Rationale." *American Forests* 87 (March 1981): 25.

NEWSPAPERS, PERIODICALS, AND REPORTS

Arizona Daily Star
Arroyo
BNA Environmental Law Update
Chicago Tribune
Colorado River Studies Office Newsletter
Congressional Quarterly Weekly Report
Conservation Foundation, State of the Environment 1982. Washington, D.C.: The Conservation Foundation, 1982.
High Country News

Inner Voice
Life Magazine
Los Angeles Times
National Journal
National Park Resource Survey
National Parks and Conservation Association Magazine
National Wildlife Federation Newsletter
Newsweek
New York Times
Tucson Citizen
U.S. Water News
Wall Street Journal
Washington Post

UNPUBLISHED DISSERTATIONS AND PAPERS

Fairfax, Sally. "RPA and the Forest Service." University of California, Berkeley.
Ganzel, Richard and Dorothy Olkowski. "The Politics of Coalition-Building:The Inholders Reach Out." Paper presented at the Western Social Science Association Meeting, Albuquerque, N.M., April 1983.
Gold, Kenneth. "A Comparative Analysis of Successful Organizations." U.S. Office of Personnel Management, 1 July 1981. Mimeograph.
Hartzog, George B. "Management Considerations for Optimum Development and Protection of National Park Resources." Paper presented at Second World Conference on National Parks, Lausanne, Switzerland: International Union for Conservation of Nature and Natural Resources, 1966.
Kirwan, Laura, and Daniel McCool. "Environmentalists, Tribes, and Negotiated Water Settlements." Paper prepared for delivery at the annual meeting of the American Political Science Association, August 31-September 3, 1995, Chicago, Il.
Leman, Christopher. "Resource Assessment and Program Development: An Evaluation of Forest Service Experience Under the Resources Planning Act, with Lessons for Other Natural Resource Agencies." Mimeograph.
McCool, Daniel. Survey questionnaire to a sample of National Park Service employees at the Albright Training Center at Grand Canyon, Arizona.

SELECTED GOVERNMENT DOCUMENTS AND PUBLICATIONS

Complete citations for the hundreds of other government documents that were consulted during this research, including appropriations hearings, may be found in the chapter endnotes.

Agency Documents

Army Corps of Engineers, U.S. "Vision 21: A Strategic Assessment of the Nation's Water Resources Needs." Draft Report, March 1990.

_____. "Environmental Activities in the Corps of Engineers Water Resources Programs: Charting a New Direction." Prepared by Leonard Shabman. IWR Report 93-PS-1. (November 1993)

_____. "National Wetland Mitigation Banking Studies." IWR Report 92-WMB-1 (July 1992); IWR Report 94-WMB-3 (January 1994); IWR Report 94-WMB-4 (February 1994); IWR Report 94-WMB-5 (March 1994).

_____. "National Study of Water Management During Drought." Draft. IWR Report 94-NDS-12 (June 1994).

_____. "Living under Constraints: An Emerging Vision for High Performance Public Works." IWR Report 94-FIS-20 (October 1994).

Beard, Daniel P., Commissioner of Reclamation. "Blueprint for Reform: The Commissioner's Plan for Reinventing Reclamation." November 1993.

Bureau of Reclamation. "Irrigation and Crop Subsidy Programs." Office of the Inspector General, Report No. 90-106. September 1990.

Bureau of Reclamation. "Strategic Plan: A Long-Term Framework for Water Resources Management, Development, and Protection." June 1992.

Fish and Wildlife Service, U.S. Report: "Resource Problems." July 1983.

_____. Report: "Federal and State Endangered Species Expenditures for Fiscal Year 1991." December 1992.

Forest Service, U.S. "RARE II: A Quest for Balance in Public Land Use." Washington D.C.: GPO, 1978.

_____. "RARE II: Final Environmental Statement, Roadless Area Review and Evaluation." January 1979.

_____. "U.S. Forest Service: Meeting Society's Changing Needs. FACTBOOK". Comp. by William E. Shands. et al. June 1994.

Helms, Douglas. "New Authorities and New Roles: SCS and the 1985 Farm Bill." In *Readings in the History of the Soil Conservation Service.* Washington, DC: U.S. Department of Agriculture, Soil Conservation Service, Historical Notes No.1. September 1992.

Higginson, R. Keith, Commissioner of Reclamation. Speech before the American Water Resources Association, Denver, Colorado, 6 November 1979.

National Park Service. "Administrative Policies for the Historical Areas of the National Park Service." Washington, D.C.: GPO, 1968.

_____. "Background Material on the National Park Service." Document 527–76. November 1976.

_____. "State of the Parks 1980." May 1980.

_____. Office of the Chief Personnel Officer. Personnel Table. 6 June 1994.

Reuss, Martin. "Reshaping National Water Politics: The Emergence of the Water Resources Development Act of 1986." Office of History, U. S. Army Corps of Engineers. IWR Policy Study 91-PS-1. October 1991.

Congressional Documents

House and Senate, Appropriations Hearings, 1900–1992. See chapter endnotes for complete citations.

House, Committee on Government Operations. Hearings before the Subcommittee on Stream Channelization, 92d Cong., 1st sess. May 1971.

_____, Committee on Government Operations, "Degradation of the National Parks." 94th Cong., 1st, 2d sess. 4 December 1975, 30 January 1976, 7 April 1976.

_____, "The Degradation of Our National Parks." 24th Report by the Committee on Government Operations , 30 June 1976.

_____, Committee on Merchant Marine and Fisheries. "Reorganization Hearings." 84th Cong., 2d sess., 1957.

_____, Committee on Post Office and Civil Service, Subcommittee on Civil Service. "Testimony of John Mumma." 23 September 1991. (Mimeo from author).

_____, Committee on Rivers and Harbors. "Pollution of Navigable Waters." Testimony of Thomas Robins, Deputy Chief of the Corps of Engineers,. 79th Cong., 1st. sess., 1945.

Joint Economic Committee. "Hard Choices: A Report on the Increasing Gap Between America's Infrastructure Needs and Our Ability to Pay for Them."Summary Report of the National Infrastructure Advisory Committee. February 1984.

Public Land Law Review Commission. *Final Report to Congress: One Third of the Nation's Land.* Washington, D.C.: GPO, 1970.

Senate, Committee on Interior and Insular Affairs, Subcommittee on Parks and Recreation. "Proposed Reservation System in Selected National Parks."93d. Cong., 1st sess. 23 February 1973.

_____. "Oversight—Park Reservation System." 93d Cong., 2d sess. 21 August, 19 September 1974.

Presidential Documents

Executive Order 9060, 23 February 1942.

Executive Order 9577, 29 June 1945.

Executive Order 12113, 4 January 1979.

Executive Order 12322, 17 September 1981.

Interagency Floodplain Management Task Force, Final Report. "Sharing the Challenge: Floodplain Management into the 21st Century." Washington, D.C., June 1994.

Office of Management and Budget. Appendices to the Budget of the United States. See chapter endnotes for complete citations.

Papers of President James Earl Carter, 1977, Vol.13, no. 17, 18 April 1977.

Other

Bureau of Labor Statistics. Current Wage Developments. Washington, D.C.: U.S. Department of Labor, March 1975.

Department of the Interior, News Release, 6 November 1979.

_____, Office of the Inspector General. "Development Status of the Dolores and the Animas–La Plata Projects, Bureau of Reclamation." Report No. 94-I-884. July 1994.

General Accounting Office. "Facilities in Many National Parks and Forests Do Not Meet Health and Safety Standards." CED-80-115. 10 October 1980.

_____."Federal Charges for Irrigation Projects Reviewed Do Not Cover Costs." PAD-81-07. 3 March 1981.

_____. "Impact Uncertain from Reorganization of the Water and Power Service." CED-81-80. 29 April 1981.

_____. "Analysis of the Powder River Basin Federal Coal Lease: Economic Valuation Improvements and Legislative Changes Needed." RCED-83-119. 11 May 1983.

_____. "Water Subsidies: Basic Changes Needed to Avoid Abuse of the 960-Acre Limit." GAO/RCED-90-6, 12 October 1989.

_____. "Water Subsidies: The Westhaven Trust Reinforces the Need to Change Reclamation Law." GAO/RCED-90-198. 5 June 1990.

_____. "Reclamation Law: Changes Needed before Water Service Contracts Are Renewed." GAO/RCED-91-175. August 1991.

_____. "Views on Proposed Reclamation Reform Legislation." GAO/RCED-91-90. 12 September 1991.

_____. "Hydroelectric Dams: Interior Favors Removing Elwha Dams,But Who Should Pay Is Undecided." GAO/RCED-92-168. June 1992.

_____. "Factors Associated with Delayed Listing Decisions." GAO/RCED 93-152. August 1993.

_____. "Wetlands Protection." GAO/RCED-93-26. April 1993.

Natural Resources Defense Council v. Morton, 458 F 2d. 827 C.D.C. Cir., 1972.

Udall, Stewart L., Secretary of the Interior. Memorandum, 10 July 1964.

Watt, James, Secretary of the Interior, Secretarial Order No. 3087, 3 December 1982.

Index